The
Grooves
of
Change

The
Grooves
of
Change

Eastern

Europe

at the Turn

of the

Millennium

J. F. Brown

DUKE UNIVERSITY PRESS

DURHAM AND LONDON

2001

Second printing, 2003
© 2001 Duke University Press
All rights reserved
Printed in the United States of America on acid-free paper ∞
Typeset in Minion by Keystone Typesetting, Inc.
Library of Congress Cataloging-in-Publication Data
appear on the last printed page of this book.
Portions of chapter 4 previously appeared in articles in *Transitions*
and in *Building Democracy* (Armonk, N.Y.: M.E. Sharp, for the
Open Media Research Institute, Prague, 1996).
Reproduced by permission of the editor,
Transitions.

For Arthur, Roley, and Louis,
unlikely musketeers

Let the great world spin for ever
down the ringing grooves of change
—Alfred, Lord Tennyson,
"Locksley Hall"

Contents

List of Maps

Preface

IN 1994 DUKE UNIVERSITY PRESS published *Hopes and Shadows: Eastern Europe After Communism.* It followed two books by me that Duke Press also had published: *Eastern Europe and Communist Rule* (1988) and *Surge to Freedom: The End of Communist Rule in Eastern Europe* (1991). This book is both similar to and different from those other three. It confines itself to the seven former communist countries of Eastern Europe—Albania, Bulgaria, the Czech Republic and Slovakia (both once Czechoslovakia), Hungary, Poland, Romania, and the successor states of Yugoslavia—but it also looks at these countries in the perspective of the twentieth century and at their prospects for the new century.

I retain the term "Eastern Europe," not only out of habit or because of its sequential convenience in following the titles of my other books for Duke. (Back in 1966, my very first book was called *The New Eastern Europe.*) Instead, I do so because the term still has its uses. It provides a suitable framework in which to discuss the abiding features of the region's modern history: its basic continuity; the prominence of ethnic and national factors; the region's dependence on great powers or combinations of powers outside it; the north-south divide between East Central and South Eastern Europe; its overall political and economic deprivation; the intense variety within it that has defied definition and generalization. Besides, many of the problems that these countries face are similar, the attempts to deal with them are comparable, their successes and failures are relevant and illustrative. I am aware, of course, of the argument that the term "Eastern Europe" should have died in 1989 with the cold war, that a one-time convenience had become an offensive inaccuracy. In keeping with this argument, I accept that "Eastern Europe" is on its way to becoming a solecism or fading into oblivion. But there is still some way to go. Take one simple fact: leaving aside the Yugoslav catastrophe, what divides East Central Europe ("Central Europe") from South Eastern Europe is still in some key respects of much less significance than what divides it from virtually the whole of Western Europe. As the one gap widens and the other narrows, then the term "Eastern Europe" will indeed become as untenable as it is now unfashionable. In the meantime, though, it survives—eroding but not erroneous.

In this regard, I am myself trapped in an inconsistency. I believe Russia is part of Europe and that it must be brought patiently into the European fold. Obviously, therefore, it is part of Eastern Europe. But I do not cover it in this book. (A review in 1995 took me to task for not doing so in *Hopes and Shadows*.) There are four reasons for my not doing so: (1) it would require more space than this volume avails; (2) precedent, since my earlier books have covered only the seven countries specified; (3) proportion, since Russia would crowd out Eastern Europe, diminishing if not demeaning it, making it "Zwischen-Europa," a totally unacceptable term; (4) ignorance, since my knowledge of Russia is "fringe"; ignorance, of course, is an impediment that seldom deters, but Russia, of all places, is not for fools rushing in.

This book is painted with a broad brush, and it is judgmental. I make no apology for either. It is, if you like, more the distillation than the extent of what I know. I hope only that too many generalizations have not become over-simplifications. I have assumed some knowledge on the part of the reader, or at least a willingness to quarry below the surface. I also have tried not to suffocate the book with a surfeit of footnotes. As to judgments, I cannot avoid them in a book like this one. I hope that they are strong enough without being too opinionated. In parts, I can be charged with repetitiveness, especially when dealing with ethnic and minority issues. Why not one chapter covering them for the whole of the twentieth century and beyond? Perhaps. But I was anxious to show how these issues have overshadowed, even bedeviled, every period that the book covers. Hence, the cumbersome chronological approach. I also sometimes quote longer or shorter passages from my earlier books. This is done neither because I think these books are the best, nor because they are the only ones that I have read. Instead, I have done so because the passages quoted fit in with the continuity of my thinking over a number of years, or they illustrate the corrections or modifications necessary to it.

Many people have helped me with this book. I am grateful to them. I name them in no sort of order, except the first: Margaret, my wife, to whom I am most grateful of all. The rest are Vlad Sobell, Vladimir Kusin, Barbara Kliszewski, Tom Szayna, Steve Larrabee, Vera Tolz, Jan de Weydenthal, Jiri Pehe, Viktor Meier, Michael Shafir, Dan Ionescu, Evelina Kelbecheva, Aglica Markova, Louis Zanga, Franz-Lothar Altmann, Anneli Ute Gabanyi, Pat Moore, "Dimi" Panitza, Mark Thompson, Stefan Troebst, and Evie Sterner. Not all of them would agree with everything I say; precious few, probably. But I owe all of them a debt.

This book had a difficult birth. It needed a good midwife. It got one in Valerie Millholland, editor and friend at Duke University Press. Yet again, my gratitude. It got a good editor, too, in Bob Mirandon, who has edited my last three books for Duke Press. Many thanks also go to Pam Morrison at the press. I couldn't have been luckier, and couldn't be more grateful.

Lynne Fletcher typed the manuscript with skill, patience, and humor. What more could a pen pusher want?

Dr. F. Stephen (Steve) Larrabee read the manuscript thoroughly and made many advantageous recommendations—in fact, saving me from minor disasters in several places. My thanks to a friend of thirty years.

Looking back beyond this book to the time when I began working on Eastern Europe, I think especially of four men: Charles Andras, a colleague, counselor, and friend; Pierre Hassner, who matches wisdom with fun and humanity; the late General C. Rodney Smith, who was an example and an inspiration; and the late Gordon Sterner, a much remembered friend.

I spent several months in 1995–96 working for the Aspen-Carnegie International Commission on the Balkans, based in Berlin, always a capital city. David Anderson was one of the commissioners. He died in 1997. He was a good, able man, much loved by those who worked for him. For me it was a privilege knowing him.

I spent the spring semester of 2000 teaching at the American University in Bulgaria. It is located in Blagoevgrad, a vibrant little town, geographically and historically just about as Balkan as you can get. My students were of a high order and from more than a few of them I learned more about Balkan experiences and attitudes than I could have from countless textbooks and endless miles of travel. I thank them, salute them, and wish them well.

The Oxford Public Library and the Maison Française in Oxford were very helpful. But the two institutions to which I have always been most indebted are the Radio Free Europe Research Department and the *Neue Zürcher Zeitung*. I joined the one in 1957 and have been reading the other since 1959. To say I am grateful gives absolutely no idea of how lost I would have been without them.

This is the last book I shall write about Eastern Europe. But the interest remains. So do the concern and the affection.

Jim Brown
October 2000

Coming into Being

THE INDEPENDENCE OF THE East European nations stemmed not so much from their own exertions, however considerable, as from the exhaustion and collapse of the empires that ruled them. The maintenance of that independence has depended mainly on the will of others. Its permanence, therefore, could never be taken for granted. That is the basic and continuing lesson of modern East European history.

But we must immediately enter a caveat. When we refer to the independence of *nations* we mean the independence of those East European nations that became nations-of-state, "majoritarian nations." Thus, we encounter another determining factor in modern East European history: its glut of nations and the relations between them.

In a book published in 1988 I wrote:

Eastern Europe has never been rich in natural resources, but it has always been rich in nations. It covers an area about two-thirds the size of Western Europe. But, whereas Western Europe is more or less exclusively covered by five large nations—the Germanic, French, Hispanic, Anglo-Celtic, and Italian—Eastern Europe has more than fifteen nations jostling within its boundaries. Nor are many of these nations compact units: many have sizable minorities of other nations in their own midst and members of their own nation enveloped by others. The patchwork quilt has been produced by historical events that still embitter the atmosphere in many parts of the region today, often evoking nationalism in its more virulent forms.[1]

What has characterized the relations of these nations is not unity or cooperation, but the struggle for mastery and survival. Some nations would have preferred being left alone in their former subjection; their older masters were better than the new. The superior status of some was reduced to inferiority overnight. Many states found that their unity under oppression melted away when the oppression was over. The end of the great imperialisms begat little imperialisms. And these little imperialisms often were more virulent than the old.

Another major theme of this book is the distinctiveness between the two parts of Eastern Europe: East Central Europe and South Eastern Europe (the "Balkans"). The two areas, many would argue, are more than distinct: they are so different as to be incomparable—even incompatible. Perhaps. But throughout their history the independent states in both these parts of Eastern Europe have shared similar experiences in state-building and in political and economic development. They have also operated in the same international setting; parts of both regions have been ravaged by the two world wars. All of them for nearly a half-century were pressed into the communist mold. These experiences are still fresh and relevant enough to warrant an overall, if discriminating, perspective. It was the twentieth century that pulled them together. Early in the twenty-first century, the ties that once bound them will drop away.

Finally, a fourth major theme is continuity. The successive phases of modern East European history—imperial subjection, precarious independence, Soviet communist domination, and now renewed independence—would seem to be so different from one another as to preclude any suggestion of continuity. But, though it is too much to see history as essential continuity regardless of change, it remains true that all change, including revolution, has elements of continuity. In Poland, until recently, citizens' habits, attitudes, even personalities, differed according to whether their forebears had lived in Russian, Austrian, or Prussian Poland during the partitions. Other East European nations show marks of their imperial histories more obviously than the Poles do. Historical and national peculiarities helped to break up the flat standardization of communism. Now, after 1989, communism itself has left some indelible footprints.

Freedom Through Diplomacy

In the Balkans the course of independence lasted a whole century, starting with Serbia at the beginning of the nineteenth century, ending with the independence of Albania in 1912 and finally the creation of Yugoslavia after

World War I. In between, Greece, Romania, and Bulgaria became independent.[2] The will to national independence was there, and so were the heroism, the effort, the sacrifice. But it was the decline of the Ottoman empire, beginning in the seventeenth century, that decisively eased the process of independence. And what finally secured it was the diplomatic interplay of the great European powers, the workings of the "balance of power."

Many attempts have been made to define the balance of power, some downright incomprehensible. Bismarck's remains the crispest definition, as befits its most skillful practitioner: "Always try to be one of three in a world of five great powers."[3] The balance of power was a fluid concept, shifting and changing according to circumstance. But it governed international relations for much of modern history, and it was the midwife of Balkan independence.

The Congress of Berlin in June–July 1878 saw the balance of power at its zenith. In March 1877, Russia had brought into being through the Treaty of San Stefano imposed on Turkey not just an independent Bulgaria but a "Greater Bulgaria." It was good for the Bulgarians, obviously, but it also was good for the Russians, greatly enhancing their power in the Balkans. Hence, it upset the balance of power and alarmed Britain, Austria-Hungary, and Germany. Those countries faced down Russia, and the Treaty of San Stefano was revoked; the new Bulgaria was drastically reduced and a certain normalcy was restored. But, as often happened in the workings of the balance of power, where one problem was solved, another emerged. The "Macedonian Question" has now straddled three centuries. It began in earnest toward the end of the nineteenth century, continued throughout the twentieth, and is still unresolved at the beginning of the twenty-first (see chapter 7).

Freedom Through Ideology

World War I marked the end of the nineteenth century and the classic concept of the balance of power. The war itself was the sign and the measure of the demise of the balance of power, which did not immediately die. The mind-set that it had shaped lingered on irrelevantly for many years. After 1945, too, a new East-West balance of power emerged in Europe, but this was a rigid security balance, not a flexible diplomatic one. As the *governing* principle for international relations in Europe, the balance of power was dead. It had been an effective principle for most of the nineteenth century because it suited the powers that conducted it. It collapsed mainly because it

1. Eastern Europe in 1914. © Bartholomew Ltd 2000. Reproduced by permission of HarperCollins Ltd, Bishopbriggs, Scotland.

did not suit the ambitions of the newly reunited Germany. Bismarck would have gone on playing the game, but Kaiser Wilhelm II had neither the will nor the wit to.

At the Paris peace treaty meetings in 1919 and 1920, ideology touched down on the European scene in the person of U.S. President Woodrow Wilson and the doctrine of national self-determination. Wilson's insistence on this principle led to a drastic redrawing of the map of Eastern Europe, which called for the re-creation of Poland, the creation of Yugoslavia and Czechoslovakia, the survival of Albania, and the drastic diminution of Hungary. "Eastern Europe," as it generally was to be known through the rest of the twentieth century, came into being.

The new Wilsonian ideology, however, came and went. Wilson's policy was repudiated by the U.S. Congress, and the United States returned to isolationism, refusing to guard and smooth the wheels it had set in motion. In the meantime, two new ideologies, lethal threats to Wilsonianism and to democracy, had appeared on the European scene: communism and fascism. Soviet communism primarily threatened Russia's internal order. But, behind it, Russian imperialism threatened the new Eastern Europe. Italian fascism was imperialist-inspired, while German fascism was racist, imperialist, revanchist, and vengeful. Eastern Europe was also threatened by the machinations of two of its own states: Hungary and Bulgaria, "losers" at the Paris peace settlements and lackeys first of Italy, then of Germany. These ambitions, combinations, and machinations led to the destruction of interwar Eastern Europe and to World War II.

Still, for nearly twenty years, this new Eastern Europe survived. Geographically, Poland was its largest state. The Polish state had been destroyed in the second half of the eighteenth century, partitioned by Russia, Prussia, and Austria. But the Polish nation, though losing its freedom, never lost its will or its coherence. World War I gave it the opportunity to again move toward freedom, and the Treaty of Versailles brought the Polish state back to life.

The most spectacular, but eventually unsuccessful, state creations after World War I were Czechoslovakia and Yugoslavia, both daringly multinational. They were not the direct creations of the Paris treaties; they were inspired and conceived locally. But it was Wilsonianism that secured them. The original inspiration for them came from the nineteenth-century Romantic notion that ethnic and linguistic similarities could override cultural and historical differences and secure multinational states. This turned out to be a destructive myth. Wilsonianism was also to founder on the complexities of European history and on the depths of ethnic prejudice. A prolonged period of peace might have secured the success of the new East European order. But a prolonged period of peace could have been ensured only by what the United States in 1920 was not ready to give: a strong presence in, and commitment to, Europe. Britain and France could not secure the new principles that the United States had pressed in the peace settlements. They were too weak; and they were less than enthusiastic about these principles, anyway. Indirectly, they even encouraged the forces that destroyed them.

Czechoslovakia and Yugoslavia were cases of self-determination vulgarized and gone wrong. In 1921, more than 5 million Czechs lived in Czechoslovakia along with slightly less than 3 million Slovaks. More than 3 million Germans (slightly outnumbering the Slovaks), more than 700,000 Hungarians, and nearly 500,000 Ruthenians (Ukrainians) made up the rest of the population.[4] These figures reflected a dangerous lack of ethnic balance, even when only measured in raw numbers. Officially, Czechs and Slovaks were lumped together as "Czechoslovaks," a presumptuous Czech insistence that symbolized their scant regard for Slovak sensitivities. (Westerners routinely referred to "Czechoslovaks" as "Czechs.") Thus, 9 million "Czechoslovaks" resided in a country of slightly more than 13.5 million—hardly a commanding majority for an alleged majoritarian nation, especially when most Slovaks saw themselves as anything but majoritarian. In multinational states, however, numbers were by no means everything. History and attitudes counted for more. The Germans in Czechoslovakia had been the master nation in Bohemia and Moravia under the Habsburgs, and, almost without exception, they bristled rebelliously over the postwar dispensation. The Hungarians, too, had been masters, the historic "owners," of Slovakia, and they were just as adamant in their rejection of the new order. Wide discrepancies also existed in the civilizational level between the nations in the new Czechoslovakia. Germans, generally, were at the highest level, and many Czechs were up to the German level; certainly, Czechs were higher than most Hungarians. Slovaks were the next lowest in order, and Ruthenians pooled at the bottom. Interspersed among these nations were more than 300,000 Jews. In the Czech provinces, Jews certainly stood at the highest civilizational level; farther to the east, however, they often were just as poor as their fellow citizens, although usually better educated and more "savvy."

Yugoslavia was to be an even more damaging case of multinational failure. At first, the Yugoslav concept was not welcomed by the Serbs, who subsequently accepted it as the best option available. The Serbs' basic aim was to have "all Serbs under one roof," a twentieth-century update of Ilya Garašanin's *načertanije* idea.[5] They were now determined to twist the Yugoslav idea in the interests of Serbia; Yugoslavia would become, in fact, an extension of Serbia. But, even without the Serb Herrenvolk complex, this hastily cobbled Yugoslavia would have been difficult to contain. Slovenia and Croatia both insisted on being considered "Central European." Then came the Yugoslav "others": the Macedonians, most of whom had little national consciousness and found themselves in "South Serbia"; the Albanians, shut out of the new Albanian state and becoming ever more numerous in both Serb Kosovo and Serb Macedonia; and then the Turks, Vlachs, Gypsies, and many others. The Bosnian Muslims turned out to be the most crucial of all these others. After being slighted, or even discounted, for most of the twentieth century, they seared into the European conscience at the end of it.

The Ethnic Dimension

For every problem solved by the World War I settlements in Eastern Europe, another was made; for every injustice removed, a new injustice was created. This ominous confusion came about because of the ubiquity and intractability of the "ethnic dimension." (See chapters 6 and 7.) The coerciveness of former empires had served as a bridle on ethnic tensions, but once Austria-Hungary, Germany, the Ottoman empire, and tsarist Russia collapsed, the bridle was gone. Similarly, after 1989, when the Soviet empire and the communist system collapsed, the bridle that had been reset after 1945 was removed again, and historic tensions revived. The ethnic dimension had never really disappeared, but now it was back with no restraints.

Ethnic problems were by no means confined to Yugoslavia and Czechoslovakia. Romania, the big winner of the Paris peace treaties, had acquired Transylvania, which had a large and proud Hungarian community, and South Dobrudja, with a large Bulgarian populace. Bulgaria still had a very large Turkish community despite the Turkish exodus after virtual independence in 1878. The new Poland had more than 5 million Ukrainians, about 3 million Jews, and at least 2 million Germans. Even Hungary still had a relatively large minority of Slovaks, many of them in various stages of Magyarization.

Different types of national minorities also abounded.[6] Among the most significant and most problematical were the contiguous minorities, those living adjacent to the frontiers of a state ruled by members of their own nation. Hungarian minorities in Slovakia, Ruthenia, Yugoslavia, and Romania fell into this category, although in Transylvania, just to complicate matters, a large swath of Romanians, the new majoritarian nation, lived still closer to the new frontier with Hungary. In Bulgaria, more than half the Turkish minority lived adjacent to Turkey in the southeastern part of the country. The Kosovo Albanians (Kosovars) and most of the Macedonian Albanians lived next to Albania, where a large Greek minority lived adjacent to the border with Greece. Nor was the situation less acute in East Central Europe. Most of Poland's Ukrainian and Belorussian minorities lived next door to the Soviet Union, which had established "self-governing republics" in Ukraine and Belorussia. Large numbers of Lithuania's Polish minority fronted onto Poland.

Germans made up a huge minority in Eastern Europe and the Soviet Union, probably about 10 million in all. Many in Czechoslovakia and Poland lived adjacent to, or very near, Germany, but most resided in Yugoslavia, Romania, and Hungary as well as in the Soviet Union. By and large, the Germans were decent and constructive citizens until many of them succumbed to the temptations of Nazism after 1933.[7]

Other characteristics of minorities were just as meaningful as adjacency or nonadjacency. Two of them, closely linked, require a brief discussion.

REVERSAL OF STATUS

Some ethnic groupings had suddenly become minorities after generations, even centuries, of supremacy; often they once had dominated the very nations that now lorded it over them. These included Germans, Hungarians, Turks, Bosnians, and Albanian Muslims. Others had always been minorities—some tolerated, but most exploited, oppressed, and victimized. These included Jews, Vlachs, and Gypsies. In addition, some tiny minorities had no historical role except to be subjugated or ignored.

MINORITY ATTITUDES

No nation takes kindly to being knocked off its perch, but some were less philosophical about it than others. The Hungarians and the Sudeten Germans in Czechoslovakia were such groups; so were the Hungarians in Transylvania. Whether they would have become more reconciled, or at least resigned, had they not been stirred up from outside is open to debate. So can a converse question be debated: would the Balkan Turks, left high and dry by Ottoman disintegration, have been less resigned to their fate had they not thought that Kemal Atatürk's new Turkey had washed its hands of them.

Finally, a sobering reminder. Some of the worst treatment of minorities is by other minorities. Looked down on by the majority nation, every minority looks for other minorities that *it* can look down on. That has been the iron law of ethnic relations not only in Eastern Europe, but also in Western Europe and the United States, despite differing contexts.

MUSLIMS, JEWS, AND GYPSIES

These three large minorities deserve special attention. It is difficult to imagine three more different groups, yet a unique characteristic defined them: they had no homeland, or, more correctly, they were perceived, or perceived themselves, as having none. The Gypsies certainly did not. Neither did the Jews. (Zionism was barely afloat in 1918, and the ink scarcely dry on the Balfour Declaration.) With the Muslims, the situation was complex. They had lost the Ottoman setting, with which they had identified and in which they felt secure. Certainly, some Albanian Muslims now had a state, but few of them thought of it as a homeland.

In Bosnia the situation of the Muslims was poignant and precarious. Bosnia was indeed their home; ethnically and linguistically they were no different from the surrounding Serbs. But in the eyes of the Serbs they had committed the sin that made them unbridgeably different: apostasy. By embracing Islam and rejecting Orthodoxy, they had not only collaborated with the Ottomans (most Serbs had done the same); they had *identified* with them, converting to their religion, which meant that they had become part of them. And, as Muslims, they had been legally, socially, and economically superior to their Orthodox kinsmen. Now the boot was on the other foot, and the Serbs were in no mood for magnanimity. Ivo Andrić has a sensitive passage in *The Bridge over the Drina* about the Muslim plight. He describes Turkish power as having vanished "like an apparition." The Bosnian Muslims "had lived to see that power, like some fantastic ocean tide, suddenly withdraw and pass away somewhere far out of sight, while they remained here deceived and menaced, like seaweed on dry land, left to their own devices and their own evil fate."[8] That was how they appeared early in the twentieth century. Later, the Bosnian Muslims were to gain the status of a Yugoslav "nation" under Tito, but after the breakup of Yugoslavia they became another victim of twentieth-century genocide. So did the Kosovo Muslims, also pressed into the new Yugoslavia after World War I.

The Jews were to become victims of genocide on a scale unimaginable. In 1930, about 6 million Jews resided in Eastern Europe (excluding the Soviet Union), mainly concentrated in Poland and Romania. No sane person was prepared for the Holocaust, but dislike of the Jews was widespread and always liable to be whipped into active hatred. In the countryside, Jews were sometimes the stewards on the estates of absentee landlords. Many country innkeepers and moneylenders were Jews. Some of them did prey on ignorant and hopeless peasants, although prejudice, innate suspicions, and galloping rumor grossly exaggerated their misdeeds. The Roman Catholic Church and the Orthodox Church not only countenanced, but often encouraged, anti-Semitism. The fact that hundreds of thousands of poor Jews resided in both town and country was often ignored.

In the cities and larger towns the "Jewish Question" was more complicated. Large numbers of Jews had lived in those places for generations, often in overcrowded ghettos. In some cities they numbered up to one-fourth, even one-third, of the population. In a few places they comprised more than a half the populace. A tiny fraction of them became multimillionaires in finance and industry. In Hungary especially, many Jews were thoroughly assimilated and ardently patriotic, as they were in Germany.[9] But it was the small-business Jews and shopkeepers who endured the worst of urban anti-Semitism. This bigotry was often dubbed "economic anti-Semitism" and held to be somewhat more respectable than other varieties of prejudice. Jews also were conspicuous in culture, science, and the "free professions," bunching there because access to some other careers was denied them. And while many Jews were successful capitalists, others became ardent communists. Hence, accusing fingers were pointed at them on two counts. With the economic depression, the rise of German Nazism, and the overall search for scapegoats, the Jews were the obvious target. What had once been a prejudice against them, or perhaps a fixation, was becoming an obsession as the restraints on public barbarism began to collapse. Anti-Semitism, in fact, was an integral part of East European culture. This bias did not preclude relations of respect between many Jews and Gentiles, and many Gentiles were truly horrified by the Nazis' treatment of the Jews. But the general prejudice existed, and the efforts of many East Europeans to mitigate or explain away their anti-Semitism have always been unconvincing. In fact, the vehemence with which some do it is often in itself a measure of the malady they seek to deny.

Finally, the Gypsies. When the Nazi pogroms were beginning, a German Jew is reported to have said that, while he knew many people disliked the Jews, he was mystified about the persecution of the Gypsies. What had they done? They had done nothing (except perhaps steal a bit—sometimes a lot—and behave "antisocially"). But they were different, very different, from the prescribed Aryan ideal. They were also free spirits, unaccountable. They had what is anathema to any totalitarian dictatorship: spontaneity. The Nazis killed about a half-million of them.

Gypsies not only are unaccountable, but they are uncountable, too. In Eastern Europe in the 1930s, Gypsies numbered probably about 1 million or even fewer. Many of them were engaged in jobs like tinkering, carpentry, basketry, horse breeding, or horse stealing. Most East Europeans regarded them as falling somewhere between a nuisance and a problem. But Gypsies formed only part of the background. East Europeans were not obsessed with them, as the Nazis became. As for the Gypsies themselves, absolutely no concept of Gypsy power, even Gypsy organization, existed among them. "Leave us alone" was their guiding slogan.[10] That demand remained the same at the end of the century, but by that time their problems had re-emerged (see chapter 8).

Groups and Nations

Ethnic groups and nations, ethnicity and nationalism, all have been studied voluminously. But so far they have escaped convincing and comprehensive definitions. Perhaps wise approximation of all four subjects will have to do since the quest for exactness might confuse rather than illuminate.

In the East European context some ethnic groups existed until well into the twentieth century without having any national consciousness. This was true in Galicia, for example, in the Kresy in what became eastern Poland, and in Macedonia. They were "natives," "people from here," *tutejsi*. Almost exclusively, they were peasants whose sense of national identity was subsequently formed by a combination of urban intellectual propaganda, modern communications, education, Christian denominationalism, war, and oppression.

What, then, were nations? Joseph Stalin, an expert in defining them as well as destroying them, saw the main components of nations in language, territory, similarity of economic system, and similarity of psychological setup or culture.[11] (Coming from Stalin, the third component was only to be expected; the fourth raised eyebrows.) One of the most satisfying definitions—practical, precise, and muscular—came from a group of Serbian rebels who went to see Lajos Kossuth, the Hungarian leader, in April 1848. (Kossuth was rebelling against the Austrians and the Serbs were rebelling against the Hungarians in a multiple national struggle.) When Kossuth contemptuously asked the Serbs what they understood by "nation," they replied: "a race which possesses its own language, customs, and culture, *and enough self-consciousness to preserve them.*"[12] These Serbs were not so much defining nationhood as showing that they were a living example of it.

What, then, was nationalism? Ernest Renan's chestnut about a nation being a "group of people united by a common error about their ancestry and a common dislike of their neighbors" not so much defines nationalism as describes it. Nationalism is nations being human, with all the negative consequences that follow.[13] It became an amalgam of fulfillment, frustration, and aggression; it also added a real dimension to the tribal suspicions that already existed. The notion of "ancient hatreds" has become unfashionable recently because of its sloppy use by Western writers and politicians during the Yugoslav wars of the 1990s. It seemed to relieve the writers of deeper analysis and the politicians of deeper engagement. But tribal suspicions and resentments always existed, waiting to be tapped, channeled, and fanned into full-blown hatreds. Dark centuries were indeed sleeping.

The most satisfying summation I have seen of the emergence of nationalism from the concept of nation is that of R. J. W. Evans:

> But what is a nation? We can identify two basic senses of the term, one older in origin, on the whole, and the other younger. On the one hand, a nation is a community bound together by residence in a given territory. On the other, it is a community bound together by ties of language, tradition, religion, or culture in general. The first kind of nation defines itself through citizenship, the second through ethnicity. In 1848, these two principles first confronted each other directly. Patriotism, allegiance to one's country, found itself outflanked by nationalism, allegiance to one's ethnic kin. From that time on, nationalism progressively became the dominant motive force, threatening the

breakup of existing states, forcing strategists of the prevailing political order to take on board its own weapons.[14]

In Eastern Europe the emergence of ethnic nationalism was eased by the sense of cultural superiority that some nations had always felt regarding others. As Eric Hobsbawm put it: "The true distinction (between ethnic groups) . . . demarcates felt superiority from imputed inferiority, as defined by those who see themselves as 'better,' that is to say usually belonging to a higher intellectual, cultural or even biological class than their neighbors."[15]

After the world war the peacemakers partly accepted the growing dominance of ethnic nationalism by breaking up Austria-Hungary; they then sought partly to reverse their action by establishing Yugoslavia and Czechoslovakia. In the erstwhile Russian empire, the triumphant communists, despite their earlier promises, stamped out the many sprouting national movements and, despite the pretense of ethnic devolution, reimposed their own imperial control. After 1989, resurgent ethnic nationalism destroyed the Soviet Union, Yugoslavia, and Czechoslovakia, and it seriously threatened Russia itself.

The International Setting

The international setting, which always has been decisive for the East European states, has changed remarkably in the twentieth century. In the few years after 1918, a power vacuum developed in Europe. Neither Britain nor France had the strength or the will to fill it. The United States helped win the war, and it then helped make the peace but then withdrew. Soon, however, Germany and Russia revived under aggressive totalitarianisms, and a series of momentous and bewildering changes buffeted Eastern Europe. In 1945, Germany lay shattered and divided. The East European states became satellites of the victorious Soviet Union. The United States, having returned victoriously to Europe, now stayed and became the West's leader in the cold war. The United States and Russia were now the two superpowers; Britain and France had lost world and Continental influence. From 1989 through 1992, the Soviet Union and the communist system collapsed. Germany now stood powerful and reunited. The United States was the sole superpower.

Although the United States had withdrawn from Europe after World War I, it continued to have a profound social, economic, cultural, and ideological impact on tens of millions of Europeans—especially East Europeans. The United States remained the land of hope for them. It offered the prospect not only of escape, but of freedom, fulfillment, and a better life. And those who did emigrate kept in touch with their many relatives and friends back home. The East European ruling and cultural elites despised or patronized the United States, as did their counterparts in Western Europe. (The United States was where the lower orders and the Jews went.) The elites smirked when Clemenceau described the United States as the only nation that had gone from barbarism to decadence without the usual interval of civilization.

Little can be said about Britain and France during the interwar period. A vigorous Franco-British partnership might have made up for the American absence. But the old mutual suspicions remained, and vigor was the last thing that characterized either nation. Britain's role was provincial and discreditable; at Munich in 1938 it became shameful. France was more active, and a French system of alliances developed in Eastern Europe.[16] This network, for a while, preserved the illusion of French power and leadership. But in the end, French policy proved to have been little more than posturing. France tried to give Eastern Europe assurance, but all the while it was losing its own.

Under its new management after 1918, Russia's official philosophy and values changed, but not its concept of national interest. In fact, its ideology, Bolshevism, gave Russian foreign policy a powerful new dynamic. Its first, most tangible impact in Eastern Europe was the establishment of the Béla Kun communist republic in Hungary in 1919. This advance, along with spectacular communist successes in Germany, aroused the fear of red revolution across the European continent. But the new Poland heroically turned back the new Russia in 1920. The Bolshevik scare soon subsided. Moscow, too, quietly dropped its strategy of world revolution and concentrated on "socialism in one country." Yet those early fears of the new Russia left their mark on Eastern Europe. Communist parties, as such, were banned in several countries. Anti-Semitism, too, markedly increased. Jews were at first seen to be associated with the new, threatening socialist movement. "Communism: Jewry's new weapon" became a rallying call for Europe's proliferating anti-Semites.

Germany was not done to as badly by World War I and its aftermath as many Germans wanted to believe. Joseph Rothschild has pointed this out:

The defeat of Germany in 1918 was deceptive. Neither in absolute nor in relative terms had Germany been weakened to anything like the extent that was often assumed in the 1920s. In absolute terms, Germany's industrial and transportation resources had been left largely intact because World War I had not been fought on her territory. In relative terms, a territorial settlement predicated on the national principle, such as now ensued in 1919–21, *ipso facto* left Germany as Europe's second largest country after Russia. . . . [17]

Strategically, too, Germany benefited from the end of the Habsburg empire and the pushing back of Russia, by the liberation of the Baltic states and the re-creation of Poland. The new small and weak states on its eastern borders were tempting waters to fish in, and Germany would take full advantage of this over the next twenty years. True, Germany was severely punished by the post–World War I treaties, but it was not punished nearly as vindictively as the Germans had penalized the Russians by the treaty of Brest-Litovsk in March 1918. In Orlando Figes's term, Brest-Litovsk reduced European Russia to a status on a par with "seventeenth-century Muscovy."[18] By comparison, Versailles was a model of magnanimity.

Finally, Italy. Unified about the same time as Germany, it thrust itself into major power status only with the seizure of power by Benito Mussolini and the fascists in 1922. Even before then, however, Italy had begun staking its claims to territory in southeastern Europe, north and east Africa, and the eastern Mediterranean. Imperialism was de rigueur in Europe, and Italy wanted to gain from it. Under Mussolini, Italy became the schoolyard bully in the Balkans, threatening Yugoslavia through intimidation and terrorism, and turning Albania first into a protectorate and then a colony. In World War II, Italy invaded Greece but was soon defeated. Mussolini had once fancied himself as the driving force in the Balkans, but he needed Hitler when he drove into trouble.

The Regional Setting

The peace treaties after World War I may have shaped the concept of Eastern Europe as a region with a regional identity, but in no sense did the treaties give the newly conceived region a sense of unity. Indeed, the principle of self-determination on which the new states were now supposedly based, even if it had been interpreted fairly and applied wisely, ensured disunity. The new Eastern Europe was a jarring mosaic; most of its pieces did not fit. It was doomed to disintegrate, either through its own incompatibilities or through outside interference—or for both reasons.

POLAND

Of the Eastern European states, Poland was among the most susceptible to outside menace. It had been re-created out of three defeated empires, one of which (the Habsburg) had passed totally out of existence, and for several years the successors of the other two were in no condition to threaten. But German and Russian resentment over the territories each had lost to the new Poland never diminished, and, though Nazi Germany and Soviet Russia were mortal enemies, they did agree on Poland's eventual destruction. The fourth partition of Poland was on the horizon, and that horizon was near. The Poles were well aware of being in the nutcracker between Germany and Russia. They first looked to France for protection. But in 1934, a year after Hitler's assumption of power, they signed a nonaggression treaty with Germany. This act was realistic in intent; it accepted the fact that no one would stand up to Germany. But it was totally unrealistic as a means of mitigating the German danger. And it gave the world the impression that Poland, a quasi-dictatorship itself, was moving toward the European dictators.

With the rest of Eastern Europe, Poland's relations oscillated between correctness and tension. It signed an alliance with Romania with which it now shared a frontier. A long-standing fellow feeling with Hungary, the other "gentry nation," also persisted. With two of its new neighbors, Lithuania and Czechoslovakia, relations were strained over territorial issues: Vilnius (Wilno) with Lithuania and Těšín (Cieszyn) with Czechoslovakia. Ethnographically, Poland had good claims to both places. It unceremoniously incorporated Vilnius in 1920, leaving the Lithuanians, who regarded it as their historic capital, duly aggrieved. Then came the Poles' turn to be aggrieved when Czechoslovakia induced the Western allies to give it Těšín in 1920; no credit was to be gained, however, by Poland's grabbing it back when Czechoslovakia was dismantled in 1939. Basically, Poland's attitude toward Eastern Europe has continually been that of a big fish among minnows; it has done itself little good when it has tried to turn from a big fish into a shark.

Czechoslovakia was a mosaic in itself, a fragile creation that could have survived only with international stability and goodwill. It had two angry minorities: the Germans and the Hungarians. But the Czech-Slovak relationship itself contained the seeds of Czechoslovakia's destruction. That relationship was characterized by Czech superiority, which, however benevolent, rankled with most Slovaks. The few Slovaks prepared to collaborate with the system and with the myth of "Czechoslovakism" were mainly from the Protestant and Jewish elites, which felt endangered and largely despised by the primitive and intolerant Catholic Slovak majority. This majority was offended or bemused by the Czechoslovak concept. For most Czechs, the idea was simply a cover or a euphemism for their own superiority. This sense of superiority continued throughout Czechoslovakia's entire history. Between the world wars, this sense of superiority showed itself in disregard, condescension, or contempt. During World War II the Czechs despised the Slovaks for collaborating with the Nazis (although many of them collaborated too). After it, they resisted the notion of greater rights for the Slovaks. Many Czechs were reserved about federal status for Slovakia in 1968, and many were flatly opposed to it. They then came to resent the Slovaks' adaptation to Gustáv Husák's "normalization" after 1968, incensed by the fact that Husák himself was a Slovak. After 1989 they were unsympathetic to the Slovaks' determination to fully assert their identity. And, after 1993, it was good riddance. Looking back, it was a marriage made, if not in hell, then certainly in haste.

ROMANIA

After 1918, Romania became more than double its former size and population. The old Regat became Greater Romania almost overnight. No one had expected it would do so well at the Paris peace settlement. But the Romanian state (unlike most Romanian citizens) had always been touched by luck. It came into being in 1861 through a masterly sleight of hand; it then got a capable and durable king (Charles I), wished on it by the European powers. In the Balkan wars of 1912 and 1913, Romania tried to get as much territory as it could with the least possible military effort. Then, in World War I, it broke its treaty obligations with the Central Powers to side with the Allies. Its armies, poorly led but fighting stubbornly, were mauled by the Germans in the war. In the war's aftermath, Romania came to the Paris peace negotiations with its reputation lower than ever. But it benefited hugely from Wilsonianism at Paris and a general desire to punish Hungary, gaining both Transylvania and Bessarabia.[19] It had already gained South Dobrudja after the second Balkan war. But Romania's bounty brought acute internal problems. Many of its new non-Romanian citizens were less than euphoric about their new status. Externally, Hungary, Bulgaria, and the Soviet Union now became its resentful enemies because of their territorial losses to it. Skillful diplomacy, centered on closeness to France, its "Latin sister," brought Romania temporary breathing space. But Greater Romania, an ethnic jigsaw puzzle rather than a coherent state, and badly governed at that, could not last. Transylvania was its brightest acquisition, one justified on both ethnographical and historical grounds. But even the Romanians in Transylvania, accustomed to a higher level of public life under Magyar rule, were dismayed by the imported standards of the old Regat. They did not want to turn the clock back; they simply wished that their compatriots were a little more advanced.

HUNGARY

With the post–World War I treaties, Romania won big. Hungary lost bigger. The treaty of Trianon, the specific Paris treaty that dealt with Hungary, stripped it of two-thirds of its former territory and of one-third of its ethnic Hungarian subjects. More than 5 million of the 8 million troops mobilized by Hungary in World War I had been killed, wounded, reported missing, or taken prisoner.[20] Of special concern to its ruling class was postwar Hungary's almost total loss of European and regional influence. Under the Habsburgs, especially after the *Ausgleich* of 1867, Hungary was a major European power, exerting decisive influence on the empire in matters of foreign policy. Now it was reduced to a self-pitying rump. No doubt, Trianon was in some instances unfair to Hungary. It suffered the loss to the new Czechoslovakia of part of Southern Slovakia, for example, which was overwhelmingly Hungarian in population, and some parts of Transylvania were also overwhelmingly Hungarian. But Hungary met with little international sympathy, even less when it subsequently became the vassal of Germany and Italy in pursuit of its irredentism. Still, Trianon not only incensed Hungary's ruling class, but it dug deep into the marrow of ordinary Hungarians. Trianon's penalties continued to engender resentment into the communist era, and they still do. But now, after all the suffering, the errors, and the guilt, the pain has lessened, the passions calmed, and the lessons of history have largely been learned. Irredentists still loudly exist (deafeningly in the diaspora), but even they know that little encouragement will come from anywhere.

BULGARIA

After the Paris treaties of 1918, Bulgaria was the other loser. However, where Hungary was mourning something that it had lost, Bulgaria was mourning something it had never had—at least not in modern times. In its efforts to win Macedonia, Bulgaria, between the first Balkan war in 1913 and the end of World War I, lost not only considerable territory but 155,000 of its soldiers lost in battle and in sickness, more than 400,000 wounded, 150,000 civilians dead as a result of various epidemics (this in a country of fewer than 5 million).[21] After the second Balkan war later in 1913, Bulgaria also lost South Dobrudja to Romania (it was regained in 1940), and its only window onto the Aegean Sea at Dedeagach (Alexandroupolis) was taken away at the end of World War I. As a result of these humiliations, Bulgaria saw the destruction of whatever internal political composure it had ever had. For well over a decade after World War I, Bulgarian public life was convulsed by political violence. Bulgaria also lost its international reputation, which it has never regained. It remains a sad country. The contrast with its neighbor, Romania, has been poignant and telling. It is best symbolized by two historic commemorative dates. After 1989, both countries quickly ditched their communist annual "national" holidays (marking their "liberation" by the Soviets after World War II). Bulgaria reverted to March 3, the day that the treaty of San Stefano was signed in 1878. Romania chose November 1, the day the Romanian nation willed the return of Transylvania in 1918. On the Romanian side, fulfillment; on the Bulgarian, pathos.

ALBANIA

Albania existed on sufferance. Except for President Wilson, it would not have survived World War I. The new Yugoslavia and Greece coveted parts of it, and after 1922 Italy saw it as an easy target. A client state from the outset, therefore, Albania's foreign policy was driven by its reading of which neighbor threatened it the most. That appeared to be Serbia, now dominating the new Yugoslavia. The Italians were undoubtedly preferable to the Serbs and the Greeks, just as the Ottomans had been preferable throughout the nineteenth century. At first, the Italians seemed to provide protection. But the price for it turned out to be too high.

Yugoslavia was conceived as a historic opportunity. But immediately it became a historic mismatch between its two strongest nations, the Serbs and the Croats, two flowers from the same stem but growing in different directions over the centuries. Serbs (and Montenegrins) more than doubled the number of Croats. Belgrade, the nineteenth-century capital of Serbia, was also the Yugoslav capital; thus, the Serb royal house became the royal house of the new state, which until 1929 was officially titled the Kingdom of Serbs, Croats, and Slovenes. The Serbs unquestionably had superior status, which was loudly proclaimed by themselves and recognized by the rest of the world—by everyone, in fact, except the Croats. The Serbs were a proud nation, full of their history, convinced of their destiny, totally unmindful of their neighbors. Their pride dated back to their medieval kingdom and was bolstered by myth, memory, and manipulation (see chapter 6). In modern times, Serbia became the first Balkan nation to strike for independence from Turkish rule. A hundred years later, the Serbs hardened their reputation for bravery and endurance in World War I. In short, the Serbs saw themselves as both heroic and deserving—deserving at the very least to be brought together in one country. This meant that the Serbs would be not just the "majoritarian nation" in the new Yugoslavia, but the nation *exclusively* in charge.

No one saw the Croats as heroic. They fell under Hungarian rule at the beginning of the twelfth century and remained there for 700 years, not exactly without a murmur, but with no epic resistance. In terms of religion, culture, and civic standards, the Croats were more Central European than Balkan. They were also Roman Catholic. Magyar rule, though hardly enlightened, was never nearly as benighted as Turkish domination. The Magyars' higher level of public life rubbed off on many subject Croats. The Serb community in Croatia, descendants of the *prečani* who had left the Old Serbia, also benefited. The Serbs in Croatia had a much higher overall culture than their kinsmen in Serbia itself, and many returned to Serbia in the nineteenth century to help run the new Serbian governmental service.

In short, the Serbs had what the Croats did not, and vice versa. But what resulted was not complementarity but conflict, not a developing mutual identity but a speedily growing alienation. "God save me from Serb heroism and Croatian culture," wrote the novelist Miroslav Krleza, himself a Croat.[22] It was a devilish mix and was to culminate in the mass slaughters of World War II and in the Yugoslav wars of the 1990s.

Failures of Regional Cooperation

The kind of cooperation that emerged in Eastern Europe after 1918 was negative: against rather than for, performed out of fear rather than hope. The Little Entente was devised primarily against Hungary, and the Balkan Entente was primarily against Bulgaria. The Little Entente was formed as early as 1920–21. It was blessed by France and consisted of Czechoslovakia, Romania, and Yugoslavia, all three of which had benefited from the dismantling of Hungary at Trianon. Though widely hailed as an example of the new European diplomacy, the Little Entente was a sham from the start. Hungary was weaker than any *one* of these three allied states. But the Little Entente's clearest weakness was that it made no provision for mutual defense against any of the three major powers—Germany, Italy, and Soviet Russia—that had designs against one or more of them and that might collude with Hungary, as Germany and Italy soon did. The Little Entente thus was a case of overkill against a shared lesser danger and of every man for himself when it came to the main danger.[23] It was practically an open invitation to Berlin and Rome to pick off the Little Entente's members individually—salami tactics on an international scale.[24]

Romania and Yugoslavia were also members of the Balkan Entente, which began to be formed in 1930. This agreement marked a more genuine effort at regional reconciliation. Greece and Turkey, also members, were being brought closer by the efforts of Eleftherios Venizelos and Kemal Atatürk, and some effort was initially made to induce Bulgaria to join. But Bulgaria wanted territorial concessions that no one was prepared to entertain. (Albania was virtually ignored.) Again, no provisions were made against interference from outside the region. No country was prepared to help a supposed ally if that ally were attacked by a major power. The Balkan Entente, therefore, like the Little Entente, was a dilettantish gesture.[25] The League of Nations was the midwife of both treaties. But like the United Nations that followed, the League was only as good as the "international community" wanted it to be, or would make sacrifices for it to be.

Dictator diplomacy was the twentieth-century reality in Eastern Europe, with Fascist Italy and then Nazi Germany setting the pattern. Both regarded Eastern Europe as an area of opportunity. In the 1920s, Fascist Italy was alone, but in the 1930s it first had to cooperate with, then follow, and later hang on to Nazi Germany. Hitler's destructive aims were directed at Poland and Czechoslovakia. For the rest, his aim was subjection. Berlin took up the

2. Eastern Europe in 1925. © Bartholomew 1998. Reproduced by
permission of HarperCollins Publishers Ltd, Bishopbriggs, Scotland.

cause of irredentist Hungary, gradually edging out Italy as the "champion of the victimized." The Nazi government subverted the loyalties of the large German minorities in Eastern Europe and encouraged the emergence of fascist or quasi-fascist governments in Bulgaria, Romania, Yugoslavia, and Hungary. It also pursued an inspired commercial policy that won support for Germany in unexpected sections of East European society. Germany was ready to buy up the entire agricultural surpluses of Romania and Yugoslavia as well as to take their mineral and oil exports. This proposal came at a time when the world economic depression was ravaging Eastern Europe, when Britain and France were doing little to alleviate hardships, and when the East Europeans were incapable of helping themselves or each other. Subversion and coercion were the hallmarks of Nazi diplomacy, but it was not without its inducements either.[26]

Domestic Debilities

"We never had a chance." One has heard that often from members of the older generation of East Europeans. They are probably right. But they usually are referring to the international situation that militated against their independence, to the external predators just biding their time. Only rarely do older East Europeans emphasize the internal weaknesses that undermined their ability and often their will to resist. They were not responsible for these weaknesses in the sense that they did not originate them. But many of them *were* responsible in that they did little or nothing about them—hence, perpetuating them. Some actually saw these weaknesses as strengths and benefited from them.

The most debilitating weakness was the class structure. True, a civic bourgeoisie thrived in Bohemia. Here, in the cities, the advanced civilization of Germans and Jews had rubbed onto many Czechs in the relaxed atmosphere of Austrian Habsburg rule. Elsewhere, strong elements of a bourgeoisie were present in Budapest, Cracow, and in Slovenia, again leavened, even dominated, by Germans and Jews.

But the peasantry remained by far the biggest section of society. It had corporate consciousness, but little civic consciousness. As they had in pre-revolutionary Russia, some urban intellectuals tried preaching a sense of patriotism to the peasants, but most peasants remained impervious to that message as well. They also were bemused by what many intellectuals tried to make of them in their search for a "national essence." However indefinable (or mythical) this national essence may have been, nationalist intellectuals often were convinced that they had found it in the peasantry. The result was that this unfortunate mass of humanity, who wanted more land, lower taxes, and fairer treatment, but whose lives remained nasty, brutish, and short, became romanticized and idealized beyond all reality, dignity, and respect.

Some peasants realized the fools that others were making of them. But only a few grasped the potential power they had. The region was overwhelmingly and inefficiently agricultural, the victim of "rural undercapitalization, underproductivity, underconsumption, underemployment, overpopulation, and pervasive misery."[27] During the interwar period, serious attempts were made to promote manufacturing industry throughout the region, but these efforts had little impact on the economy as a whole. The extractive industries were largely foreign-owned. On the eve of World War II, the economies of every country except Czechoslovakia were still dangerously one-sided and unproductive. Their fates were still being determined by each year's weather. In 1938, Eastern Europe produced only 8 percent of the industrial output of all Europe, minus the Soviet Union, and one-third of this total was produced in Czechoslovakia.[28] The situation called for radical change.

At the other end of the social spectrum from the peasants, and increasingly hated by them, were the nobility, the landowners. Some of the nobility were poor, scarcely better off than some of the peasants. What counted, however, was not fat purses but long lineages. Some of the biggest landowners preferred loafing in the capital or abroad and only rarely saw their land. They often were cultivated, multilingual, and exhaustively au courant. Just what use they were was open to debate.

The East European states were mainly governed by their bureaucracies. These bureaucracies were generally ethnically "native" (Jews need not apply) and recruited from the intelligentsia, a large, inchoate group of people, almost invariably men, who had some kind of university degree or diploma. Many bureaucrats were lawyers; many others had read in the humanities, while only a few were engineers or had some practical qualification. Members of the intelligentsia who were not absorbed into the bureaucracy tended to be drawn into the two most radical political movements of the time: fascism and communism. In neighboring countries, with many similar problems, they could be drawn to opposing extremes. In Yugoslavia, and certainly in Serbia, the magnetic pull was generally to communism; in

Romania, to fascism. The bureaucracies developed their own corporate sense and became the East European governing class (almost caste) during the interwar period. They were decimated by World War II and by the communist takeover, when they were replaced by generally much less competent successors.

The military played a key role in some of the East European states—for example, in Poland after 1926, increasingly in Bulgaria in the 1930s, in Yugoslavia, where the officer class was predominantly Serbian, and in Romania. In Poland, mainly because of its victory over the new Red Army in 1920, the army became the most highly regarded section of society, a distinction it kept throughout the century. On the other hand, in Czechoslovakia, where civil rule predominated, the army was less respected. Taking the region as a whole, the military was nationalist and tended toward fascism. It usually remained in its barracks, but it sometimes preferred the corridors of power.

The constitutions of the East European states were Western-inspired and usually modeled on specific Western examples. They were almost totally ornamental, rather like waxed fruit selections in glass domes that once adorned family sideboards. They certainly had little bearing on the political behavior they were supposed to mirror and determine. The free elections stipulated by them were often travesties, the results cynically manipulated and cynically accepted. In Hungary there was not much even to be cynical about: the electorate was restricted, and voting in the countryside was public. (Eighteenth-century England seemed more the model here.) Czechoslovakia was again the shining exception, but ballot-box stuffing and vote intimidation was not unknown in Slovakia and Ruthenia. Still, it was not unknown in the West either.

Balkan constitutions were monarchical, while those in East Central Europe were mostly republican. The first constitutions were drafted when monarchies were the fashion, the second when republicanism was challenging it. Two royal houses, the Yugoslav and the Albanian, were local; the Bulgarian, Romanian, and Greek stemmed from Western or Central Europe. They were no worse, and much less dull, than their Western counterparts. Politically, most monarchs definitely preferred authoritarianism to constitutionalism, and in the 1930s "royal dictatorship" became the norm throughout the Balkans. The pick of all the monarchs was probably Charles I of Romania, who died at the beginning of World War I, thereby missing the spectacular gains his country garnered from it. The biggest disaster—though by no means the least able—was Ferdinand, prince and then king of Bulgaria, "Foxy Ferdinand," who was deposed after his country's calamities in the Great War. Although a tragic failure (and perversely romanticized by the likes of Rebecca West),[29] Alexander II of Yugoslavia did try hard to give his country some meaning. So did Zog I (Ahmed Zogu, the "bandit king" of the Albanians). But it was Charles II of Romania (King Carol) who grabbed the headlines. His private life was enviably dramatic, but it was his desperate machinations, too clever by half, as royal dictator that remain in historical memory. For convoluted reasons, Hungary was a regency. The regent was Miklós Horthy, a former admiral, "a regent without a kingdom and an admiral without a sea." His status epitomized one aspect of interwar Hungary: its operettalike absurdity. Horthy, though, was not without decent instincts; had he lived in better times, he might be better remembered.

In Eastern Europe as a whole, only two great political figures stepped forward during the interwar period: Thomas Masaryk and Józef Piłsudski. Masaryk is still remembered, even revered, by many Czechs (by many others, too) as a great liberal democrat and constitutionalist (Václav Havel is of his tradition but not his stature). "Democracy means debate" was one of his favorite maxims. None of this rhetoric appealed much to Piłsudski, who was far from being a democratic role model. But he secured Poland's independence, saved it, and worked tirelessly for its consolidation and coherence. Subsequently, he was to appeal to Poles of all generations and persuasions. (Both Lech Wałęsa and Wojciech Jaruzelski regarded him as their hero.) Masaryk and Piłsudski personified a telling political contrast between Czechs and Poles—certainly at the time, perhaps less so today. For Masaryk, freedom was primarily for the individual vis-à-vis the state. For Piłsudski, freedom was primarily the freedom of the nation vis-à-vis the predators surrounding it.

The East European states began, as their constitutions provided, with representative institutions. The question was whether they themselves could become genuine states and whether their institutions could become truly representative and eventually democratic. The more perspicacious East Europeans knew that this outcome would take time, that progress would have to be solid and consolidated, that neither magic wand nor sleight-of-hand could play a part. Still, during the 1920s, with the startling exception of Poland after Piłsudski's coup in 1926, Eastern Europe generally seemed to be on a slowly staggering democratic path. The Great Depression, beginning in

1929, blew them off that pathway. Every country except Czechoslovakia, soon to be doomed anyway, turned to authoritarianism. The Depression was destroying democracies in Western Europe, too, most notably in Germany. There, Hitler and Nazism emerged triumphant. It was the Depression therefore that undermined the democratic will in Eastern Europe and set in motion events that were to destroy its freedom.

The first distinct period of East European existence ended with the onset of World War II. Not a single state and not a single nation escaped its impact. The Jews were virtually annihilated, and the Poles and Yugoslavs suffered immense losses. The material and moral damage done to some countries was enormous. And, although some states had been less innocent than others, none had caused the harm that befell all of them. What the interwar period and then the war underlined was that none of them was the master of its own fate. But no one was prepared for the riveted dependency into which they were forced after the war.

2

Communist Rule: La Longue Durée

WORLD WAR II CLOSED DOWN the first phase of Eastern Europe's independence in modern history. The war began in Eastern Europe, just as World War I had begun there. But the East Europeans were to blame for neither war. It was the fault of Central European predators: first, the last imperialist gasps of the Habsburg monarchy, and then the all too vigorous expansionism of Nazi Germany.

Nowhere was World War II more complicated than in Eastern Europe. Much of the fighting there reflected the ethnic and territorial conflicts that had traditionally beset the region (briefly discussed in chapter 1). Germany's aims were Lebensraum, genocide, and subjugation. Soviet Russia's aim was first to recover territories lost after World War I, then to resist the German invasion, and eventually to take over Eastern Europe for imperialistic, security, and ideological reasons. The motives of these two Great Powers were, therefore, simple. The motives of those "lands between" were much less simple, and their fates varied widely.[1]

The Polish nation, faced with enslavement, fought for its very survival. Many Czechs reluctantly collaborated with the Germans. The Slovaks were allowed their own clerical-fascist puppet state. The Hungarians, their irredentism partly satisfied, drifted ineluctably toward the German camp and then crossed ignominiously into it. Romania, forced at the beginning of the war to shed some of the gains it had made after World War I, fought initially against the Russians in the hope of not losing any more, then changed sides when the Russians had virtually won the war. Bulgaria backed Germany to regain South Dobrudja and grab as much of Macedonia as it could. But its government, mindful of its public, never formally declared war against the

Soviet Union. The Albanians were not too unhappy under Italian and German occupation; it was better than being overcome by Serbia or Greece.

In Yugoslavia the ethnic tensions that had been growing since the state was created burst into hatred. Under German occupation, Croatia, like Slovakia, became a clerical-fascist puppet, but infinitely the more murderous one. Slovenia was divided between Germany, Italy, and Hungary. Many Muslims supported the Germans, as did many Albanians in Kosovo and Macedonia. The Macedonians took a closer look at their Bulgarian "brothers" and decided they were better off without them. The Serbs, initially the targets of Hitler's wrath, were far from united against the German occupation. Some produced their own version of Marshal Pétain and his collaborationist regime; others, though unquestionably patriotic, found themselves fighting along with the Germans; and many others, as they had done under the Turks, settled for as quiet a life as possible. Tito's Partisans eventually did constitute a red thread of unity through all of these Yugoslav divergences. But the civil war, which they eventually won, killed more Yugoslavs than the struggle against the original German enemy.[2]

The impact of the war was as mixed as the motives of those involved in it. It devastated Poland and Yugoslavia in terms of human and material losses as well as economic dislocation. Hungary, Bulgaria, and Romania suffered severely, although some branches of their economies were less affected than at first was thought. Relatively little harm befell the Czechoslovak economy.

When the war ended, most East Europeans were united on one thing: there could be no return to normalcy, that is, the status quo ante bellum. But what kind of change would occur? What was the alternative to normalcy? The victorious Russians and the local communists had no doubts. But the voters' preference, as long as it was allowed to express itself, was more democratic than communist. It was, ironically, in the Czech Lands of Czechoslovakia that procommunist sympathy was strongest. There, where democracy had been embedded and political culture was highest, the communists initially won the support of a strong minority—nearly 40 percent of the voters in the local elections of 1946. (In Slovakia it was 30 percent.) In one sense, this vote marked a return to the prewar past, when communism had always played a considerable role in Central Europe—not only in Czechoslovakia, but in both Germany and Austria before fascism, or neofascism, took over. But other reasons can be identified for the Czech "exception": the sapping of public morale over the country's poor war record; the disgust at Britain and France after the betrayal in 1938; a corresponding respect for the "liberating" Soviet Union. Nor was this respect shaken by the savagery of most Soviet troops in Eastern Europe. The Czechs saw relatively little of it. But the rest did suffer from it (many Germans and Austrians, too). That was enough. It only confirmed the image of Russia as the "inhuman land."

The East European distrust of communism was reflected in several early election results after 1945—in Hungary and Bulgaria, especially, where traditional peasant parties polled well. But the communists were indirectly helped by the urge for change; revulsion against right-wing authoritarianism; and their own effective propaganda. Communist propaganda was seductive at first. Stalin himself was telling East Europeans that their fears were groundless. Private agriculture would flourish, but more equitably than before; the "commanding heights" of the economy—the big extractive industries and big manufacturing—would be nationalized (this was popular) but not the lower levels of the economy; democratic choice would be respected; so would national traditions, and national paths ("own roads") to socialism.

Many East Europeans, whatever their politics, felt that the East wind was blowing stronger. The Soviets were there. Nothing could be done about that fact, and the West apparently wanted to do nothing. True, many East Europeans were bitter about Western cynicism or naiveté at Yalta. (The controversy over Yalta still bubbles, more than a half century later.) But many East Europeans knew that historical circumstance, more than Western indifference, had sealed their fate; it was illusion to pretend otherwise. Finally, most East Europeans were physically exhausted, emotionally drained, and materially destitute. Life had become a matter of surviving, sustaining, and rebuilding. Their forebears had been through much, and now it was their own turn. Fatalism, not fancy, ranked uppermost.

Eastern Europe, though hardly ripe for communism, was resigned to its coming. Where fancy did exist was in the hope that the communism descending on them would be more moderate, civilized, and "European" than the brutish, "Asiatic" variety that Stalin had visited on Russia. And the local communists, beginning their unavailing quest for legitimacy, set about trying to give this assurance. Unlike Stalin, not all of them were insincere: some of them did want their form of communism to be different. They soon had to learn better, or be taught better.

3. Postwar Population Movements in 1947. © Bartholomew Ltd 2000. Reproduced by permission of HarperCollins Publishers Ltd, Bishopbriggs, Scotland.

Stalin, for whom ideology meant more than some Western observers realized, seems to have assumed that the "liberation" in Eastern Europe would be accepted as such by the "liberated." When their ingratitude became evident, he did what came naturally to him: look for "traitors." There followed in Eastern Europe a combination of systematic Soviet terror and outbursts of local social hatred, the kind that had characterized both the French Revolution and the Russian Revolution of 1917. The definition of "class enemy" became broad indeed, and the revenge taken was universally brutal and often fiendish. But what alarmed Stalin the most was the spontaneity in some of the East European communist parties, a spontaneity that he first appeared to have overlooked. He decided to establish the Cominform (Communist Information Bureau) in 1947 to replace the old Comintern that had been disbanded in 1943.[3] It was time to show his minions the shape of things to come.

Phases of Communist Rule

The first meeting of the Cominform took place in a small resort in southern Poland. Anxious to prove its orthodoxy, the Yugoslav delegation was the most aggressively conformist group at the meeting. The Yugoslavs also saw themselves as having a special authority, a privileged place, among the satellite ruling parties. But Tito's days as favorite son were rapidly coming to an end.

The founding of the Cominform and the Stalin-Tito break the following year ushered in the first real phase of communist rule in Eastern Europe. It also marked an end to the public relations pretense of the previous two years. This was now the Stalinist period in Eastern Europe's communist history, and it lasted until 1956, despite the modifications after Stalin's death in March 1953. Its main characteristics:

> A sharp increase in systematic terror against enemies—real, imagined, or construed—among the population and within the ruling communist parties themselves. This "party terror" was accompanied by the rooting out and, in the most prominent cases, the show trials and executions of some "home communist" leaders in the satellites and their replacement by "Muscovites," East European communists who had spent periods in the Soviet Union. The Muscovites (many of whom, though by no means all, were Jewish) were considered safer than the home communists who, Stalin suspected, could be too local in their outlook and loyalties. (Romania was the tantalizing exception; the Muscovites were purged and the home communists strengthened.)
> The proliferation of Soviet "advisers" in all branches of government. Total conformity with Soviet foreign policy, which became even more stridently anti-Western following the Berlin blockade in 1948, the start of the Korean War in 1950, and unsuccessful attempts at subversion in Western Europe.

Massive heavy industrialization programs at the expense of light industry and living standards, with rapid agricultural collectivization.
Political exclusivity; the party, knowing the path and the goal, arrogated power, responsibility, and trust to itself.
The massive, morbid cult of the personality of Stalin himself.

Stalin's death resulted in major changes in the Soviet Union. It began with the partial lifting of the pall of terror, intimidation, and fear—the hallmarks of Stalinism. Within the Soviet regime itself, it started a struggle for power that lasted three years. It also led to some changes in Moscow's policy toward Eastern Europe and the West. Some of the most hated of the previously installed Muscovites were deposed. Some imprisoned home communists were released, and calls for the rehabilitation of those executed began to be raised. Many of the Soviet advisers were withdrawn, and their more zealous local pupils began to feel uneasy. Heavy industrialization ("Sector A") was slightly modified in favor of more consumer goods ("Sector B"); agricultural collectivization was generally slowed and, in Poland, virtually abandoned.[4]

But something both profound and spectacular was needed to "make assurance double sure" that the Stalin era was over. It came in March 1956 when Nikita Khrushchev, now apparently secure in the leadership of the Soviet party, denounced Stalin at the Twentieth Soviet Party Congress. It purported to be a secret speech, but it was heard around the world.

Khrushchev's speech began the second phase of Eastern Europe's communist history, although for the rest of 1956 it appeared that it might have caused its early end. Revolution occurred in Hungary, and a national uprising was narrowly averted in Poland. Elsewhere, the situation remained relatively calm, but the mood was tense. The revolution in Hungary was severely repressed; bloodshed in Poland was avoided by Polish skill and nerve—and by Soviet restraint (no bloody repression was wanted on two fronts). Even so, the events in Hungary and Poland must have come close to losing Khrushchev his position. The ultimate charge of "hare-brained scheming" could so easily have been brought forward from eight years hence when Khrushchev was eventually toppled. But Khrushchev, gambler throughout, not only survived this near-disaster but persisted with the loosening-up policy in Eastern Europe that had initially caused the blowup to happen. The new "socialist commonwealth" still consisted of a sun and its satellites, but the satellites could now opt for an autonomy that, by the Stalinist yardstick, was treasonably unsafe, especially in the context of the cold war.

Just how much autonomy became available was never specified. The bolder pushed their luck, the timid held back. Determined to carry out reforms at home, Khrushchev was not alarmed by the innovative spirit in Eastern Europe. He could also stretch the ideology to allow for the unorthodox becoming orthodox. He formed alliances of purpose with the newer East European leaders, especially with János Kádár in Hungary. Although insisting on the primacy of Moscow and of communist party authority, Khrushchev allowed a broad construction of both aspects of power. Finally, Russian bully boy though he was, Khrushchev's style and personality ("the closest thing they've had to a regular fella," as one U.S. politician enthused) was so different from Stalin's that the contrast itself became an important political sign. Many Russians distrusted him because they could not fear him, and his buffoonery made them blush. For many East Europeans, he was the kind of Ivan that they knew—primitive but human when scratched.

The second phase in Eastern Europe's communist history, the Khrushchev era, finished not in October 1964, when he was overthrown, but in August 1968 with the suppression of the Prague Spring. The era's most notable characteristics were less party exclusivity—the emphasis, in fact, was on inclusivity, more togetherness and a sense of belonging, with a stress on legitimacy—and concessions to nationalism. Its most notable events can be listed:

> Kádár's new course in Hungary, which, with interruptions, lasted right up to the downfall of communism itself.
> The rustle of the Prague Spring, its flowering and its trampling.
> The comprehensive reforms in Yugoslavia during the mid-1960s, independent of Moscow but very much in the Khrushchev spirit.
> The momentous Sino-Soviet dispute, the main offshoots of which in Eastern Europe were the defection of Albania to China in 1961 and the start of Romania's progressive edging away from Moscow at the end of the 1950s.
> The Polish retreat from reform after 1958. Having been pushed to the brink in 1956, the Polish party edged back as close to orthodoxy as the situation in Poland (strong church, private peasantry, incorrigible population) would allow. Władysław Gomułka deceived everyone (who

did not know him) by not being a broad-minded socialist but a narrow-minded "Calvinistic" communist.

Khrushchev was forced from power in October 1964, ousted by an appa-ratchik backlash that propelled Brezhnev into eighteen years of rule—"the years of stagnation," as Gorbachev subsequently called them. By this time, however, the Kádár reform process in Hungary was well under way, and the Prague Spring was coming. The momentum of the Prague Spring con-tinued largely because of the uncertainty and disunity in Moscow. But Warsaw and East Berlin were as one in recognizing the danger in Prague. Both regimes felt themselves directly threatened and urged intervention. When intervention finally did come, the Khrushchev era in Eastern Europe ended and the Brezhnev era began.

The invasion of Czechoslovakia was necessary from the Soviet point of view. If left to gain further momentum and become more comprehensive, the Prague Spring, despite the protestations of its leaders, would have spawned some form of genuine democracy, partial capitalism, and in-creased national independence. These developments soon would have en-gulfed Hungary and Poland, fatally isolated the German Democratic Re-public, and caused uncertainty in Ukraine. The Soviet position in East Central Europe, therefore, would have deteriorated to the same extent, if not in the same manner, as it had already deteriorated in the Balkans (see p. 46). Prague would have done in 1968 what Budapest tried to do in 1956: declare or practice neutrality. No Soviet leadership could have allowed it. This line of thinking in no way condones the Soviets' action; it actually shows how shallow their support was in Eastern Europe.[5]

The third phase in the region's communist history received an early shock in December 1970 when workers in several Baltic ports in Poland rioted over a sudden sharp increase in basic food prices, a reflection of the regime's incompetence and lack of credibility. Officially, the riots left nearly fifty dead; actually, the number was much higher. General Wojciech Jaru-zelski made his major debut on the political scene as minister of defense, the official responsible for restoring order and—ultimately—for the killings.

A bad end, therefore, for phase two and a bad start for phase three. But ironically, it was the Polish worker riots that pointed to a possible way for Moscow to retrench and then save the system. The direct cause of the Polish riots was not ideological, as the Prague Spring obviously was; it had to do with wages, prices, working conditions. If these could be visibly and permanently improved, perhaps not communism itself but at least the communist regimes might be safe. Never mind ideology! Shore up the status quo—and the power, privileges, and perks that went with it! Not acceptance through conviction, but sufferance through *consumerism!*[6] That became the aim. The Brezhnevian social contract was unveiled (see chapter 3).

In both the Soviet Union and Eastern Europe the social contract opened the floodgates still wider to cronyism, corruption, and cynicism. It actually hastened the end of the system rather than preserving it. But it kept the pacesetting Poles quiet for five years, during which Edward Gierek flattered to deceive, bamboozling many of his countrymen as well as many Westerners. Some Western observers even began to accept the notion that communism was now "delivering the goods," not just in Poland but everywhere. The GDR was even claiming that its per capita national income was higher than Great Britain's. (British Marxists and masochists believed it.) The future was at last working!

But the bubble soon burst, and it burst because of the inefficiency of the economic system (see chapter 3). What the Poles, the Hungarians, the East Germans, the Yugoslavs, and eventually the Bulgarians used to keep their consumerism going, and to shelter themselves from worldwide economic storms, was Western capitalist credits. In the end, these resulted in nothing but crippling debts and more disillusion.

Nothing crowned the illegitimacy of communism more dramatically than the election of Karol Cardinal Wojtyła, archbishop of Cracow, as pope in October 1978. In Poland the Catholic Church had continued its historic role of keeping the faith and holding the nation together. However surprising, it was nonetheless fitting that a Pole should mount the throne of Saint Peter. Perhaps it was not God's judgment on communism, but it was certainly history's.

The election of Cardinal Wojtyła, now John Paul II, had four results. It galvanized the Polish nation;[7] stiffened anticommunist feeling throughout East Central Europe; renewed world attention toward Eastern Europe; and further bemused, depressed, or alarmed communists everywhere. It came just three years after the Conference on Security and Cooperation in Helsinki in 1975 (CSCE, later O—for Organization—SCE). Rather than being the sellout to communist rule in Eastern Europe that many initially thought, the "spirit of Helsinki" considerably stimulated free thinking in Eastern Europe. It had no direct connection with election of a Polish pope three years later, but both developments helped further the erosion of communist rule.

This erosion hastened the founding of Solidarity in Poland in 1980, the shipyard workers' union in Gdańsk that defied government threats and spread rapidly among workers throughout the country. Even more important, it was reflected by *recognition* of Solidarity (however reluctant and insincere) by the communist government in Warsaw.[8] Recognizing a free trade union struck at the very heart of the system; in retrospect it signaled the end of the system. But Solidarity was not just a trade union; it immediately became a national movement. For the third time in less than a quarter-century the Poles had mounted a major rebellion against communist rule. This rebellion, though nonviolent, was the strongest one of all, and it both mirrored and compounded the weakness of the entire communist system. The system already was clearly failing. In the Soviet Union, moribund leaders sat atop a moribund regime. In Poland, the system was shipwrecked; throughout the Eastern bloc "real existing socialism" had simply become degeneracy with slogans.

But it was the German Democratic Republic that was immediately threatened by Solidarity, not just the GDR's communist system, but its very existence. The threat from Poland in 1980–81 was even much greater than that from Czechoslovakia in 1968. And since the division of Germany and the existence of the GDR were the basis of the entire Soviet position in Europe, Solidarity was a strategic as well as a systemic threat to Moscow. Poland was the GDR's link to, and lifeline from, the Soviet Union. Therefore, the trade union that began life in a Gdańsk shipyard became as much a threat to East Berlin and Moscow as to the government in Warsaw.

Solidarity, therefore, had to be crushed. But how and by whom? In the event, it was submerged quietly, not crushed, and with minimum loss of life, by Poles and not Russians. It lived to fight—and win—another day, because the mass of the Polish people supported it, and the communists in 1989 had not the spirit to resist it. In the meantime, the *fourth* phase of communist rule in Eastern Europe had begun. This fourth phase, beginning after December 1981, was also the last, ending in the autumn of 1989. When it began, no one reckoned that it would be the last. Rather, it seemed as if a new period of communist repressiveness was setting in, with Moscow still determined *and able* to hold on to what it had.[9] The Brezhnev Doctrine still seemed set in stone.

But it was obvious—and characteristic of communist rule's fourth phase—that all of the East European regimes were becoming totally demoralized. Except for the Poles, by the early 1980s they all had long-standing leaders. Erich Honecker had been the East German party leader since 1971; Nicolae Ceauşescu, the Romanian ruler since 1965, Gustáv Husák, the Czechoslovak leader since 1968; János Kádár, the Hungarian head of government since 1956; Todor Zhivkov (doyen of the Soviet camp leaders), the Bulgarian leader since 1954. Outside the Warsaw Pact, Tito died in 1980, and Hoxha would die in 1985. Tito had been the Yugoslav party leader since 1937, Hoxha the head of the Albanian party since 1941. Except for Tito and Hoxha, all of these leaders were ultimately Soviet puppets, but each had his own personality and developed patterns of rule strongly influenced by domestic considerations and national backgrounds.

Honecker's rule was based on the interaction of four dependencies: the Berlin Wall to keep his citizens in; the Soviet Union for survival; the secret police (Stasi) and the large East German army for internal order; and West German largess for warding off economic misery and political discontent.

Zhivkov was a formidable power politician, striking down aspiring crown princes almost before they surfaced. He was also a keen (but orthodox) experimenter. But his experiments went wrong. He was demonstratively loyal to Moscow; hence, he was allowed a degree of surrogate nationalism in the Balkans.

Husák's aim after the Prague Spring was simple: "never again." But he was milder in his repression than many communists demanded, and in his native Slovakia, where the Czech connection was rapidly withering, he had a considerable following.

Kádár had presided over a successful reform program in Hungary that made Hungarians better off and freer than other East Europeans. He had always skillfully managed his relations with Moscow. By the 1980s, however, he was becoming vulnerable rather than masterful. His economic reform was now acquiring a momentum of its own, approaching and even crossing the border with capitalism.

Ceauşescu was still trying to graft North Korea onto Romania. Fanaticism, "familialization," and fantasy had become his hallmarks. Once he had been a real embarrassment to the Soviets; now he was an embarrassment to everybody. To his own people, though, he was more than that: he was their ruler.

Jaruzelski was, and remains, an enigma. His great problem after his coup in December 1981 was in convincing the Polish people that it had been necessary and that he was as good a Pole as they were. He succeeded in neither goal. His rule during the 1980s was undermined by (1) his countrymen's resistance; (2) the West's disdain; and (3) the galloping debility in Moscow.

After Tito's death Yugoslavia spun out of orbit. The trajectory had been socialism with federalism, the socialism tinged with bogus experimentation. In the 1980s, Yugoslavia headed for disaster and demise. Tito had clearly failed, although the task of melding Yugoslavia was almost certainly an impossible one. Two things motivated him: power and a primitive Leninism. But he was a real leader, remembered nostalgically by those in former Yugoslavia who have since been oppressed and by those who are still fearful. Hoxha almost literally drove Albania into the ground. After him, the problem was picking up the pieces. They could not be (and still have not been) reassembled into a state. Hoxha, though, is still considered by some Albanians—Kosovars mostly—as a good national leader who "went wrong" through paranoia and megalomania. They see him through an ethnic, not a civic, prism. (Ceauşescu is viewed similarly by some Romanians.)

Discontent, Dissent, and Accommodation

Communism fell in Eastern Europe because of economic, political, and nationalist dissatisfaction. It failed to deliver the goods, it spurned civic freedom, and it wounded national pride. It also massively insulted the intelligence of most of its citizens. (The "uneducated" were often quicker to see through it than many of the educated.) The confluence of these dissatisfactions led to 1989. The few make revolutions. They can do so because the many support them, or the many no longer think that the status quo is worth defending. The revolutions of 1989 also occurred—and succeeded— only because the Soviet Union had lost the will to defend the gains of 1945. In 1992 the Soviet Union lost the will to preserve itself. Without Soviet power, East European communism could not exist. Everybody knew that to be the case. But without East European communism, the Soviet Union could not exist, either. The interaction had become mutually weakening, and then mutually ruinous.

Much discontent was evident throughout the communist period. Only rarely, however, did discontent become opposition, open resistance, or even active disaffection.[10] Most of the time it was a matter of putting up with it, making the best of it, and that meant dealing, even cooperating, with "them," however grudging that cooperation might be. Historically, it had always been that way. At just what point cooperation became collaboration was difficult to discern. The issue was subjective, part of the broad no-man's-land between rulers and ruled.

This was the case even with Poland. Nowhere was communist rule weaker, or opposition to it stronger. But for eleven years, from 1957 until 1968, neither riot nor revolution occurred there. Some experts had even begun explaining why the historic rule of Polish intellectuals was fading and that of the apolitical technocrats beginning. Others were suggesting that the workers were becoming resigned to communist rule and were being "softened" by it. In the early 1970s the Polish United Workers' (Communist) Party had more than three million members out of a total population of 36 million. Prolonged resistance began in Poland with the strikes and riots of 1976, when the five-year honeymoon between Edward Gierek and the workers came to an end. From 1976 to 1978 the alliance between workers and intellectuals, broken after 1956, was reshaped. Then in 1978 came the miracle that no one expected: the election of a Polish pope. In 1846 Metternich had bargained on everything except a "liberal pope," and Brezhnev could have been excused for bargaining for everything except a Polish one. The conspiracy theories that have been woven around the Ronald Reagan–John Paul II "secret alliance" to undermine communism may be exaggerated; "coincidence of active interest" may be a better term. But the regenerative effect that Karol Wojtyła's election and the force of his personality had on his countrymen can hardly be exaggerated. For them, communism became not just unpopular but irrelevant. All the regime had was armed force, which it used with apparent success in December 1981. But it was the pope who, after all, had the divisions that really counted. By the mid-1980s a large-scale opposition had formed, underground this time and largely equipped from abroad. Photocopiers were more useful than tanks. The revolution of 1989 came quickly, almost unavoidably. The coup of December 1981, aimed at saving communism in Poland, only helped accelerate its demise.

In Hungary the revolution and in Czechoslovakia the Prague Spring were traumatic events in the histories of their countries. Both were defeated, then immediately followed by introspection and inaction, periods when self took priority over society, private over public, recriminations over loyalties. From that point, however, the histories of Hungary and Czechoslovakia diverged remarkably.

In Hungary the Kádár era set in—the breakthrough for inclusivity. "He who is not against us is with us."[11] Kádár sensed the national mood and responded to it with political genius. After World War II, the Stalinist terror, and then the revolution, Hungarians wanted some peace and quiet. Kádár gave it to them and then more: virtual free speech, travel to the West, higher standards of living, and general relaxation of political and social strictures. But a growing number of intellectuals became repelled by what they saw as Kádár's cynicism, his "corruption of the soul of the nation." In this growing intellectual opposition the prewar intellectual division between urbanists and populists became discernible again. Historically, those contrasting groups had often disliked each other intensely, and their historic divisions were to reemerge after 1989. But many of them became united in their opposition to the Kádár regime. Politically, they had little impact. They had no support from the workers, and the peasants had begun to do well under the regime's imaginative agrarian policy. The fact was that most Hungarians became resigned not so much to communism as to Kádárism. It was only by about 1985, when the entire communist system was in crisis, and Kádár himself in personal decline, that majority opinion changed.

In Czechoslovakia, most Slovaks made something of their new federal status and were far from ashamed at seeing one of their own, Gustáv Husák, at the helm in Prague. The Czechs, on the other hand, showed their customary susceptibility to *l'itost*, the masochistic dredging up of earlier and current misfortunes. Their own quiescence stemmed from the same sources as did that of the Hungarians: as a way of escape from recent tragedy. There the similarity ended. The national moods were entirely different. While Prague became a slough of despond, Budapest became fun city.

In 1977, Prague gave birth to Charter 77. It was an extraordinary movement because of the courage and quality of some of its signatories, one of whom, Václav Havel, captured the admiration and imagination of the Western world. Charter 77 eventually became an important symbol of Czech resistance and of the nation's universal aspiration for freedom and tolerance. But for years Charter 77 had little impact on the Czech public and practically none on the Slovak. It was not so much a response to the public mood as an indictment of it.

In Romania, opposition was minimal by the standards of East Central Europe. Many individual cases of heroism occurred in the face of regime persecution, but only rarely was resistance organized or dissent sustained.[12] Within the communist party and in the armed forces, considerable opposition developed toward the maniacal course that Ceauşescu's rule took, but that opposition never amounted to much. Key sections of the working class, most notably the miners, sometimes challenged the regime with strikes or demonstrations. Some intellectuals were prepared to buck the sycophantic trend and try to redeem the honor of their position. They were pitifully few, however. Only at the death rattle of Ceauşescu's rule did dissatisfaction broaden into dissent and dissent into resistance. In 1989 it exploded into revolution.

In Bulgaria, some peasant resistance to collectivization had occurred at the start of the communist regime, and some discontent became apparent among factory workers. After that, minor cases of dissatisfaction were evident among the ruling party and in the military, and Turkish resistance to Zhivkov's repressions in the 1980s became fierce (see p. 59). But, as in the case of Romania, resistance worthy of the name had to wait until the very end. In 1989, dissident groups proliferated, the most significant of which, *Ecoglasnost*, was ostensibly an ecological pressure group backed by establishment figures.[13] The party itself then took up the fashion, and Zhivkov's thirty-five years at the top were over.

In Albania, with the regime red in tooth and claw, overt, covert, or suspected dissidence meant death or disappearance. In Yugoslavia opposition was of an order different from that of other East European countries. It began as political dissent in the famous case of Milovan Djilas in the early 1950s. It broadened in the 1960s to become economic, political, and national. Then it deepened into a nationalist disaffection that destroyed not just the Yugoslav system, but Yugoslavia itself.

Authoritarian or Totalitarian?

Looking back on communist rule in East European history, one is struck by the inaccuracy of several terms that Western observers used to describe it. "Totalitarian" was the most obviously inaccurate one. Kádár's Hungary after 1960 was anything but totalitarian, or even "totalitarian aspirant." For many years, the same was true for Poland. Despite the disappointing backsliding after the heady months of 1956, the Roman Catholic Church in Poland remained relatively free, as did most Polish peasants. In both countries, travel to the West was relatively unimpeded. At the other end of the spectrum, Hoxha's Albania was indeed totalitarian. Romania for the entire period remained a terror-driven state; Bulgaria less so. And in both countries the communist party sought to penetrate every nook and cranny of public life and society. But both countries had large ethnic minorities. Real totalitarianism demands that minorities be either assimilated, cowed, or expelled. Zhivkov in Bulgaria in the 1980s seems to have played with all three alternatives, and Ceaușescu would have liked to assimilate the Hungarian minority. But that effort would have created a casus belli for both Hungary and the Soviet Union. In Yugoslavia, multinationalism would have made totalitarianism impossible, even if Tito had not become more relaxation-minded in politics, economics, and culture. Successive Czechoslovak leaderships aspired to totalitarianism before the reformist reawakening in the 1960s, and after 1968 it looked as if totalitarianism might be reimposed. Instead, Czechoslovakia became a good example of the whole totalitarian failure in Eastern Europe. A kind of social contract emerged between the regime and society; most citizens became openly contemptuous of ideology. Slovakia kept its federal status and drifted away from the Prague center. These, in retrospect, were the longer-term results of August 1968. Finally, except in Albania and for the Ceaușescus (husband and wife), the regimes simply lost their inspiration to govern. They were hanging on. And totalitarian regimes do not hang on.

The Soviet Union and Eastern Europe

Eastern Europe was part of the Soviet Union's ideological, political, and economic system. It also was part of its power system, part of its empire. Looked at from a historical perspective, almost every territorial ambition that Russia had ever had in Europe was attained by its domination of Eastern Europe after World War II. Indeed, this domination now exceeded its historical ambitions. It covered a considerable part of Germany, and the GDR became the cornerstone of the Soviet empire in Eastern Europe. But now this domination had become different. It also meant imposing the conqueror's *ideological system* on the acquired territories.[14] Stalin attempted to achieve this goal in his own inimitably brutal way. He was still doing it when he died in March 1953.

The Stalinist system in East Europe was mainly designed to further a dual process of *Gleichschaltung*: at the national level through the imposition of leaderships trusted by Moscow, and at the domestic level through a revolutionary transformation that would lay the foundation for socialist development. Stalin's successors were soon made to realize that his way had to be modified. The East Berlin revolt, riots in Pilsen in Czechoslovakia, and minor disturbances elsewhere, all in 1953, were quick to bring this fact home. Then, three years later came the Polish October and the Hungarian Revolution.

In a paper written for RAND and published in November 1975, I developed the simple concept of *cohesion and viability* as the Soviets' twin post-Stalin aims in Eastern Europe. Cohesion meant a situation where, allowing for a degree of diversity caused by different local conditions, a *general* conformity existed in domestic and foreign policies as well as a cross-identification of the institutions developing those policies in both the Soviet Union and the Eastern European countries. Viability was a degree of credibility, confidence, and capacity in each East European country that would increasingly legitimize communist rule and, as a consequence, reduce the Soviet need for a preventive preoccupation within the region.[15]

The problem, though, was that during neither the Khrushchev nor Brezhnev eras could these two imperatives be brought into balance. Thus, the aim became the dilemma, and this dilemma formed the root of the Soviet failure in Eastern Europe. Under Khrushchev, the emphasis seemed to be on viability, which brought on the Hungarian Revolution, the Polish October, the Prague Spring, and, within the shadow of the Sino-Soviet dispute, the Albanian defection and the Romanian deviation. Under Brezhnev, after the near-disaster in Czechoslovakia and in keeping with the very character of his leadership, the emphasis shifted to cohesion. Cohesion led to stagnation, however, which partly paved the way for the final collapse. The balance always remained elusive.

The bedrock of the Soviet system in Eastern Europe was the network of comprehensive bilateral alliances between the Soviet Union and each member of the East European alliance as well as among the East European states themselves. But the two multilateral alliances, the Council for Mutual Economic Assistance (Comecon, CMEA, or CEMA) and the Warsaw Treaty Organization (WTO, or Warsaw Pact), became the chief instruments for alliance coordination ("togetherness"). Comecon was founded in 1949 by Stalin as a response to the Marshall Plan, but it remained largely symbolic for several years, each member hellbent on an autarkic policy of heavy industrialization. Khrushchev saw its potential for an "international socialist division of labor," which involved a degree of specialization among the

East European economies. The Warsaw Pact was founded in 1955, ostensibly as a response to the inclusion of West Germany in NATO. Although primarily a military security institution, the WTO, like NATO, also became used for political and other forms of coordination.

Comecon quickly mirrored the historical north-south division of Eastern Europe. Pressure was brought to bear on Romania and Albania and initially on Bulgaria to trim their heavy industrial ambitions and concentrate on what they supposedly did best: light industry, the food industry, and agriculture. This division offended the socialist aspirations and national pride of all three countries. With Bulgaria, the idea seems to have been dropped early. With Albania, it might have been one reason for its defection to China, although fear over Khrushchev's steady wooing of Tito was certainly uppermost in Enver Hoxha's mind. In Romania's case, it was certainly one reason for its subsequent pursuit of semi-independence from Moscow.

After 1958, Comecon had to face the European Common Market, which Soviet leaders first dismissed as a supranational, capitalistic, exploitative monster that would soon either collapse of its own weight or be strangled by its own contradictions. But when it became obvious that the Common Market was a going concern, this dismissive tone became muted. Although still denouncing the Common Market's supranationalism, Moscow began trying to introduce the same thing, but by the backdoor, into Comecon through suggesting various coordinating mechanisms. But nothing much was ever achieved. Comecon's particularism remained largely intact, and its autarkism, though softened at the edges, remained the core.[16]

The Warsaw Pact will be remembered mainly as the only alliance in history that attacked its own members rather than its ostensible enemies. Twice, member countries were invaded to eliminate threats to socialism— first Hungary in 1956, then Czechoslovakia in 1968. And it seems certain that in late 1980 or early 1981, the Soviets, supported by East Germany and Czechoslovakia, came within an ace of invading Poland to put down Solidarity. In the event, General Jaruzelski did the job for them.

Both Khrushchev and Brezhnev tried to use the Warsaw Pact, not just for military cooperation, but for institutionalized, supranational, foreign policy coordination. They never really succeeded, just as they never succeeded in making Comecon a supranational organization. This lack of success should be remembered when Soviet-East European relations are looked back on. None of the communist regimes in Eastern Europe could have existed without the Soviet Union, yet Moscow had to take them into account, and because the satellite states opposed Comecon, Moscow failed to achieve its aim of greater unity. Nor was Romania alone in balking at supranationalism. It may have been Eastern Europe's most open spoiler, but Poland and Hungary occasionally balked, too. The GDR sometimes turned its basic weakness to account; and Bulgaria parlayed loyalty into a form of surrogate nationalism in the Balkans. None of these relations and conditions turned the alliance into a conciliar movement. Moscow dominated through its own strength and the others' weakness. But Moscow continually faced constraints that forced it to seek consensus and compromise. And none of its junior partners was unaware of this fact.[17]

Moscow's East European policy after 1956 was one of shoring up the Soviet position rather than consolidating it—holding rather than extending. But by 1965, that position in the Balkans was in tatters. It had completely lost control over Yugoslavia and Albania and partly so over Romania. Bulgaria was the only reliable subordinate. Added to this lack of leverage was the fact that Greece and Turkey, which many had feared would fall under Soviet control after World War II, stood as members of NATO after 1952. Yet East Central Europe, of course, was more crucial to Soviet interests; the Soviets' grip there was tighter and its determination to retain its position much stronger. The GDR in 1953 and 1961 (the Berlin Wall), Poland in 1956 and 1981, Hungary in 1956, Czechoslovakia in 1968—all were examples of that determination. But the very fact that it was necessary to show this determination at all was in itself a massive political, ideological, and psychological defeat. And the Sino-Soviet dispute challenged Soviet communist hegemony on a global scale. To say, therefore, that Soviet policy had been a failure would be an ineffable understatement. Gorbachev began to comprehend this reality soon after he came to power. But in Eastern Europe, as well as in the Soviet Union itself, he tried to repair the irreparable, and his efforts made the system still worse.

The United States and Eastern Europe

U.S. policy toward communist Eastern Europe began to develop in 1948 when Washington backed Yugoslavia's independence against Stalin's attempts to destroy it. For the period, it was a remarkably unideological action on the part of the U.S. and other Western governments. Yugoslavia not only was communist, but zealously and oppressively so, and it remained

4. Eastern Europe in 1949. © Bartholomew Ltd 2000. Reproduced by permission of HarperCollins Publishers Ltd, Bishopbriggs, Scotland.

rigidly communist for several years after 1948. But Tito's split from Stalin was seen as a step that checked and therefore weakened the Soviet Union. As such, the U.S. move should be seen in conjunction with Washington's decision a year earlier to take on Britain's role in Greece and to defeat the communist forces there as well as to guarantee Turkey's independence against Soviet threats and territorial demands.

Eisenhower's "Roll-Back" declaration in 1953—rolling back the "tidal mud of communism"—reflected in a clumsy way the ideological anticommunist militancy, not so much of himself as of his secretary of state, John Foster Dulles. It generated hope and then bitterness in Eastern Europe, especially in 1956. In that year, rollback became rollover, as the Soviets, without let or hindrance, put down the Hungarian Revolution. After that terrible chain of events, Americans and East Europeans (especially Hungarians) became more realistic.

U.S. realism after 1956 became evident not in attempts to overturn Soviet control over Eastern Europe but in efforts to erode it.[18] The policy of the United States came to have two-sided aspects: state and societal. The policy was essentially one of "differentiation" before that term became widely used. It aimed to conduct as normal a relationship with the East European communist governments as their behavior toward Washington, Moscow, and their own populations would allow. Obviously, these three criteria—state, societal, differentiational—were difficult for the Americans to balance. With Yugoslavia it was relatively easy; Belgrade, despite its serious ethnic difficulties, scored relatively highly on all three criteria. It also was easy with Albania; Tirana hated virtually everybody, its own population not excluded. Bulgaria, too, with its hard domestic regime, general boorishness toward the United States, and its sycophancy to Moscow, presented few problems. But things were more difficult for the Americans with Romania and Hungary. Romania was steadily—sometimes stirringly—independent of Moscow. The corollary of this posture was its sidling up to Washington. But Ceauşescu became tyrannical, and the Romanians suffered. Kádár, on the other hand, ruled Hungary with a light touch. But he always maintained the needed amount of subordination to Moscow. This tightrope act often mean crossing Washington, but Kádár did this, too, with an enviable finesse. Poland in some respects was the most difficult of all. Spells of domestic reform were followed by rigidity, and loyalty to Moscow was punctuated by genuine displays of distinctiveness. The U.S. government also had to keep its own ethnic lobbies in mind. How the administration's

Polish policy would play in Chicago often meant more than how it might play in Bielsk Podlawski.

Five specific features and phases of the U.S. policy toward Eastern Europe need mentioning. (1) It had a moral thread. The East Europeans had a right to liberty. The Pax Sovietica notion had its supporters but, compared with Western Europe, they were few. (2) However "moral" it might be, the policy was never without its cold war calculations. For Moscow, Eastern Europe was a vast buffer zone that added to Soviet security; for Washington, it was a source of Soviet weakness to be exploited with care. (3) Kissinger's "un-American realism"—that foreign policy and morality do not mix!—also became a dominant feature. If a comprehensive deal could be struck with the Soviet Union, Eastern Europe could remain within its sphere of influence. This option was a card to play in the global game that must not be lost through New World sentimentality. (4) For Ronald Reagan, Eastern Europe became the stage for his anticommunism, American "exceptionalism," and democratic decency. He did not win the cold war: the Russians lost it. But Reagan shortened it. (5) George Bush's handling of the cold war's demise made him a European statesman. But his "Chicken Kiev" speech in 1991, backing the Soviet Union's survival, the wishful thinking over Yugoslavia, and the early unawareness over Czechoslovakia, suggest that the "ethnic dimension," the salient feature of twentieth-century Europe, was not fully grasped.

Generally, U.S. policy in Eastern Europe worked well between 1945 and 1989. But it was the very existence, the image, and the strength of the United States that most sustained hope in Eastern Europe. The links that the United States had made with the East European peoples over more than a century remained intact. And the East Europeans' faith in the United States was vindicated.

Germany and Eastern Europe

No one put it better than Josef Joffe in 1987: "There was never, nor is there now, such a thing as a neatly compartmentalized [German] policy toward Eastern Europe as a political, geographical, entity separate from the GDR and the Soviet Union. . . . The driving factor was and remains *Deutschland-politik*"—the issues relating to, or arising from, the division of Germany.[19]

At first, the Federal Republic of Germany (West Germany) virtually turned its back on Eastern Europe, refusing diplomatic relations with any country that recognized the GDR. That policy may be described as negative. Then came tentative Ostpolitik in the mid-1960s, which began a policy of cautious rapprochement, dangling economic enticements aimed at isolating the GDR. This new policy was also influenced by important changes toward Eastern Europe in the policies of both the United States and France, Bonn's two closest allies. It was attractive to some East European states as well, most notably Romania, but also, initially, to Bulgaria and Hungary. It was strongly opposed by the GDR's neighbors, however—Poland and Czechoslovakia—and by the Soviet Union. The alliance was therefore called to order by Moscow, but Romania, in a dramatic act of defiance, accepted Bonn's overtures and opened diplomatic relations with West Germany in 1967.

The alliance was called to order more painfully and comprehensively by the Soviet-led invasion of Czechoslovakia in August 1968. This action prompted an important shift of emphasis in Bonn's policy. The road to Eastern Europe now lay through Moscow. Changing the status quo could be done only through accepting the status quo. With these parameters signaled and understood, the full Ostpolitik under the Social Democratic-led government of Willy Brandt now got under way. It caught the imagination of both halves of Europe. West Germany recognized the GDR and removed the main obstacle to better relations with Poland by recognizing Poland's post-1945 Western frontier on the Oder and Neisse Rivers (the Oder-Neisse line). Multilateral relations with all of the East European countries began, with economic relations especially prominent. Trade with, and aid from, West Germany assumed some importance in most East European economies. German-Soviet relations also markedly improved. Moscow now felt it could gain rewards without incurring costs.

The Soviet Union was particularly reassured by Bonn's change of strategy on the GDR. Unification, though never officially repudiated, was in effect dropped. "Re-association" became the policy—"two states in one nation" the watchword. And in view of the apparent impregnability of the Soviet position in Eastern Europe and the Soviets' determination to maintain it, re-association seemed a more realistic course. Besides, as most Germans were aware, the Western alliance strongly opposed the very notion of re-unification. Concern over that possibility was always less in the United States than in, say, Britain and France; nonetheless, it was strong overall. And there was no burning enthusiasm for it in West Germany itself.

Ostpolitik was well conceived. It greatly enhanced the Federal Republic's reputation, did much to rehabilitate the German image, and brought considerable indirect benefit to the populations of Eastern Europe. Like the Helsinki Initiative in 1975, Ostpolitik did not "legitimize" Soviet domination, as many of its opponents argued, but it took a realistic path toward easing that control. That path, not confrontation, seemed the best way to travel forward.

But the policy of Ostpolitik had its dangers. And the German governments in the 1970s, under both Willy Brandt and his successor, Helmut Schmidt, aggravated them. As Bonn's relationship with the regimes in Eastern Europe grew cosier, its concern for the East European peoples diminished.[20] Accepting the status quo became all too evident; changing it was virtually ignored. Poland was the clearest example, and it came to the fore because the Poles kept endangering the status quo. They would not lie down and be walked over. Bonn's official attitude toward Solidarity was a mixture of coolness and caution, with more than a touch of Teutonic condescension. Brandt seemed convinced that the Poles were being "stirred up from outside," and Schmidt, proud and provocative in his unsentimentality, was as disdainful as only he could be. Ostpolitik seemed to many to have become *Anpassungspolitik* (accommodation policy). As for *Deutschlandpolitik,* both the Social Democrats and their successors in power in the 1980s, the Christian Democrats, could claim success in improving relations with the GDR. *Deutschlandpolitik* did help bring West and East Germans closer together. It also emboldened dissident elements in East Germany, increasing both their esteem and their following. Just as important, it made the East German regime more and more nervous, both in East Berlin itself and throughout the provinces. But despite these stirrings, it still would take chutzpah for Bonn to claim credit for the GDR's collapse. Clearly, this breakdown took place in the context of the broader failure of the Soviet system—a failure in which West Germany's role was secondary. True, Chancellor Helmut Kohl brilliantly grasped the opportunity for reunification. But that opportunity had been created mainly by others, most notably the United States. And backing from the United States enabled him to take the initiative.

The Persisting Ethnic Dimension

The communists claimed that they had made ethnic tensions irrelevant. Even their adversaries agreed that the Soviets had submerged such differences. But how effectively had they done so? Not nearly as thoroughly as they claimed. The ethnic cauldron bubbled, and its lid was never tightly shut. "Ethnicity," ethnic divisions, and suspicions continued to be the dominant elements of the life of Eastern Europe throughout the century. The brief listing to follow illustrates its continuation during the communist period. And it excludes Yugoslav cases; these were prelude to the carnage of the 1990s and are discussed in chapters 6 and 7.

Nationalism under communist rule deserves a bigger, fuller study than the following discussion. For many years its significance was underrated. But it provided one of the most important links between precommunism and postcommunism. Indeed, nationalism soon proved a much stronger ideology than communism and permeated all communist institutions. True, Soviet power submerged the excesses of nationalism, but because it refused to confront nationalism, those excesses became worse when communism finally collapsed.

First, though, a backward glance toward World War II. From 1939 until 1945, East Central Europe and the Soviet Union suffered the most massive human slaughter, deliberate extermination, ethnic cleansing, and population dislocation that has occurred in European history. The suffering there was incomparably greater than that in South Eastern Europe. But this incredible carnage greatly eased East Central Europe's ethnic problems. It is worth remembering this carnage and this ethnic cleansing when comparing the two parts of Eastern Europe since 1989, certainly before expatiating on the "primitive Balkans" as a way of explaining the Yugoslav slaughter. (And the East Central European catastrophe in World War II was mainly the responsibility of the Germans, a West European or Central European nation.) Taking the twentieth century as a whole, the Balkan record, compared with the rest of Europe, looks relatively humane.[21] As for the argument that (believe it or not) is occasionally still made—that the genocide in East Central Europe was better and more scientifically organized, hence reflecting a higher civilizational level—the only answer to that is an eight-letter barnyard epithet, as the *New York Times* was once wont to say.

But one crucially relevant point needs to be made, namely, that in East Central Europe genocide, ethnic cleansing, and racial strife took place over a half-century ago. Postcommunist East Central Europe could now concentrate almost solely on political and economic transformation. The civic factor was in the ascendant. In South Eastern Europe, however, the ethnic factor still predominated because so many ethnic questions remained unsettled. So the civic factor has had to wait. The emphasis on a civic versus an ethnic factor is probably the basic difference between these two parts of Eastern Europe.

Anti-Semitism

Poland started the post–World War II era with a serious Jewish pogrom in the southwestern city of Kielce in 1946. This was neither communist- nor Soviet-inspired; it was pure Polish. Later, in 1968, much officially inspired, as well as spontaneous, anti-Semitism occurred in the anti-intellectual campaign of that year. Solidarity, too, in 1980 and 1981 had a vocal anti-Semitic element.

From 1948 to 1953, anti-Semitism was rife in several East European countries, sanctioned, it seemed, by Stalin's final paranoid excess. The Slánský trials in Prague, where the defendants were almost exclusively Jewish, saw a most primitive display of anti-Semitism. In Poland, too, and especially in Hungary, some of the most conspicuous Stalinist leaders were Jewish, which gave popular anti-Semitism a specious excuse. In Hungary, with its relatively large surviving population of Jews—about 100,000—anti-Semitism simmered among rulers and ruled throughout the communist period. In Romania, periodic purges of Jews were generally welcomed by the populace. Later, mainly to gain U.S. approval and U.S. dollars, Ceauşescu relaxed emigration policy toward Jews. Many of them moved to Israel as the Jewish population in Romania dwindled to a few score thousands. But Romanian anti-Semitism has remained widespread and intense. After 1989, whatever constraints had been felt about expressing it fell completely away.

Transylvania and the Hungarian Minority

Hitler forced Romania to return northern Transylvania to Hungary in 1940. It was handed back to Romania after World War II, when Hungary had to return all the former territories it had recovered through its alliance with Nazi Germany. The Romanians, for their part, were even more sensitive about Transylvania after World War II than they had been before.

But in 1952 Romania was forced by the Soviets, ostensibly "in the spirit of Leninist internationalism," to create a Hungarian Autonomous Region in part of Transylvania. Its population was not exclusively Hungarian, but it came to include about 600,000, about one-third of the total number of

Hungarians in Romania. This region was not fully autonomous but enjoyed a certain administrative freedom. Above all, its creation and status symbolized that it was *special*. To Romanians, it meant that they were not fully masters in their own country. They strongly opposed its establishment, and, after Stalin's death in 1953, the Romanian communist regime worked toward its demise. The Hungarian Revolution, which had considerable nationalist impact on Hungarians in Transylvania, only added to Romanian indignation and underlined the regime's determination to do something about the autonomous region. It proceeded to change its boundaries, moving two heavily Romanian-populated districts into it, thus diluting its Hungarian population. It also changed the region's name, giving it a Romanian flavor. Its official title was now the Mureş-Magyar Autonomous Region. Earlier, the Hungarian university in Cluj (Kolozsvár) was merged with (actually, submerged by) the Romanian university there. Later, in 1968, the autonomous region was dismantled altogether. Now, just two counties out of a total of thirty-nine in the country as a whole, had large Hungarian majorities. No trace remained of Hungarian territorial or higher educational autonomy. Integration was virtually complete. Assimilation was now on the agenda.

These moves against Hungarian autonomy ran concurrently with the so-called Romanian deviation, the distancing from Soviet control, the climax of which was Ceauşescu's stand against the Soviet-led invasion of Czechoslovakia in 1968. Unquestionably, a link could be drawn between the two processes. Probably they were mutually reinforcing. Had Romania remained a conventional Soviet satellite, it would not have destroyed the Hungarian Autonomous Region; it would not have been allowed to do so.

Many members of the Hungarian minority at first had looked with hope to Ceauşescu (during his early, brief, "unsullied" phase), but later the minority as a whole suffered severe discrimination. In Hungary, indignation over this bigotry mounted among the public and inside the communist regime itself. A special anti-Romanian alliance between Budapest and Moscow developed. The Hungarians were prompted by Romania's minority policy, the Soviets by its independent-mindedness. The Soviets also became irritated by Romania's muted irredentism regarding Bessarabia, which they had regained in 1940. Three-way sniping, therefore, continued throughout the 1960s and 1970s with the Romanians (Ceauşescu, himself, at times) matching the Soviets and the Hungarians shot for shot. In 1985 the situation of the Hungarian minority was raised at a Hungarian communist party congress for the first time ever. But the Romanian regime—and on this point the nation supported it—was little affected. It continued restricting the rights of its Hungarians to be educated in their own language. The long-term aim was to de-Magyarize (assimilate) them.

A word on the German minority. About 250,000 ethnic Germans were living in Romania in 1939. Many of their ancestors began arriving in Transylvania eight centuries earlier. During World War II, many of them collaborated with the Nazis, and after 1945 the German minority as a whole suffered severe discrimination. Many people were sent to Soviet labor camps, from which few returned. But about 170,000 were still left in the mid-1970s when Ceaușescu, this time seeking German favor and German deutsche marks, began letting them go, with a hefty price on their heads. After 1989, another swell of migration carried minority Germans back to Germany. By the end of the twentieth century, fewer than 17,000 were left. A small segment of East European civilization had vanished.[22]

Hungarians in Slovakia

In 1964 a conference was held in Czechoslovakia between Slovak and Hungarian historians. The aim was fraternalism, the result fiasco.[23] What emerged was that anti-Hungarianism was the historic mainspring of Slovak nationalism.

Similarities were present in the situation of the nearly 2 million Hungarians in Romania (some 8 percent of the total population) and the 600,000 in Czechoslovakia (about 12 percent of the population of Slovakia). The most important similarity was their general discontent; many wanted, or yearned for, reincorporation into Hungary. Another was their sense of superiority to the Romanians and Slovaks, historically subservient, but dominant after 1920. However, sharp differences also existed. Slovakia had been part of Hungary for a thousand years (Upper Hungary). Transylvania had always enjoyed a distinctiveness. Slovaks began to be nationally conscious only in the nineteenth century, while Romanians had had to be nationally conscious for several centuries. After the middle of the nineteenth century, Romanians also had the Romanian state, the Regat, for identification and support.

But the Hungarian-Slovak relationship, however unequal, was personally closer than the Hungarian-Romanian relationship. Both Hungarians and Slovaks were mainly Roman Catholic, and they generally understood each other. But the Slovaks had none of the supports that the Romanians could fall back on in Transylvania, and in the second half of the nineteenth century they were subject to a massive exercise in Magyarization, mainly through education. The words of Béla Grunwald, adviser to Count Kálmán Tisza, the Hungarian prime minister from 1875 to 1890, are worth quoting. "The secondary school is like a huge machine, at one end of which Slovak youths are thrown in by the hundreds and at the other end of which they come out as Magyars."[24] Slovaks in Hungary were being thrown into school at about the same time that Slovak national consciousness was beginning to stir. This contrast led to most educated Slovaks becoming bitterly hostile toward Hungary. After World War I, with Hungary dismembered and Slovakia now part of Czechoslovakia, the Slovak-Hungarian relationship in Slovakia changed completely. The Slovaks were now in the coach. Many Slovak communists also were strongly anti-Hungarian, not least among them Gustáv Husák. Nationalism was a mainspring of communism in Slovakia.

During the communist period a strong similarity existed in the official forms of discrimination used against the Hungarian minority in both Romania and Slovakia. Just as the Romanians eroded and then disbanded the Hungarian Autonomous Region, so the Czechoslovak government, at Slovak insistence, moved systematically against administrative-territorial structures that gave (or seemed to give) consolidated power to sections of the Hungarian minority. In 1948 and again in 1960, reorganizations were carried out that broke up the compactness of the Hungarian community in south Slovakia.

The only tangible reform of the Prague Spring that survived 1968 was Slovakia's federal status. Through their government in Bratislava, the Slovaks now had even more freedom to deal with the Hungarian minority. More active discrimination was bound to come. The main target now became the Hungarian minority's educational facilities in their own language. Minor encroachments were made that caused increasing unease in Budapest and among the minority itself. Finally, a proposed law on Slovak education in 1985 was opposed so strongly because of its provisions restricting the teaching of the Hungarian language that the bill had to be withdrawn. This action marked a considerable victory for both the Hungarian minority and human rights. But it was a victory the Slovaks only reluctantly conceded.

Czechs and Slovaks

The restoration of Czechoslovakia after World War II was universally welcomed by Czechs. Many Slovaks, too, were ready to give Czechoslovakia another chance. But the mistrust that had bedeviled Czech-Slovak relations resumed almost immediately after 1945. Once again, the reason was the status of Slovakia. Thomas Masaryk had reneged on his original promise of federal autonomy for Slovakia after 1918, and now in 1946 an unholy alliance between the communists and the Czech democratic parties denied Slovakia much of the autonomy it had been promised toward the end of the war. Then, when the communists seized power in 1948, whatever genuine autonomy the Slovaks' political institutions still retained was neutered; Slovakia was ruled from Prague. Red "Czechoslovakism" and "Prague centralism" were now the order of the day. Slovak opponents of centralism, including prominent communists, were ruthlessly cut down.

Most Czechs supported Prague centralism. They assumed Czech superiority and saw little reason why this superiority should not be reflected in the ways in which Czechoslovakia was run. Most Czechs also felt betrayed by Slovak behavior in World War II. Most Slovaks, however, highly resented the reimposition of Prague centralism. To them, it was a betrayal of promises. The Slovak Question was reemerging. In the early 1950s, Vlado Clementis, the Czechoslovak foreign minister, was executed, and Gustáv Husák and the famous Slovak poet Laco Novomeský were sentenced to life imprisonment, all for "bourgeois [Slovak] nationalism." In the early 1960s the Slovak Question became the catalyst for change throughout Czechoslovakia. The Slovak reform agenda, though, was different from the Czech. The Slovaks wanted what the Czechs wanted, but above all they wanted home rule for Slovakia. Czech and Slovak priorities, therefore, not only diverged, but the Czechs saw an element of antagonism between them. They deemed the Slovak demands to be not just secondary but as undermining the main thrust of democratic reform. The old struggle, therefore, had been renewed between liberalism and nationalism. For the Slovaks, nationalism was of the essence; for the Czechs, it was secondary.

Some Czechs sympathized with the Slovak case and readily conceded that a healthy Czechoslovakia depended on a satisfied Slovakia. But majoritarian nations seldom like devolving power, let alone sharing it, especially when they themselves have been a subject nation for centuries, as had been the case with the Czechs. Somehow it was symptomatic that federal status for

Slovakia was left as the Prague Spring's unfinished business, finally enacted only in October 1968, two months after the Soviet-led invasion. Slovak federal status survived the Prague Spring, but during it was never high enough on the reformists' agenda. And federal status only survived because it was the sole aspect of the Prague Spring of which the Soviets approved.

Most Slovaks were not dissatisfied with their status after 1968. They did not like communism, but they were pragmatic; they did not like Russians, but they were realists; they did not like Husák, but he was a Slovak. Moreover, except for the more militant Catholics, they now were ruled with a fairly light touch. Economically, the Slovaks began to get new inputs of heavy industry, which meant more jobs and higher wages. Above all, their national pride was no longer being insulted. Many Slovaks saw themselves as having no friends, not even interests—only enemies. Were the Czechs enemies, then? Militant Slovak nationalists had, after 1918, regarded them as such. Most Slovaks would never have gone that far. But many older Slovaks had an inferiority complex about Czechs. After 1968, though, younger Slovaks had few such complexes. They began regarding Czechs not as superior but as irrelevant. They no longer needed them.

All through their history together, Czechs and Slovaks accused each other of bad faith—even betrayal. The Slovaks charged Masaryk with going back on his promise. The Czechs saw the Slovaks' conduct from 1938 till 1945 as betrayal. Many Slovaks saw post–World War II Prague centralism as a betrayal. In 1968, Czechs accused Slovaks of thinking only about themselves. After 1968, the Czechs resented the Slovaks for having it so good. Then, after 1989, in negotiations for the new Czechoslovakia, the two groups talked past each other. Even since the "velvet divorce" in 1993, they still have not started talking *to* each other.

The Turks in Bulgaria

Bulgaria has generally had a good record in its treatment of minorities. There had never been many Jews in Bulgaria, about 50,000 in the interwar period. The royal government, though allied with Nazi Germany in World War II, saved Bulgarian Jews from deportation. (It did not do the same, though, for about 11,000 Jews in those parts of Macedonia that its armies occupied.) After the establishment of Israel, Jews were allowed to go there.

The Turks, settlers during the Ottoman period, have constituted by far the biggest minority, except now for the Roma (Gypsies). The Turks numbered about 800,000 in the 1970s, living mainly in the country's northeast and southeast. Also living in Bulgaria were about 160,000 "Pomaks," ethnic Bulgarians whose ancestors converted to Islam; they still spoke Bulgarian. The Turkish exodus from Bulgaria back to Turkey had begun after the Congress of Berlin in 1878. From 1912 until 1940, more than 340,000 Turks left, but a large minority, with its high birth rate, remained. In the late 1940s vague plans were advanced to expel all the Turks from Bulgaria, but such ideas were shelved. Bulgarians and Turks generally kept to themselves. Some villages were entirely Turkish, and some Bulgarians rarely saw a Turk. The towns saw some interaction and a fair degree of mutual tolerance, even respect. Many individual Bulgarians trusted individual Turks more than they trusted some of their own. But, as in the case of ethnic relations generally, good individual relations were seldom broadened. The tinder was dry and waiting. In Bulgaria, as in the rest of the Balkans after the Ottoman demise, the descendants of Turkish settlers wanted to be left alone.

They were not an arrogant minority, as German and Hungarian minorities tended to be. Still, many Bulgarians resented them as residuals and reminders of the Turkish Yoke. From the end of the 1950s (again the timing was virtually the same as in Transylvania and Slovakia—national reemergences after the Stalin ice shield) some of the rights of the Turkish minority began to be whittled away, especially in education and journalism. This restrictive policy continued, albeit unevenly, through the 1960s and became increasingly evident in the 1970s. But no one was fully prepared for Zhivkov's massive denationalization or Bulgarization campaign of the 1980s. Too conspicuous to go unnoticed, this effort received much adverse attention in the world press. The Bulgarian government argued, by way of justification and with some academic backing, that the Turks were actually descendants of Bulgarians who had been converted to Islam in Ottoman times and had then begun using the Turkish language.[25] It was time, therefore, to reassimilate or "re-Bulgarize" them. They had to assume Bulgarian names and stop speaking Turkish in public. Many refused, which led to bloody encounters with the police, many more confrontations than were actually reported. Later, in an apparent reversal of policy, several hundred thousands were "encouraged" to leave for Turkey (see chapter 8). Zhivkov's measures were supported by most Bulgarians, but some intellectuals, either genuinely or with an eye on the international response, opposed them. This token opposition was an early example of the growing Western influence on East European public life. This influence would increase.

Economics 1945–2000: Behemoth

A RESORT TO WEBSTER'S DICTIONARY tells us: "Behemoth: (1) in the Bible, a huge animal, assumed to be the hippopotamus"; Job 40: 15–24; (2) "any huge animal." But the *Chambers 21st Century Dictionary* has "*loosely,* something huge and monstrous." That is precisely what the social-ist, Soviet-type economy was—something huge and monstrous. And much of that economy still remains. Hence, this chapter straddles both commu-nist and postcommunist eras. It does so because, although it may be dying, Behemoth still blocks the road to eventual prosperity and is incredibly hard to transform or redirect.

The Basics of Behemoth

Briefly, the characteristics of the socialist economic system—or Soviet-type economy (STE)—comprised:

A central planning agency (GOSPLAN was the legendary Soviet model). These agencies developed disproportionate bureaucracies that controlled every aspect of the economy. The planning system involved longer-term (usually five years) and shorter-term plans.
A central state bank that controlled data on the value of inputs and outputs of individual enterprises.
A state monopoly of foreign trade conducted in a way that segregated domestic prices from world prices.
Prices and wages established by the state.
State provision of housing, health services, transportation, and

educational facilities. The state also subsidized basic foodstuffs, transportation, housing, and clothing.

The state guaranteed full employment, not on economic grounds, but on ideological and social ones. Full employment soon became massive underemployment.

Economic planning became almost obsessed with the priority of heavy industry, which itself became synonymous with socialism. Heavy industry became not only ideologically correct, but a matter of national pride. The escape from backwardness! Huge industrial complexes became the flagships of these industrialization drives, and it was not entirely incidental that this same mania for heavy industry in Eastern Europe led to increased dependence on the Soviet Union for supplies of raw materials and fuel.

Heavy industry was "fed" by an increasingly larger industrial proletariat that mainly emanated from the forced collectivization of agriculture.

In both the Soviet Union and the socialist East European countries (and by many countries in the West), this centrally planned heavy industrial drive was credited with achieving basic economic expansion at a rapid rate. But the speed and methods of this expansion subsequently caused crippling dislocations and distortions.[1]

Almost every aspect of the Soviet-type economic system and its operation was lined up against the consumer in a chronic sellers' market. Although improvements occurred, the overall standard of living remained depressed. The discontent caused by this state of affairs was only partially assuaged by the social benefits that the system offered. In the end, this discontent was a principal cause of the collapse of communism. (After communism, however, the specter of massive unemployment and the curtailment of social benefits created widespread discontent against the rigors of nascent capitalism.)

At the apex of this economic system stood the communist party. Vlad Sobell succinctly describes the situation:

> The ultimate political power rested with the party, and the party ran the economy as its fiefdom, appointing nomenclature officials, including company directors. These people were not interested in maximizing the economic gain, but in maximizing their political kudos and leverage with the political bosses. This was ultimately also the only

access to economic welfare. They aimed to fulfill the plan (at least on paper) drawn up (or rather sanctioned) by the party, but cared little whether the plan actually made any economic sense. This is why human and natural resources could be wasted over decades on constructing and maintaining vastly inefficient industrial plants.[2]

Efforts at Reform

Beginning in the 1960s, and becoming common in the 1970s, much was made of "the decisive shift" in communist economic policy from "extensive" to "intensive" methods. The extensive methods had done their job, it was claimed; they put heavy industry and socialist agriculture in place. But material and human resources, once plentiful, were becoming scarcer (some official sources even admitted that profligacy had been involved). It was time, therefore, to switch to intensive methods. Economic policy reforms or reorganizations were introduced throughout the region. The most notable reforms were the brief series in Poland in 1955 and 1956, the Prague Spring reforms that budded early in the 1960s, and the Hungarian New Economic Mechanism, beginning in 1968, but prepared well beforehand. Also beyond the Soviet pale were the Yugoslav reforms of the mid-1960s. Bulgaria displayed little reforming zeal but almost a mania for reorganization—the most notable example in the early 1970s being the Agro-Industrial Complexes, a refurbished version of a classic Bolshevik notion.[3]

It should be added that just two and one-half years after the crushing of the Czechoslovak reforms, communist regime establishments suffered another shock through the worker's riots in Poland in December 1970, which caused the downfall of Gomułka. That uprising was followed by the *political* decision to divert more investments to consumer goods. The "age of consumerism" thus began, and overall living standards actually did improve. But the distribution of goods did not increase because of any conversion to reform; everywhere, except perhaps in Hungary, consumerism was basically an attempt to dodge reform. Hence, it could not last; it was not sustainable. What it did was whet popular demand, disappoint rising expectations, and bring the communist collapse closer.

The early 1970s were unquestionably years of economic hustle and bustle. A new formula for success seemed to have been devised. The sequence hewed to this design: imports of Western technology; use of cheap Western credits to pay for them; export-led economic growth; repayment of credits;

use of the consumerism bromide to lessen political lusts. The international situation, too, seemed promising for the new look in economics. Détente was in the air; the German Ostpolitik was in action; the Western money markets were awash with petrodollars; and Soviet energy supplies were still cheap. In fact, everything was set for fair sailing—except for Behemoth itself, the economic system. It simply could not use the technology that came its way. In both theory and practice, it remained embedded in the kindergarten socialism of the 1950s. Poland under Edward Gierek was probably the most egregious example of this approach, but even a more sophisticated economy like Hungary's could not cope. An aura of make-believe hovered over the first half of the 1970s.[4]

The make-believe dreams turned to smoke toward the end of the 1970s. Harsh reality did not return because of the world explosion in oil prices, which forced the Soviets to increase their export prices to the East Europeans. That certainly did not help, but the real reasons were the "system-specific" defects of the socialist model itself.[5] Exports of technologically based products to the West simply did not happen, Western debts accumulated, consumer expectations were disappointed, popular discontent mounted. Perhaps one cause was the most crucial of all. As technological development in the West accelerated into the computer age, the Soviet Union and its satellites fell further and further behind. Vlad Sobell sums this up well:

> Application of technological change demands an even greater degree of commitment to efficiency and profit-seeking than normal economic activities. It also demands freedom and openness to influences from outside, including, of course, free access to information and participation in the research and development process. It is simply inconceivable that the most recent expression of technological progress—the expansion of computers, information, technology and the productivity gains made possible by this revolution—could be applied under the conditions of the communist system. The information and data processing technology revolution perhaps delivered the final blow to the communist economic systems.[6]

1989: Groping Toward Rationality

During the communist era, Czechoslovakia and the GDR were sometimes described as having advanced socialist economies. The notion was that, generally, communist economies were on an upward spiral with these two leading the way. The truth was that the spiral was downward, and what was advanced about the Czechoslovak and East German economies was the capitalist legacy that the communists steadily dissipated. Or, as Václav Havel frequently described the Czechoslovak economy after 1989: "It was not just a house badly needing repair, but a ruin." He was talking about an economy that in the first forty years of the twentieth century, when it was outside the Soviet orbit, had been in the world's top half-dozen.[7]

What was certain after 1989 was that the escape from socialism into a market economy would be difficult.[8] It was easiest, of course, for the East German economy. That was taken over by the former West Germany. But it proved a millstone the sheer weight of which few Germans had suspected. Escape was difficult for three main reasons:

1. Behemoth itself, the all-encompassing monstrosity. Even when clinically dead, it was massively resistant to burial.
2. No way of escape was known from state socialism to a market economy. A half-century earlier, it had been much easier to go from the market to socialism. Nationalization was relatively simple; much of the capitalism in Eastern Europe had been state capitalism, anyway; the Soviet model was already in place; compulsion, rather than persuasive inducement, was the means used. Now, introducing capitalism was like pinning the tail on the donkey.[9]
3. The astonishing technical progress made in the West (and in parts of Asia), especially in the previous fifteen years, had made efficient modernization—catching up—all the more daunting.

The drive toward market reform centered on two notions: shock therapy, a tactless but descriptive term, and gradualism. The first involved a package of measures including privatizing business and industry; liberalizing or even abolishing price controls; effecting macrostabilization, which included wage controls and other enterprise spending; and reducing the budget deficit. Gradualism involved the same measures but, as the term implies, more gradually, mainly to mitigate social unrest.[10] It therefore took political and historical considerations into account. The shock therapists, though some of them were conscious of such considerations, emphasized that speed was crucial. Delay, they argued, meant failure.

In a study published in 1994, Nicholas Barr and his colleagues cited Leszek Balcerowicz, later deputy premier and finance minister of Poland

and the father of his country's radical economic reform, on the three broad components of market transformation: stabilization, mainly through macroeconomics policy; liberalization, such as that of ownership options, prices, and wages; and structural reconstruction.[11]

Performance: The North-South Divide

Already by 1994, Poland, the Czech Republic, and Hungary had begun achieving impressive economic results. Poland, in particular, began making spectacular progress. In 1995 and 1996 the Polish economy was expanding five times faster than the average growth rate in the European Union, and the Czech Republic was not far behind. The living standards in these two countries, as well as in Hungary, became both optically and statistically better. Generally speaking, this improvement was brought about through measures that allowed prices (at first, mainly those of goods and services) to become determined primarily by market forces; also brought under control were inflationary pressures, whether inherited or newly generated. The essential measures were macroeconomic, involving control of wages and other enterprise spending, slashes in subsidies, and reduced budget deficits.

In the mid-1990s the East Central European reform economies began to falter after their good starts (see chapter 5). By 1995, the Hungarian economy was ailing from twin deficits in its budget and current account; to avoid them, a drastic change of course had to be made. The initial price to be paid was a slowing down in Hungary's economic growth rate, higher inflation, and lower real incomes. The result: marked improvements in virtually all economic indicators. For some time the Czech economy, under Premier Václav Klaus, had continued confident, even buoyant. But confidence became complacency, and in 1997 it suffered similar, though more severe, misfortunes than Hungarians earlier had endured. Gross Domestic Product (GDP) slumped; inflation and unemployment rose. Neighboring Slovakia, though at a considerably lower level, was beginning to have the same problems, but the increase in its GDP continued impressively. In Poland, the economy kept growing robustly.

If East Central Europe therefore appeared still on course, South Eastern Europe was nowhere near it. As a Western newspaper reported: "Bulgaria, Romania, and Albania must realize in quick succession that their early upturn was based on all-too-shaky ground and that the timidity of their reforms was avenging itself."[12]

While the collapse of the various Pyramid schemes in Albania and the chaos resulting from it (see chapter 5) were unique, the economic transitions of most of the former Yugoslav republics were directly or indirectly affected by conflict. The debilities of the Bulgarian and Romanian economies, however, were due to basically similar reasons. True, Bulgaria had been much more dependent on the Soviet economy, and, especially in the 1980s, its debt to Western lenders had grown enormously. But both economies had suffered serious mismanagement under communism, and both were later exposed to dislocations caused by the UN embargo against Iraq, then against Serbia, and by the conflict in Kosovo. Both countries also suffered grievously from the inertia and the mistakes of domestic economic policy. Incompetence played a big part. But no consensus existed for comprehensive reform in either country. Even worse, a large element of their former communist bureaucracies soon realized that it could benefit from no reform or only a semblance of reform. In doing so, the bureaucracies paved the way for mafia interests to invade both politics and the economy (see chapter 4).[13]

Structural Reform

The gap between East Central and South Eastern Europe was widening. But much remained to be done in East Central Europe. It could all be subsumed under microeconomic adjustment or structural reform. The Czech Republic's much-vaunted voucher privatization scheme had led to nothing like the "stake-holders' economy" that was originally promised. Both ownership and control passed to remote financial institutions, some of which were susceptible to blatant corruption.[14] In Poland, several privatization schemes were tried out, some ill-conceived, others deliberately delayed. Hungary made the most progress in sound privatization (see chapter 5) and in the development of a credible banking system. By contrast, the deficiencies and corruption in the Czech banking system led to serious financial crises in 1997. Poland, though, after a series of false starts, began a consistent policy of bank privatization under Balcerowicz in 1998.[15]

In East Central Europe, too, there remained the problem of the "red elephants," the huge heavy industrial state factories and extractive industries still employing disproportionate numbers of workers. It was a problem likely to persist. Some successful downsizing and reinvigorating as had occurred, for example, in parts of Nowa Huta, in Poland, and parts of the Dunaujváros complex in Hungary. But the problem—as much political as economic—was still there. The Czechs had ducked it under Klaus, but they knew that they could not keep ducking it. Premier Mečiár in Slovakia had depended on heavy industrial workers and managers for some of his political support, and in Poland the issue began to cause strife in the governing coalition. In Romania and Bulgaria, assuming their economies got back on the road to macrostabilization, pressing problems of structural reform awaited. Until they were tackled, no sound economy could be achieved.

These problems differed in degree from country to country, but they had some basic elements in common. The large coal and steel district in Upper Silesia in Poland reflects the regional problems and the possibilities.[16]

According to estimates being made in 1998, by 2003 the coal industry in Silesia, with its population of about 4 million centered in Katowice, expected to have laid off about 100,000 miners. Imaginative and generous (but costly) schemes were adopted to soften the blow: early retirement, high severance pay, retraining, development of new industries and services through privatization, tax concessions, etc. The Polish authorities were pinning considerable hope on younger miners becoming small businessmen, using their severance pay to start up on their own or with others.

Most Katowice officials were not predicting catastrophe in 1998. All told, they expected about 300,000 jobs to disappear in the steel and mining industries and in the ancillary industries that serve them. But, with luck, they thought that they could cope with, or at least mitigate, the damage. From 1991 through 1998, 170,000 jobs had been trimmed in the coal industry alone, but the unemployment rate in Katowice remained well below the national average.

The relative optimism of officials was based on three facts:

1. In its communist heyday, industry in Upper Silesia, with good pay and perks, attracted many thousands of workers from all over Poland. Now, many of these workers probably would return to their original homes, helping to ease Katowice's problem (but hardly helping matters elsewhere).

2. As a huge socialist concern, the Silesian coal and steel industry had almost every possible ancillary: canteens, equipment, machines, hospitals, transport facilities, trade union offices, a gamut of sports

facilities, vacation services, administrative offices, etc. Some of these ancillaries, it was hoped, could become private concerns offering new employment.

3. New industries and a new infrastructure were coming to the Katowice district—some of them high tech. A new freeway, for example, was under construction. Here again, new jobs would come on-line.

But those 1998 estimates—which were characteristic for predictions about heavy industry throughout the former communist bloc—were proving too rosy by the turn of the century. The Katowice coal mines were incurring huge losses in 2000. There was still far too much overproduction, costs were increasing, and further reductions in the labor force were essential. An altogether new, leaner and meaner approach was imperative. A "reform of the reform" was being talked about; the reform of two years earlier had proved totally unrealistic. But *who* would reform the reform? This question also applied to the rest of Eastern Europe. The truth was that the political courage to make the required economic changes would be regarded as political lunacy. Revamping heavy industry was now Eastern Europe's biggest problem.

The Future of Social Welfare

Despite the general tendency, for sociopolitical reasons, to duck real structural reform, by the end of the century much punishing economic change had affected the standard of living of a great many East Europeans. Yet these changes had not been greeted with the angry popular opposition that many expected. True, massive outrage in 1997 was set off by the Pyramid fiasco; in Romania, too, the mining fraternity flexed its muscles several times; and in Bulgaria, tens of thousands of citizens, driven to desperation by government corruption and incompetence, demonstrated in 1996. But, by and large, moderation, not mayhem, prevailed. This calm probably stemmed from basic historical, psychological, and cultural causes, but one immediately obvious reason was the *enrichizzez-vous* opportunity that the emerging capitalist economic order was giving to a large and increasing number of younger East Europeans. And these were the most spirited and activist members of the community, the ones most likely to exert influence on the population as a whole (see chapter 4).

Another reason for the relative calm was the retention of a protective safety net, a social welfare system centered on retirement and disability pensions, unemployment assistance, and the easing of poverty. Mark Kramer in 1997 described how relatively impressive that social net was.[17] Although it was nothing like even the most threadbare of West European nets, it did soften economic blows and take the edge off people's anger.

While the benefit system may have made for immediate calm, however, it could be the cause of future problems. Payments to provide it could become a serious impediment to further financial stabilization, economic growth, and general prosperity. They are, in fact, deemed *too* generous from an economic point of view. So are other aspects of the welfare state inherited from the communists. It is the *universality* of welfare that is so costly.

Kramer relates a telling quotation from Lajos Bokros, Hungary's former finance minister, when he still held that position: "A country as indebted as Hungary cannot afford to spend the equivalent of 29 percent of annual GDP on welfare and social services. It cannot afford universal child-care benefits, two years of maternity pay, and free higher education for all. The universal entitlement will have to go. We have to limit social assistance to those in need."[18] Bokros was putting his finger on a problem that could not be avoided. At the turn of the twenty-first century, anger was beginning to mount. In Poland, and especially in Romania, serious strikes and intra-government bickering were growing, and the former socialist proletariat were spearheading the disturbances, egged on by political opportunists.[19] Reforming governments, even timid ones as in Romania, could be voted out of office, or even blasted from it. The skill and restraint of domestic politicians, the European Union, and the international financial community would be needed to prevent economic reform, and eventually democracy, from being derailed.

Globalization and Emigration

By the end of the twentieth century no subject was being more widely discussed, hotly debated, or vigorously opposed than globalization. Its worldwide impact and ramifications cannot be discussed here. What can be discussed briefly is its impact on Eastern Europe, which has been relatively slow but is quickening. Globalization is being recognized as the biggest opportunity (or the biggest danger) for the region in generations—more comprehensive in some ways than the collapse of communism, more complex in many ways than the transition to capitalism and democracy.

For East Europeans globalization means that most of their industry worth having, now or in the future, will become Western property, run mainly for Western private profit. And "Western property" is now beginning to mean *100 percent* Western property. Joint ventures between Western and local concerns seemed to be the way forward for most of the 1990s, but more Western investors are now favoring total ownership for themselves. Total ownership is seen as more efficient and better able to manage the local workforce, whose educational standards have surprised many Westerners by being so good.

It is not surprising, therefore, that globalization has provoked wrath, suspicion, or unease. From Polish Catholic nationalists, to Czechs like Václav Klaus, to former Bulgarian communists, the perceived dangers of globalization have been weapons used to influence and frighten people, for obvious political ends. They have been a boon to reactionaries, "nostalgics," conspiracy theorists, and America-haters. Some genuinely concerned environmentalists have also inveighed against globalization, as have many intellectuals alarmed at the possible flattening of national identities by this new multinational juggernaut. And in many parts of Eastern Europe these opponents have been given much ammunition by many Western entrepreneurs, whose arrogance and local ignorance are sometimes compared unfavorably by older East Europeans with the behavior of the Soviet advisers who invaded their country after World War II. These new arrivals could take to heart Goran Lindhal's warning that "the pursuit of profit alone cannot hold societies together."[20]

The *Economist*'s judgment seems particularly sound: "Multinationals should continue to listen, to try to do no harm, to accept the responsibilities that go with size and wealth. Yet, in the main, they should be seen as a powerful force for good. They spread wealth, work technologies that raise living standards and better ways of doing business."[21] But the point is that Eastern Europe has no choice. If it is to have any chance of economic recovery and political progress (i.e., toward meaningful democracy), then globalization must be accepted and made to work. The alternative is isolation, destitution, and some form of fascist/nationalist politics—something like Serbia under Milošević, but eventually worse. Western Europe might have the luxury of doubting and delaying globalization but Eastern Europe does not.

And the good that globalization can do is already evident. Some Western-owned companies are transforming for the better the economics, way of life, and psychology of the areas where they operate.[22] More Western companies will certainly come if foolproof property laws are enacted and bureaucratic regulations are reduced. One huge benefit they will bring is the elimination of much economic corruption and the reduction of mafia control throughout the region. As for "McDonaldization," "Coca Colonialism," the emergence of the "denationalized eunuch," or other threats intoned by many local intellectuals, the only possible answer is this: It is hard to imagine, say, the Poles, who have survived four partitions and successive efforts to annihilate the flower of their nation, or the Bulgarians, who have endured five centuries of alien rule but have kept their identity, their language, and their religion, throwing in the towel for the sake of a Big Mac or a small Coke, even with a free order of french fries.

Emigration is also a subject that needs fuller treatment than can be given here. Almost 2.5 million East Europeans have left their native land since 1989,[23] usually the youngest, the brightest, and the best. In South Eastern Europe, particularly, a large part of which has recently been engulfed or directly affected by war, the numbers emigrating have been proportionally very large.

The mass exodus is certainly worrying, but several aspects about the whole issue need to be taken into account. Briefly, they are:

1. Emigration is a reality. It cannot and should not be stopped.

2. There is a need for fairness. Any man or woman has the right to go when and where he or she will. The right to emigrate was denied to practically all East Europeans for almost half a century. And this fifty-year denial made the post-1989 tide of emigration all the greater and swifter.

3. Most young East European emigrants will, by their exertion and example, do their native countries proud in the countries where they settle. They will be excellent ambassadors, immeasurably improving the image of, and knowledge about, their countries—an even more important contribution than the financial remittances they send home. An improved image may not be necessary in the case of Poland, but for Romania and Bulgaria it is.

4. A sense of perspective about the flow of emigration is needed. After people were so long denied an opportunity to emigrate, and were then bombarded by Western glamour, their rush for the exit was only natural. This rush will ease, and the consequent losses will be tangible but not necessarily crippling.

5. Some emigrants, for whatever reason, will return. They will be better-rounded and more useful citizens than they would if they had not emigrated.

But the most important factor in the whole emigration equation may well be the migration *eastward* through Western investment. Here the link between globalization and emigration becomes clear. If numerous successful, state-of-the-art Western companies set up shop in Eastern Europe, more promising East Europeans will stay and emigrants will be tempted to return. These Western companies will pay wages that are not only consonant with human dignity (and many wage "scales" in Eastern Europe are not) but stimulating and competitive; they will also provide opportunities for local talents and skills, thereby restoring pride in local capabilities.

Emigration is a serious problem, without doubt. But it is no excuse for wallowing in melancholy and self-pity. Globalization might be the best answer to emigration. It could build a West-East link to bring tangible benefits to East Europeans—not least a sense of worth coming from high-level participation and contribution.

4

Democracy: Stumbling Forward

NEW YORK YANKEES' MANAGER Joe Torre, a survivor from the days
when baseball meant something special to American civilization, was once
asked his golden rule of managing. "Always tell the truth," he said. Asked to
explain this seemingly ruinous precept, he replied: "If you tell the truth, you
don't have to remember what you said."*

This homespun wisdom reverberates far beyond the clubhouse. It should
serve as a cautionary reminder to politicians, policy analysts, academics,
and sundry others who claim that they saw 1989 coming in Eastern Europe
and spotted the Soviet collapse from afar. A few, it is true, can cite chapter
and verse. But even the best that most pretenders can do is point to a "just-
might-be" paragraph or an occasional sibylline aside. Most egregious of all
are those who try to reinterpret past utterances, crystal-clear at the time,
with a mixture of casuistry and breathtaking sangfroid.

Rather more reassuring is the candor of a man like Christoph Bertram.
Reviewing a book about the fall of the GDR, Bertram confessed:

> I was persuaded that the Soviet Union, with all its tanks, missiles,
> warheads, party bosses and raw materials, was there to stay. And what-
> ever steps it might take towards internal reform, it would never permit
> its German creation, the German Democratic Republic, to go down
> the drain. Hence the GDR, economically the most successful of Mos-
> cow's satellites, was also there to stay, under a leadership which seemed

---

*Bob Mirandon, of Duke University Press, has told me that Mark Twain said the same thing
over a hundred years ago. This may detract a little from Torre's originality but tends to
reinforce his wisdom and awareness.

to enjoy a measure of domestic support despite the fact that it continued to shoot anyone who tried to escape to the West.[1]

In explaining why he (and almost all of us) were wrong, Bertram puts his finger on the crucial factor: the Soviet Union. Practically everybody who had followed developments in Eastern Europe knew by about 1985 that "real existing socialism" was facing collapse. But practically all of us were convinced that, as long as the Soviet Union was there, the East European regimes would be propped up. And propping them up meant insisting on a recognizable structure of communist rule. Besides, we were all fatalistic about the Brezhnev Doctrine and Moscow's capacity to enforce it. August 1968 in Prague had taught us that much, and it had been confirmed in December 1981 when Jaruzelski acted as Brezhnev's proxy in Poland.

What we of little faith did not understand was the true condition of the Soviet Union. It was not just weak, but incurable; death itself was inside the house. Gorbachev had the honesty to recognize this degeneration and the courage to act. But he could not see that the system had so rotted as to be incapable of regeneration. And he *would* not see that the doctrine on which the system was based was profoundly flawed. He had made his "Leninist choice," and he stuck to it. This was what made him a great failure. In terms of the task he set for himself—the redemption of Soviet socialism—he could have been nothing else. And nowhere was his failure more predictable and more complete than in Eastern Europe.

Gorbachev thought socialism was redeemable not only in the Soviet Union, but also in Eastern Europe. And because of this faith, he believed that nationalism was basically irrelevant. This was his greatest misjudgment. True, from 1987 till 1989 he modified his views about Eastern Europe. His speeches before 1987 were generally orthodox Soviet dogma, banal not only on socialism's permanence in Eastern Europe, but also on its natural roots. Hence, nationalism was steadily being squeezed out of the body politic and out of citizens' consciousness. (A touch of Khrushchev here.)[2] Later, Gorbachev showed signs of learning, but he still could not face the nationalist reality in Eastern Europe, in the Baltic republics, or elsewhere in the Soviet Union.

In *Surge to Freedom,* I quoted some remarks about "socialist cooperation" that Gorbachev made to intellectuals in Warsaw as late as July 1988. That date marked a time when Poland was in renewed ferment, and Solidarity, after seven years out of open politics, was pushing its way into power. Those remarks are worth repeating:

> We have noticed in Poland that you have the same concerns. I feel that we are following the same road even more confidently, taking into consideration the specific differences, which is obvious and clear. It was a great error to ignore specific differences; at last the dispute about the model of socialism is at an end. It is scientific socialism, and it must be realized in concrete conditions of every state, taking into consideration tradition, level of development, political culture, and the potential of each country. This is my view of the model of socialism. Nevertheless, acting independently, following the chosen road, we feel how much we need each other, perhaps as never before. . . .[3]

Gorbachev's line went: no matter how free the East Europeans become—and freedom was their birthright—they would opt for the socialist "essence." In fact, the freer they became, he thought, the more they would opt for socialism. The common essence would be recognizable and indestructible, no matter how distinct each country became. And this essence would reduce national differences and strengthen the voluntary socialist alliance, for which eventually no formal structures would be needed.

Just what this socialist "essence" was could be endlessly discussed. No one doubts that in the Soviet Union's final few years it was endlessly discussed there. Moscow and other cities were the scene of intense, high-level ferment, centering on the nature and the future of socialism, on economic, administrative, educational, and governmental reform, nuclear and conventional disarmament, the Soviet alliance, the Soviet role in Europe, Soviet-American relations, Sino-Soviet relations, and more—much more. And the ferment was more public than it had ever been in Russia's history. Communists—some nominal, some opportunistic, and some sincere—were at the heart of the ferment.

For East Europeans, the substance of this discussion was much less relevant than its possible implications. They had had enough of socialism and too much of the Soviet Union. Gorbachev was popular among many of them—but as a symbol of hopeful change. In their view, this change should not strengthen socialism and the socialist alliance, but it should undermine them. For them, Gorbachev was not the way to an equal and dignified "partnership," but a possible means of escape from any sort of partnership.

And the main reason for his popularity was that they knew he would not use force (at least outside the Soviet Union). He had ditched the Brezhnev Doctrine because he honestly believed that true socialism would make it irrelevant and unnecessary. Now it was the "Sinatra Doctrine," as Gennadi Gerasimov trendily put it: "Doing it their way."[4] But the "it" was socialism, which they did not want. And "their way" was *out*, not *in*. As for Gorbachev's catchword, "our common house Europe," Europe was *their* house, not Russia's.

The last, saddest words about Gorbachev and Eastern Europe were written by Gorbachev himself in a letter to Jacques Lévesque in July 1995. He said that he continued to believe that "the socialist idea, as the idea of freedom, democracy, and social justice, cannot die or disappear." He added that "the objective course of events, including the most recent elections in a whole series of East European countries, fully confirms this conclusion."[5] The elections he referred to were those in Poland, Hungary, and elsewhere that had returned or retained postcommunist parties in power, parties that were actually introducing capitalism into their economies. Gorbachev was still out of touch, as he had been about Eastern Europe all along.

The Revolutions in Retrospect

This book is appearing more than ten years after the great upheavals of 1989. In the light of what we now know, or think we know, about events in the different countries, do we need to make basic changes in our early assessments of what happened? Basic changes no; modifications, yes.[6]

The modifications center on the question of whether events in 1989 indeed constituted a "surge to freedom" (as I called my book published by Duke in 1991) or a communist *sauve qui peut*. Certainly what happened in 1989, and what has (or has not) happened since, can lend support to *sauve qui peut*, but everywhere in Eastern Europe a genuine surge to freedom took place. As in most revolutions there were mixed motives and different emphases, hence different interpretations. But in no way was 1989 a gross deception or a great illusion. Accompanying it, though, came a degree of communist "adaptation": brazen, knowing, and successful.

Those who have insisted on basic changes in the early interpretations have usually been the conspiracy theorists, a brotherhood that grabs attention wherever it goes, whatever it mystifies, and whomever it confuses. But because of the vagaries of Eastern Europe's history, the conspiracy zealots tend to get a wider hearing there than elsewhere. Romanians, in particular, have been both avid purveyors and consumers of conspiracy schemes. In Romania, politics are seldom allowed to be what they seem to be.[7]

Romanians staged two coups against dictatorships in the twentieth century—one in 1944 against the pro-Nazi Antonescu regime, and the other in 1989 against Ceaușescu's communist government. Both coups were courageous, and both were successful. But both became the subjects of controversy, deception, and misunderstanding. Certainly the 1989 revolt against Ceaușescu was not the "popular uprising" against tyranny that it was at first depicted to be, and realization of this fact spawned many attempts to tell the "real" story. None of these accounts, then or in retrospect, have turned out to be convincing. The most sensible analysis remains that of Nestor Rateș's short book, *Romania: The Entangled Revolution*.[8] Entangled it certainly was, but genuine nonetheless.

The conspiracy theories mainly rest on Moscow's role in the 1989 revolutions, and genuine controversy certainly still surrounds this notion. How directly, and to what extent, did the Gorbachev leadership intervene, if at all, to get rid of East European leaders it regarded as blocking change? In Romania's case, Soviet leaders, from Brezhnev to Gorbachev, wanted to get rid of Ceaușescu. Some of them may have tried. But by 1989 the Soviet leadership must have known that Ceaușescu was doomed. The wisest among them also must have understood that the best way to assure his fall was not to risk being seen as hastening it. The rotten apple would fall without the tree being shaken.

In any case, because of Ceaușescu, Romania was exceptional. Poland was exceptional, too, though for markedly different reasons. Virtually in a state of siege ever since Solidarity was founded in the summer of 1980, it was obvious by 1988 that this abnormal situation could not continue. Poland was in ferment yet again, and the threat to communist rule was becoming more direct. Gorbachev was aware that Jaruzelski was a symbol of communist repression. Yet Gorbachev also knew enough about Poland's history to make him reluctant to give Poles completely free rein to "do it their way." He further understood that Poland was crucial to the GDR's survival, the division of Germany, and the Soviet position in Europe. Thus, it was Jaruzelski *faute de mieux*. Hope for the best![9] But soon enough, the worst happened. It would have happened sooner if the Polish democrats had realized that the Brezhnev Doctrine was fast lapsing into desuetude. After all, it was only a few years since Poles had been the indirect victims of it. That was why, in retrospect, Wałęsa and his allies seem to have been so hesitant. They thought the lights were still red, or at best yellow, when in fact they had turned green. That is why the conspiracy theorists have seen promise in Poland, too. The hesitation, delay, and magnanimity toward the communists across the negotiating table—all of it seemed suspicious.

The two other Northern Tier states, the GDR and Czechoslovakia, had several similarities. They both bordered onto West Germany and the NATO alliance; they were both heavily industrialized and relatively advanced economically; by East bloc standards, they were Western. They both had veteran leaders, Honecker and Husák, who had come to power after momentous political and international upheavals. Both were basically nervous leaders, opposed to meaningful change at home, increasingly suspicious of, yet obviously dependent on, the Soviet Union, and distrustful of détente. The "years of stagnation" had suited them perfectly. Gorbachev was their nightmare turned real. Indeed, both leaders must have been high on the Soviet leader's list of undesirables. But as the anticommunist crisis in both countries developed—more quietly in the GDR than in Czechoslovakia—Gorbachev could hardly have been seen as *directly* hastening their departure. He chose the indirect—the most effective—way. He kept silent and shrugged his shoulders. Nothing to do with him! Everybody understood, especially the East Germans and the Czechoslovaks; Honecker and Husák were finished.[10]

Hungary and Bulgaria had few similarities. János Kádár and Todor Zhivkov had little in common except their having been more than thirty years in power. But it was precisely those thirty years that worried Gorbachev. They were part of a history he could not repudiate, but that he hoped would recede. Kádár, of course, had been a dramatic reformer by the standards of his time. But his mind-set was in the past, and he was not the man to whom Hungarians wanted to entrust their future. As for Zhivkov, he had never had much beyond a sense and a taste for power. But the more he clung to power, the more his authority dwindled, and in the end it did not take much to be rid of him. The Soviet embassy in Sofia may not have been the control room for a plot that ousted him, as some Bulgarians claim, but it was no longer there when Zhivkov needed it.

Continuity and Overthrow

The year 1989! Not so much *what* happened, as *how* it happened, will continue to be debated. But as the East European states and their politics push into the new century, *how* will become irrelevant. What will count is the here and now, the progress toward liberal democracy.

Perhaps the word "progress," however, conveys the wrong impression of developments since 1989. What has characterized those developments has been the mixture, the struggle, and the compromise between *continuity* and *overthrow*—the survival of people, practices, and attitudes from the communist period and the efforts to repudiate the past and create something new, specifically a system modeled on that of the West. Continuity has never meant or threatened reversal; since 1989 a communist restoration has been unimaginable except to paranoids. But many pillars of the old order have survived safely, even grandly. And many East Europeans who hated the old order have wanted to retain some parts of it. Thus, different ambitions, aspirations, and fears have formed the confluence of this stream of continuity and overthrow that has characterized postcommunist history.

The stream is both broad and deep. This is because 1989 (except in Romania) witnessed a nonviolent, negotiated revolution. Most revolutions, far more violent and antagonistic than that of 1989, also have had these twin elements of continuity and overthrow. The big exception was the totalitarian revolution in Russia in 1917, completed by the Stalinist revolution and terror. This book, though mainly concerned with the moves toward change, is also strewn with instances of continuity. Its very title is intended to convey the interaction of continuity and change.

IRREVERSIBLE CHANGE

Seven basic requirements of change were being met: (1) freedom of speech; (2) free media; (3) freedom of association; (4) free, fair elections and acceptance of their results; (5) dismantling of communist institutions; (6) introduction of competitive politics; and (7) movement toward a market economic system. Partial exceptions could be found in the Balkans. In Albania, democratic development was perverted, not so much by the former communists as by the militant anticommunists under the former president Sali Berisha. In Serbia, the occasional false promise of democracy was never fulfilled; Slobodan Milošević saw to that. What he thrived on was a state of siege, and he slipped from this condition into a state of war.

But in the rest of Eastern Europe, it was surprising how fully these seven basic requirements were being met. Even in Bulgaria and Romania, democratic elections, though not without fault, were generally free and fair. Just as important, the results were accepted by the losers. In the elections in

Romania in November 1996 and in Bulgaria in April 1997, the former communist incumbents, now the Socialists in Bulgaria, and the Party of Social Democracy in Romania, were unseated. In Poland, too, the postcommunist incumbents were the clear losers in the parliamentary elections of September 1997. Some of those defeated candidates and their followers even managed a show of good grace in their discomfiture. The same happened in Hungary in May 1998. Most East Europeans were finding that changing their governments was as natural as changing their clothes.

It was a development greatly to be encouraged. But at the very turn of the new century, fears were present in several countries that the next elections could result in governments that, while not reversing change, would slow it or tamper with it. Stagnation would result, with opportunities lost or shelved. The former communists in both Romania and Bulgaria, few of whom had genuinely come over to social democracy, were gaining in the opinion polls. (In Romania they looked set for victory.) Vladimir Mečiár was emerging (or reemerging) as the most popular politician in Slovakia (see chapter 5), and even in the Czech Republic, the communists, who had changed neither their name nor their complexion, were winning more favor with the public. Specific local issues caused these shifts, but the overall one was the economic hardship, primarily unemployment, resulting from structural reform. In Poland, too, economic difficulties were becoming a big political issue. The next major test for democracy was coming—not for its survival, but for its fulfillment.

The Underpinnings

So far, so good. But for democracies to be full, rounded, and safe, more than these seven criteria were still needed. To be precise, four essential underpinnings were called for: (1) minimum material standards; (2) rule of law; (3) civil society and the growth of a civic class; (4) a strong (enough) state.[11]

MINIMUM MATERIAL STANDARDS

Minimum material standards are essential to democracy because they are vital to private morality. "Minimum" defies definition, but much of the region falls short of achieving it. Well into the 1990s, even the East Central European countries lagged well back among the world's top seventy countries in GDP per capita. Hungary was fiftieth, the Czech Republic fifty-second, Slovakia sixty-fourth, and Poland sixty-sixth.[12] If each country can be seen in terms of two escalators—one going down, the other ascending—the up escalator would be packed with young people, overwhelmingly men, impatient at the snail's pace of their climb. The descending escalator would be chock-full of shabbily dressed, tired old people, as well as the unemployed of all ages, simply not knowing how low they were going to descend. Obviously, the upwardly mobile were the key to the future. But those descending had to be considered—and soon; if unemployment increased and welfare provisions were reduced, their lot would grow worse. They would still be entitled to vote, of course. But would they even bother? Why take part in what for them had become a ruinous sham? Could a citizenry develop?[13]

(National) independence, (personal) liberty, (economic) security—the trinity of postcommunist imperatives! Since 1989, all East Europeans have enjoyed independence and liberty; many have enjoyed security, too, and their numbers are increasing. But many more—and their numbers are not decreasing fast enough—have lost the economic security that they had under communism, and they are stuck on that downward escalator (see also chapter 10). The blessings of independence and liberty mean little or nothing to them. A reporter for the *Economist* vividly captured the plight of the dispossessed in Łódź, Poland's second most populous city:

> It is a cold, grey autumn morning ten years after the collapse of communism. A lorry is delivering a winter's supply of coal to a retired widower in a poor district of Lodz (pronounced Woodge), Poland's second city. The widower stands outside her tiny terraced house, arms folded, glowering fiercely. The coal costs too much, she moans. "Life was much better before 1989." Work was easier, and she had a free holiday at the seaside every summer. Coal was free too, she adds.
>
> The coalmen, three of them, steam in the frigid air from all the shovelling and carrying. "She's right about one thing," one of them says. "Life was much easier ten years ago." He leans on his shovel and wipes his blackened brow. "There's not much in the new Poland for people like me and her." Like you? "You know," he says bitterly, "the old, the thick, the working man." . . .
>
> To make a living, the men drive their decrepit Soviet-era lorry through the night selling coal by the bucket. They cannot understand why life is so hard for them, while others, especially young people, seem to have it easy. "Its like magic," says one. "We're struggling just to survive and all these kids have money to spend on music and clothes."[14]

These two escalators and their different passengers symbolize two apparently contradictory imperatives in postcommunist Eastern Europe: the development of the market economy and the continuing need for state intervention. (These two imperatives, however, are not necessarily contradictory.) The disasters of socialism only pointed up the virtues of the market. For the creation of wealth, the market has no known rival, and, since 1989, millions of East Europeans have needed little convincing of this fact. But the market creates misery, too, a fact that millions of East Europeans know firsthand. The state is needed more than ever to ensure some balance between the winner taking all and the devil taking the hindmost.

But the state can (and should) do only so much. It can do little (what or who can?) about one of the intractable dilemmas in Eastern Europe today: the consumerist urge, the general inability to satisfy it, and the social consequences of that shortcoming. After centuries of material deprivation, the vast majority of East Europeans have suddenly come face to face with the wonders of Western capitalist consumerism—indirectly through television, and directly through its burgeoning presence in their own midst. Presence, however, is not the same as availability—at least not for large sections of the population. They can only sit and gape. But many of these have-nots, too, determined not to be denied "their share" of the new bonanza, succumb to dishonesty, corruption, and then to petty—or not so petty—crime in their efforts to get it. The same debility exists in the West, of course, but Western citizens have become inured to consumerism. In the East, they are still blinded by its dazzling suddenness. This massive, unconditional, and exclusive preoccupation with it worries many observers—all the more so because no end seems to be in sight. No one doubts that a "clear positive correlation exists between economic reform and the consolidation of democracy,"[15] but eventually the right balance has to be found between market exuberance and market restraint. Self-restraint is always to be preferred, but an intelligent, imposed restraint is more realistic.

RULE OF LAW

Many good laws were passed in communist Eastern Europe. But there was no rule of law. Good laws were debased because all law was imbued with— and hence vitiated by—the ideological system. One of the new Eastern Europe's greatest problems is developing and ensuring the rule of law. It is a mammoth task not only because of Eastern Europe's remote and recent past, but also because of the overall urgency in dismissing the old and

5. Eastern Europe in 1995. © Bartholomew Ltd 2000. Reproduced by permission of HarperCollins Publishers Ltd, Bishopbriggs, Scotland.

summoning in the new. Speed is the natural enemy of lawfulness; not getting things done—but getting them done lawfully—is difficult anywhere.

By 1998, all of the East European countries had new constitutions. These were essential. For several years all but a few of these countries had limped along with amendments to the old communist constitutions, which became patched up beggars' garments, better than nothing but tattered and worn. Ironically, Bulgaria and Romania, two of the sluggards of postcommunist change, were the first to enact new constitutions. But, slowly and painfully, the others followed. The first essential had been achieved.

The problem now was to make the constitutions relevant and respected. On this score, so far, the overall record has been encouraging. The efforts of most constitutional courts to do their duty—to become part of the checks and balances of democracy—have been commendable. The constitutional court in Hungary has become an indispensable element in public life. The Slovak court showed courage several times in defying Premier Mečiár's populism. In Bulgaria, though wavering occasionally, the court asserted its authority in key situations. Even in Albania, it tried to stand up to President Sali Berisha's bullying. But at the end of the century, understanding was sketchy among the publics in Eastern Europe about what judges were supposed to do. Relatively few people understood that their obligation was not to do what was popular (or even what seemed right), but to do what the law laid down. However, with better and more open procedures and better judges, confidence in justice at all levels should increase.

CIVIL SOCIETY AND THE GROWTH OF A CIVIC CLASS

Few subjects have been discussed more widely, fervently, and piously than civil society. That range and depth of feeling reflect both its importance and the wishful thinking that goes with it. The very concept of civil society, though, also has had its doubters. They were common and vociferous in both the United States and Britain in the 1980s. In Eastern Europe, the Czech premier, Václav Klaus, also took up the cudgels against the notion of civil society. In 1994, Klaus debated the issue on television with Václav Havel in one of their periodic punchups that reflected their differences of opinion and sense of values.[16] Most serious actors on the postcommunist scene, however, are convinced of the necessity of a vigorous civil society.

In *Hopes and Shadows*, I used a passage by George Schöpflin to recall that elements of civil society existed in precommunist Eastern Europe. I also defined civil society as "a 'third realm of pluralistic political, social, and cultural collectives' existing between the level of the individual and the level of the state." I went on to amplify this definition: "Civil society, therefore, involves more than free elections, civil liberties, representative institutions, and an independent judiciary: it also involves the . . . development of civil, religious, and professional associations and trade unions . . . that lie beyond the control of the state and are safeguarded by the rule of law.[17]

The communists perverted several institutions of civil society by making them transmission belts—trade unions, professional organizations, cultural societies, etc. Churches were used as well. The Orthodox churches were heaven-sent for the role; so were some Protestant leaders; and in Czechoslovakia about 15 percent of all priests belonged to Pacem in Terris, the pro-regime Catholic organization. "Peace" was the insidious temptation that the communists used. They—the communists—were defending it; the West was alleged to be its threat.

One manifestation of communism's decline was the slow rebirth of civil society in Eastern Europe, especially in the 1980s. Since 1989, an apparent explosion of civil society has taken place. This change has been healthy enough, and inevitable; but it has been partly deceptive, too. The sweeping epidemic of nongovernmental organizations (NGOs) is a case in point. They are so numerous, and so many have been so short-lived, that it is impossible to keep up with either their birth rate or their death rate. Most of them have been admirable in their aspirations. But not all of them have been an expression of a burgeoning civil society. Some have been esoteric to the point of whimsy, others clearly on the make. Many have had impressive letterheads, often with lists of purported "patrons" that stretch credulity. In all, too many NGOs seem distractions from, or substitutes for, civil society— a playground for dilettantes, not a field for doers.

What must emerge—and this will take time—is a middle class with an influential, civic-minded outlook. First, though, a middle class itself is necessary. Historically, the notion and the mentality of a middle class were relatively little known in Eastern Europe. Aristocrats, gentry, and peasants populated the countryside, and only the towns boasted a small "burgher" element, most of which consisted of Germans, Jews, or, in South Eastern Europe, Greeks and sometimes Turks and Armenians. Except in the Czech Lands, an indigenous middle class was slow in developing. Nazi persecution and then the results of World War II saw the virtual disappearance of Jews and Germans. Communist ideology disowned the very notion of a middle class, and the communists set about destroying peasant society as well. In

Kádár's Hungary, a rudimentary middle class did develop; the private sphere was enlarged, material standards improved, travel abroad was permitted, and a live-and-let-live attitude developed. But neither in Kádár's Hungary nor anywhere else under communism did any notion exist of specific middle-class rights and responsibilities. Subjects existed, but not citizens.

Many observers have pointed out that, since 1989, a middle class has been emerging throughout Eastern Europe. But this perhaps oversimplifies a complex economic and social development. Elemer Hankiss, the Hungarian sociologist, thinks that several social groups have emerged, which he divides into "winners" and "losers." Hankiss specifically refers to his own country, but his differentiations also have a regional relevance.[18]

Hankiss divides postcommunist society into three groups. The first is a new property-owning upper middle class. Obviously "winners," members of this class include entrepreneurs, managers, senior bank officials, stockbrokers, top lawyers, and technical specialists, as well as former communist party functionaries who found their way around the new environment. The second group comprises the middle or lower-middle class—skilled workers, petty bureaucrats and *beamter,* and small-scale entrepreneurs in both town and country. This group is slowly declining, many already on the down escalator mentioned earlier—baffled and embittered. The third group, described by Hankiss as the "losers," are presumably most of the aged and the *lumprenproletariat,* many of whom are unemployed. Hankiss specifically mentions the Gypsies, most of whom obviously have little or no chance in postcommunist society. There is also, of course, another group, outside society but very much battening on it. This is the mafia-and-gangster class with the neckless brotherhood of bodyguards, easy to pick out, best to avoid.

Since 1989, a middle class has been developing throughout the region. But how quickly and how substantially will it develop? The signs are often depressing. One great danger to civil society in Eastern Europe, Russia, and the Soviet Union's successor states is the selfishness and lack of public spirit in society at large. After communism, it was perhaps not surprising that a strong, individualist, Social Darwinian reaction emerged, often among the fittest and brightest, those well-fitted to help society as well as help themselves.

Such individualism, if it spreads unrestrained, will pose a serious threat to future hopes for "civicness." What Eastern Europe could do with today is the public spirit that Robert D. Putnam describes in the medieval cities of northern Italy, in the public concern of the Hanseatic League, or, coming forward in time, to the working-class cooperativism in northern England in the nineteenth century. By way of warning, Putnam points to the grim lesson of the Italian *Mezzogiorno,* with which he contrasts the history of the northern Italian cities: "Without norms of reciprocity and networks of civic engagement, the Hobbesian outcome of the *Mezzogiorno*—amoral familism, clientelism, lawlessness, ineffective government, and economic stagnation—seems likelier than successful democratization and economic development. Palermo may represent the future of Moscow."[19] And not only Moscow, but Kiev, Sofia, and Bucharest, not to mention Tirana. As will be discussed, organized crime is a powerful element in the public life of several former communist countries, and crime's grip is tightening, not slackening.

Some Westerners along with some East Europeans have argued that robber barons and rugged individuals are essential, constructive elements in the evolution of a respectable middle class. That was the way of the West, so now it must be the way of the East! But must this necessarily be so? And can Eastern Europe, after centuries of backwardness and a half-century of communism, withstand the rigors of a free-for-all likely to sweep away whatever political, social, and legal progress has been made? The West is an essential role model, guide, and benefactor. However, parts of its history must be avoided, not emulated, and the West itself can bring its power to bear to ensure this path of development. A middle class, of course, is never ready-made off the shelf. It takes time, and it has its delays and setbacks. Its evolution can be crafted, though, its emergence hastened, and its civic sense strengthened. It is the prerequisite and concomitant of democracy.

Whatever their future spiritual role might be in Eastern Europe, it would seem that the different churches and other religious communities could play an important part in helping to restrain the self-serving materialism and in promoting "civicness." Churches and religious groups have a tradition of good works, service, and social conscience. Now, as they receive material restitution for the losses they suffered under communism, they also have some means at their disposal. The Roman Catholic Church, in particular, has never had much time for laissez-faire capitalism. Pope John Paul II has routinely lambasted it. A historic opportunity exists here, along with an avenue for the churches to continue their public relevance.

The Political Culture

If minimum material standards, the rule of law, and civil society underpin democratic society, a high level of political culture must pervade it. What is political culture? This question has become almost as complex as asking what truth is. No diagnosis or dissection will be made here, only a plea that political culture is too important a subject to become intellectually modish.

Ivan Siber has listed these characteristics of a high political culture.

A sense of mutual identity with the community resulting from a specific historical development.
Loyalty and trust as the basis for human relations.
Acceptance of authority; interaction and communication with authority.
Readiness of the government to listen to its citizens.
Willingness to share values with others and act jointly, thereby promoting civil society, which is the complement to democratic government and the check on it.
Tolerance of different values and origins, the breaking down of rigidity and dogmatism.
A trust in the social environment and support of others.
Absence of anxiety.
Skills in, and procedures for, conflict management.[20]

Again, a tall order for societies that have struggled through centuries of alien rule, followed by the wasteland of communism. Some Western societies with generations of freedom behind them hardly measure up to it. *All* the former communist countries, especially those of South Eastern Europe, not to mention the former Soviet Union, will find it difficult going. But what their citizens should realize is that it is *in the consistency of the attempt that the achievement lies.* Democracy always is—and must be—an aspiration. Wherever it is judged to have been realized, it is already in decline. Bear in mind Gandhi's answer to a London journalist who once asked him what he thought of English civilization: "It's a very good idea," said Gandhi. The same holds true for democracy.

The Extremist Temptation

The Jörg Haider imbroglio in Austria in early 1999 and the reaction in Eastern Europe to it is discussed in chapter 9. But the sympathy for Haider throughout the region reflected the overall strength of what can be called "right extremist" tendencies, especially on the issues of race, minorities, and immigrants that were becoming apparent throughout the 1990s. They were becoming apparent in Western Europe, too, often in an ugly form. In both parts of Europe they would get stronger and more vicious. It is therefore worth setting out a few "markers" or defining characteristics of extremism as they apply to Europe in the first few years of the millennium. They were drawn up by Urs Altermatt in a book titled *Rechtsextremismus in der Schweiz,* published in 1995 in Zurich by the *Neue Zürcher Zeitung-*Buchverlag (for "Schweiz" read "Europa"). The characteristics are:

Aggressive nationalism and/or "ethnocentrism" showing itself in xenophobia and hatred of foreigners.

Racism that proceeds from a biological worldview and/or an ethnic/cultural demarcation.

Anti-Semitism, manifesting itself in open or hidden enmity of Jews and in the playing down or denial of Nazi crimes.

Authoritarianism with demands for a strong state and a "führer" figure.

An anti-egalitarian view of society, promoting "natural and organic" divisions and a hierarchical social order.

Emphasis on a "Volksgemeinschaft" based on cultural, ethnic, and social homogeneity.

An antipluralistic political and societal standpoint, distrustful of democratic educational and decision-making processes.

Acceptance of violence reflected in social and political conflict.

A demagogic style showing itself in confrontational speech and the vilification of opponents.

Dogmatic insistence on a self-correctness that rules out societal tolerance.

Obviously anybody getting full marks in terms of these criteria would qualify for the distinction of "extremist's extremist." Fortunately there are a few who would. But there are many in both Eastern and Western Europe who would make a respectable showing. Their number is growing and the damage they do to society is always disproportionately great. And in Eastern Europe there are many former communists among them—another sign of red-brown togetherness.

Decommunization: Law, Psychology, and Practicalities

Since 1989, a close interaction between law, decommunization, and crime has taken place. In different forms and with different emphases, this interaction is likely to continue well into the twenty-first century.

By now, the importance and difficulty of establishing the rule of law should be beyond question. The law must protect the individual and restrain authority. In these regards, Eastern Europe is no different from anywhere else. But the decommunization issue has given the upholding of the law a special dimension and urgency. The old order has been overturned, but what is to be done with those who served it? For some, the case seemed clear-cut; criminals must be brought to book. But on closer inspection, even this aim was not so clear. What body of law should decide what was "criminal"? The law prevailing at the time—i.e., communist law? Precommunist law? Natural law? Many anticommunists in Eastern Europe became impatient with such niceties. The law's delay was not what most of them had been brought up on; in fact, many of them were not even aware of legal procedures. To them, the law was now a protective device to prevent real, *democratic* justice from being done. It was being used as a tactic to soften, or rule out, any punishment for the "obviously" guilty. Julian Barnes in *The Porcupine,* referring to Todor Zhivkov's hours in the dock, brings out the complexities as well as the absurdities of these problems.[21]

But taking the region as a whole, the Zhivkovs and their underlings were not the real problem. Nor were the officers of the communist security services. The actual criminals among these officials were easily identifiable. The continuing privileges of many of them (pensions, good accommodation, etc.) were particularly galling, but the fate of these people hardly affected the future of society as a whole. However, two classes of people did exist whose fate would be directly relevant: the hundreds of thousands of "ordinary" citizens who had collaborated full-time, part-time, or just now and then, with the security services; and the tens of thousands of political and economic apparatchiki who had constituted the backbone of the old regime. What should be done about them?

Decommunization was a burning issue in the early 1990s, so much so that I wrote in *Hopes and Shadows* that it was "likely to remain the most divisive and dominant issue in Eastern Europe for many years."[22] Declamations like this one were hardly testament to my prescience. Even as the book was being published, decommunization was losing its momentum. Indeed, in a short time it was "recommunization" (so-called) that was becoming the strongest political fact of life, not bringing communists to justice but bringing them back to power. True, many former communists were going through different phases of political metamorphosis, but they still were clearly recognizable for what they had been.

Still, when my ill-starred words were being penned in 1993, the decommunization issue was paramount—at least in Poland, the new Czech Republic, Bulgaria, and Hungary. I described it as "a multifaceted problem involving matters of law, moral and political justice, excess or moderation, governmental efficiency and expediency, mass psychology, social cohesion, and political demagogy." "Some see it," I wrote, "as the rigorous pursuit of justice, others as the perpetuation of injustice; some maintain it is essential for a new beginning, others that it vitiates democracy right from the start; some see it as a breakthrough, others as a massive diversion."[23]

Decommunization was not identical with *Vergangenheitsbewältigung*—the overcoming of the past. *Vergangenheitsbewältigung* was a much broader and deeper process set in motion in Germany after World War II to exorcise the demons of Nazism. Despite many grotesque inconsistencies, it was generally successful. The basic difference between it and decommunization lay in the assumptions that prompted each effort. Most Germans, it was assumed, had been infected with Nazism; most East Europeans had been resistant to communism, if not actually resisting it.

Proponents of decommunization were either moderate or militant. Stephen Holmes describes the attitude of the moderates:

> The only way to begin a rule of law system was to bring guilty parties to account. Besides, a shake-up of personnel was the fastest way to reorientate the regime toward Western values. Only the torturers and those who gave and followed shoot-to-kill orders should be imprisoned, but high party officials and collaborators with the security apparatus should be banned from important public office, at least for a time.[24]

This attitude was eminently reasonable and entirely consistent with the rule of law. The militant decommunizers would have spread their net more widely and would have been more "summary" in their methods. Many supporters of the Confederation for an Independent Poland, for instance, would have been ready to see Jaruzelski hanged first and then asked questions. On a more everyday level, a solid Czech burgher, chafing at the law's likely delay, suggested getting round it by stringing up three communists out of every thousand. (This was said during a chat with me in 1991. He was not entirely serious, of course, but neither was he entirely joking.) Not Western justice, but Wild West justice, was more in keeping with what some East Europeans had in mind after 1989.

Nowhere were the dangers of decommunization more evident than in the lustration (purification) process—using security police files to expose those who had collaborated. The manifold and manifest unreliability of many police files, however, often led to serious injustices being done. Either way, the process brought out the worst in large sections of the population. Distrust and denunciation, by no means unknown in the precommunist era and further nurtured by communist repression and police pervasiveness, spilled over. Some East Europeans were not much bothered by this state of distrust. Catharsis (a new buzzword) would purge, cleanse, and energize. It all sounded reminiscent of fascism and its variants in the first half of the twentieth century and of communism in the second half.

The fact was that after 1989 many of the more militant decommunizers throughout Eastern Europe were anticommunist, not democratic. (This point is clearly brought out in Tina Rosenberg's excellent *The Haunted Land*.)[25] Many people throughout Eastern Europe actually identified anti-communism with democracy, which was understandable after the Manichean atmosphere of the cold war. Certainly, the cold war itself was being made to look simple by comparison with the complexities that succeeded it.

Hungary was probably the most restrained in its approach to decommunization. But first in Czechoslovakia and then in the Czech Republic, the "cradle" of lustration, the whole process was badly botched. Police files turned out to be highly unreliable, and application of the information found in them was sometimes grossly unfair. But lustration also was often inefficiently and unfairly carried out in the Czech Republic. Many people against whom the case seemed strong remained in their public posts without even needing to defend themselves.[26]

Nowhere, though, was decommunization or lustration handled as crudely as in Poland, at least at the beginning. It became squalid farce in the summer of 1992 when the Polish interior minister, Antoni Macierewicz, in an attempt to discredit President Wałęsa, presented the Sejm with a carefully chosen police list of alleged former communist collaborators. Most of them happened to be opponents of the Olszewski government in which Macierewicz served. It was the low point of the campaign against Wałęsa.[27] Wałęsa, though, later compounded the sordid atmosphere in a similar attempt to discredit his victorious political opponents after the presidential elections of November 1995.

Lustration was handled better in East Germany. It was bound to be different there, with the GDR now incorporated into greater Germany. The

Gauck Authority (named after the East German pastor Joachim Gauck), which administered the former Stasi (secret police) files, was run fairly and was well-supported logistically.[28] The Gauck Authority first would give a report to the "guilty party's" employer, who then could sack the person or keep him. But although this may have been a better system, it still led to many unfair and damaging results.

In Bulgaria, a lustration statute came into effect in the early 1990s in an atmosphere of victimization and revenge engendered by the dogmatically anticommunist government of Philip Dimitrov. Considerable controversy arose over the numbers of people affected by the law. But when the Dimitrov government fell in 1992, eventually to be replaced by a postcommunist Socialist government, the official anticommunist fever soon subsided. Still, it was encouraging to note that, even when lustration was at its height, the new Bulgarian constitutional court had ruled against certain aspects of the legislation. The court did so again in 1999 when the new democratic, government was trying to renew decommunization.

What immediately became obvious about decommunization in Eastern Europe was its principal use, not as a means of justice, but as an instrument of politics and a weapon for satisfying personal grudges. It often cut across basic tenets of the rule of law. Herman Schwartz, a foremost Western expert on the subject, wrote in 1994:

> There is the danger of imposing collective responsibility and guilt by association. Many people are being purged today just for being part of a now condemned group or class, such as former officials of the Communist Party, or for having attained certain high administrative positions, even if they did nothing wrong and many even may have done much good. In some of these countries, merely having been a member of a particular group or organization forty years ago is enough to imply guilt, regardless of subsequent behavior. Even when Lustration is used properly, for the best of reasons, and not to win political battles or settle old scores, such a law always imposes some form of collective punishment of people not as individuals but as members of a group.[29]

Decommunization and lustration captured big headlines, but they caught only little fish. What about the big fish, the former communist leaders? In Romania Nicolae and Elena Ceauşescu were executed immediately after their capture. After a quarter of a century of tyranny and popular suffering, and after two weeks of bloody revolution in December

1989, their deaths somehow seemed a fitting climax. Emotionally, the executions were satisfying, but emotion and legality seldom mix.

Elsewhere, attempts to bring the top dogs to book led to fiasco, frustration, or obvious perversions of justice. Germany witnessed the failure to convict Erich Honecker and the decision to move against the moribund (now dead) Erich Mielke, the GDR's security chief, for the murders of German policemen in the early *1930s*. In Poland, more serious proceedings were begun against Jaruzelski for his declaration of martial law in December 1981, more specifically for the killing by police of several striking miners in Silesia that month, and the numerous deaths in Gdánsk more than ten years earlier during the crisis that led to the overthrow of Gomułka. None of these efforts came to fruition because declaring martial law could not legally be counted as a crime, and on the two more specific charges it was at least a case of inadequate proof. As for Edward Gierek, the country's communist leader for more than a decade, he remained free and uncharged and wrote two profitable volumes of memoirs. (Memoir-writing became a minor industry among former communist leaders.) In Bulgaria, a whiff of farce entered into attempts to nail Zhivkov. He was finally convicted on a charge of embezzlement and sentenced to seven years in prison, none of which he served because of the medical certificate that he produced. He died in 1998, mourned by some, missed by few, but still dodging his pursuers—also having published his memoirs.

But Zhivkov apart, signs indicated that from 1990 through 1992 Bulgaria's first anticommunist government was also planning indictments against the entire former communist leadership. A former premier was tried and convicted, but the fall of the prosecuting government in 1992 spared the rest of his colleagues. It also spared Bulgaria from the international opprobrium that was heaped on Albania for its treatment of its toppled communist chieftains. In Albania, the spirit of the blood feud lingered vindictively in the anticommunist excesses of Sali Berisha and his associates. Both Enver Hoxha's widow, Nexhmije, and his successor, Ramiz Alia, were tried and sentenced. So was Fatos Nano, the leader of the Socialist (formerly Communist) Party, whose real crime was presenting a democratic threat to Berisha. In a short time, the entire surviving Hoxha leadership was behind bars—an infamous roll call, no doubt, but still one that deserved more legality than it received. After Berisha's fall in 1997, Nano became prime minister for a time, and the imprisoned communist leaders were released from confinement.

Finally, to turn to Czechoslovakia and its successor states. It was perhaps surprising that the Czechs, generally so keen on both bringing to book and settling scores, held back from prosecuting their former rulers. Miroslav Stepán, the Prague party leader, got a short jail sentence for the police brutality against protesting students in 1989. But none of the prominent leaders were immediately arrested. This was partly the result of President Václav Havel's insistence on magnanimity, the usual difficulties in formulating legal charges, the fact that Gustáv Husák was virtually on his deathbed, and the birth of an independent Slovakia after 1993, which provided a haven for top Slovaks. Despite the occasional demands for action, nothing was done. Then in May 1997, nearly nineteen years after the event, charges were preferred against three septuagenarians—Miloš Jakeš, Jozef Lenárt, and Karel Hoffman—for plotting to aid and abet the Soviet-led invasion of August 1968. Another fiasco was avoided when the charges apparently sank into the sand.

Summing up, wholesale and indiscriminate decommunization had five main dangers:

1. It jeopardized the establishment of the rule of law, strengthening the notion of collective guilt and rejecting the canon of due process.
2. It divided society rather than healed it, bringing out the worst in far too many people.
3. It was potentially a diversion from democratic reconstruction.
4. It could have deprived societies of badly needed expertise in the bureaucracy, the professions, the military, and the economy.
5. From the start, it became a political or personal, not a judicial, instrument.

Decommunization had seemed to be petering out in the mid-1990s. The postcommunists were back in power in several countries, and no great public appetite remained for it, anyway. (Had there been resistance, the postcommunists would not have got back into power.) But toward the end of the decade, anticommunist governments were in office in Poland, Hungary, Bulgaria, and Romania. Signs were clear that decommunization was being revived. In Poland and Hungary, such signs had become unmistakable, with politics, not justice, being the obvious leitmotif. But over the longer run, these indications probably would not amount to much. Generations were changing; so were priorities. Memories were shortening, and

new challenges were concentrating people's minds. The new decommunization wave would have its victims, but eventually those victims would be
discredited less than decommunization itself.[30]

The Varieties and Dangers of Crime

Crime can exercise a morbid fascination; it easily becomes a hobbyhorse,
even an obsession. One need not be paranoid, however, to argue that crime
could undermine democratic development in some East European countries and delay it in others. East Europeans (Russians, Ukrainians, et al. are
included here) know this to be the case, but many Westerners do not. Some
political scientists seemed at first to find the subject demeaning, deserving
of a catchy label but not much more. Some wiseacres affected a bored
imperturbability. "We have the same in New York City," opined one American luminary.

Before we look at postcommunist crime, it should be pointed out that
breaking the law or "evading" it under communism had become a necessity,
a way of life, often an art form. Black marketeering was the norm; so was
bribery and petty corruption. Factory directors and their underlings spent
much of their time dodging directives from the center. At the center itself,
corruption, large and small, prevailed. Trade union officials looked after
themselves and their cronies. The communist system by its very nature
reinforced the historically ingrained East European tendency to cheat and
steal from the authorities or the landlords. This tendency was strongest in
the Ottoman lands, but under communism it evened out over the region as
a whole. Plenty of "free enterprise" of a sort, therefore, existed under communism. It created a habit of mind that was later to be transmuted into
either legal, constructive capitalism or into various shades of illegality. And
often permeating this illegality was the upsurge of violent crime.

Vladimír Kusin in an excellent unpublished paper points out how unprepared the first postcommunist leaders were for the upsurge in violent
crime:

Ideological, political, economic and cultural emancipation were for
them so much more important. History was being made and a key
moral deficiency righted. When it became obvious that postcommunist crime not only existed but was burgeoning, it was argued that
crime had always existed. Certainly under communism it had, but

then it had been papered over, as unemployment, nationalism, and sin generally were. Tackling this nasty new postcommunist reality was also inhibited by the new ruling elite's attitude to the constabulary they had inherited from the previous era. It was somehow felt that the old constabulary's main duty had not been to arrest criminals, dish out parking tickets, and deal with boisterous soccer crowds, but to enchain a whole population yearning to be free. Obviously, you couldn't now fire *all* the police in a fever of decommunization, but you couldn't trust them either. The police noticed this: many became corrupt, many more corrupt than they had been, and most just began sitting on their truncheons. Besides, their pay and perks noticeably shrank. In short, their morale plummeted. At the same time, the legal codes passed on from the communist era had to be examined, amended, or replaced. Inevitably this work was slow, while the increase in crime was very fast.[31]

Common crime and violence had been relatively rare under communism. Ordinary people minding their own business felt safe on the streets. After 1989, many of those same people no longer did. This turnabout resulted from the breakdown of the physical and psychological restraints of the communist period and to Eastern Europe's new exposure to the West. Kusin again:

> The West had made the street-wise underworld in the East worldwise. . . . The four major [Western] export commodities have been drugs, serious fraud, syndication and trans-border linkage. All of them [had] caused problems [for] the communist law enforcement agencies but nowhere near the present level. . . . The old regime had kept serious common crime in broadly manageable proportions. Only the mixing of Western imports, with the watered down legal antidotes (after 1989), and the "cheat and steal" sub-culture, could produce today's powerful brew.[32]

So much for "common" crime, the first broad category of crime, and in the former communist states the most obvious to the population. The second category comprises corruption and serious fraud. By no means were such acts unknown in the communist era. The Soviet Union, especially during Brezhnev's reign, lapsed massively into them. The Caucasus republics, parts of Soviet Asia, Russian cities like Perm and Pinsk, all became notorious for them. Eastern Europe saw much less of this kind of crime, but it, too, had its little Perms and Pinsks. After 1989, corruption and fraud became endemic. Kusin once again:

> In whatever currency you choose to count . . . billions have flown out of public, semipublic, and private purses into the pockets of cunning crooks. Western experts, bewildered by the incredible size and diversity of the illicit transactions, are yet to put together a record of what had really happened. The fact seems undeniable that the *enrichissez-vous* mentality (known from other postupheaval periods in history) was sorely underestimated by the makers of postcommunist financial laws. . . .[33]

The privatization process was one of the broadest avenues to corruption. Nomenklatura capitalism has become a standard term in both the former communist countries and among Western observers studying them. It reflects the process whereby communist managers and economic officials siphoned off for themselves the juiciest bits of those branches of the economy being privatized and engaged in violence to prevent "outsiders" from muscling in. The old-comrade network was thus carried over from the communist era to the democratic one. Most communist managers basked in the assurance that practically nobody could take their place. They assiduously set about making capitalism work—but only for themselves. In many way, such pillage was unavoidable. But it was overlooked, apparently, by many blinkered economists, local and Western, who saw the urgent need for privatization, but not its dangers.

The third criminal category is mafia-like gangsterism. It is partly born out of the second category; the one easily melds into the other. But its distinct characteristics are its organization, its often murderous violence, and its foreign connections, or often foreign dominance. Local mafias, national mafias, Russian mafias, Caucasian mafias, Soviet successor-state mafias, and Western mafias, all engage in frequent turf wars. They deal in drugs, prostitution, weapons, cigarettes, and now emigrant smuggling. And almost everywhere, the former communist security services have played a dominant role. In several countries, mafias have strong links with government. Many citizens suspect that they form a shadow government, or, indeed, the real government. At the end of the century, this assessment may still be an exaggeration. But it is becoming less so, and early in the twenty-first century it might become a reality. The EBRD Transition Report 1999 (pp. 117–19), in undramatic language, gives a dramatic account of the mafia role in the economic transformation process in Eastern Europe and the former Soviet Union. Referring to a "state capture by private interests" (i.e., mafia), the EBRD publishes an accompanying chart showing the percentage of companies claiming to have been affected by mafia influence or activity. The number for Bulgaria—between 40 and 50 percent—was just slightly below the Russian, and a bit worse than the Romanian. Slovenia had the lowest East European figure, closely followed by Hungary. Late in 1997, Peter Stoyanov, Bulgaria's new president, had said that organized crime was his country's most serious problem—more serious, evidently, than the huge economic mess that confounded Bulgaria. Several Bulgarian counties were indirectly under the control of organized crime groups.[34]

This mafia gangsterism often makes headlines in the West, especially when a prominent individual becomes one of its victims. One such figure was Andrei Lukanov, the "wily grey fox," who was murdered in front of his house in Sofia in October 1996. Lukanov was the scion of a famous Bulgarian communist dynasty. His father had been foreign minister from 1956 to 1962, his grandfather a prominent prewar communist. Lukanov himself was once considered "crown prince" to Todor Zhivkov, but he was subsequently dropped by his master. Lukanov spent several years in educative exile in Geneva, picking up Western ways, learning capitalism, and sharpening both his linguistic skills and his formidable intelligence. After Zhivkov's fall, he was prime minister for a short time. Then he became Bulgaria's best-known private entrepreneur. American businessmen, especially, went for his can-do attitude. What he did do, therefore, is worth reporting in some detail:

> The system Lukanov engineered was neither communism nor capitalism but a mutant hybrid combining the worst of both. It allowed the Nomenklatura to acquire wealth unshackled by the ideological and legal limits of the old regime and unchecked by normal competition.
>
> It was brutally simple. Until Lukanov's spell as prime minister ended in November 1990, his friends and associates took up key positions in state banks and industries and—under the guise of reform—diverted resources into dozens of new trading companies, banks and brokerage houses, which dominated the commodity and currency markets, transferring much of their profits to foreign bank accounts. Privatisation, which might have created genuine competition, was continually delayed.[35]

The *Economist* added some details on this kind of racket: "By supplying raw materials at market prices to state firms run by friends, and then buying back the finished products cheaply, companies can make money twice, first on the raw materials, and then by selling the finished goods. The state firm takes a thumping loss—but that is passed on to the government."[36]

What Lukanov and his associates did was being done throughout the former Soviet Union and the whole of Eastern Europe. The next step was for various companies to become organized into groups determined to protect their turf. This involved corrupting politicians and trials of strength with competing groups. Then came the ultimate: liquidation of competitors. Such was Lukanov's fate. Chicago, Palermo, Sofia! And not just Sofia. So far, though, only Bulgaria has offered up a man of such versatility as Lukanov, a communist aristocrat, a democratic leader, finally a gunned-down tsar of the capitalist underworld.

In Eastern Europe as a whole, the Balkans experienced this kind of organized crime at its most dangerous. The wars in former Yugoslavia, the black-marketeering that they engendered, the porous international embargoes, the profusion of weapons, the cheapness of human life, the overall cynicism and weakness of state authority—all contributed to the Balkan mayhem. But no one in East Central Europe could be complacent. Rampant corruption existed there, too, even in the Czech Republic, for all its traditions of public probity. In Hungary, where corruption had been largely under control, gang warfare threatened in 1998.

Crime, then, is a terrible dilemma. So is the problem of combating it. Mussolini, of course, submerged the Italian Mafia, and many today in Eastern Europe and the former Soviet Union would not mind using his methods. But once the East European authorities started implementing the methods of dictatorship, they would be well on the way to restoring dictatorship itself. Crime had to be fought, but the rule of law had to be maintained and strengthened. The West could mount a massive program of help in law prevention and law enforcement. Such assistance is just as necessary as Western economic help—and it would, incidentally, stop much of Western economic help from being thrown to the winds.

The Role of the State

The rise in crime is a challenge to both society and the state. In some countries, neither has been strong enough to resist it. The need for a vibrant civil society has been discussed. Earlier, I included the state among the four essential underpinnings of a democratic order as well as of a sound economy.

What Eastern Europe largely ignored after 1989 in its healthy rejection of *communist statism* was the need for *civic statism*.[37] It was soon to learn that the state must play the crucial role in pulling democracy back from anarchy and freedom back from license. It was indeed the weakness of the state after 1989, especially in the Balkans, that led to the revival of family clan and local loyalties, which in turn gave a real impetus to organized crime. A capable and ordered governmental bureaucracy, positively led, checked by the judiciary, and subject to the legislature but armed with the necessary means of coercion, must exist and be able to carry through democratically approved policy.

During the 1990s the need for a strong state became obvious in different countries and in different spheres of public life; the lack of it spelled disaster. Take Albania and the Czech Republic. It is hard to imagine two more different countries. Yet they both needed state intervention, and both of them lacked it. The total collapse of the Albanian state led to the disasters of 1997. In the Czech Republic the disorders were much more sophisticated and less harmful to life and limb, but they did serious economic, political, and psychological damage. The lack of any meaningful state regulation in banking, fiscal affairs, and the desocialization of the general economy caused not just corruption but a major financial and political crisis. In contrast to Albania, a Lilliputian country with a once Brobdingnagian state that quickly melted away, the Czech Republic still had a state apparatus that could easily have provided the necessary regulation. It did not do so because of administrative sloth, the mountain of work required, and because adequate regulation was deemed ideologically unacceptable.

In South Eastern Europe, outside Albania, the state exists—in Bulgaria, Romania, and Macedonia—but it is a "weak state," one where the elected government finds it increasingly difficult to exercise its executive functions and implement its policy projects. (Pockets of the former police state still exist, too, throughout the Balkans.) This lack of strength is most evident in the case of crime, but weakness exists in other spheres of government, especially the economy. In former Yugoslavia, the federal state apparatus and authority began diminishing many years before the federation broke up. In the successor states, the performance of their central authorities has been varied. Macedonia's has been a "weak" state, while Serbia's has been strong in political repression but weak in other respects. Croatia, too, has had similar problems, but the state there is much more constructive than is Serbia's. The Croatian state under President Franjo Tudjman was also repressive (see chapter 5), but, again, not as repressive as Serbia's. In Bosnia-Hercegovina, virtually no state exists. Each of its two "Entities" has state machinery of sorts, but in both cases it is disunited and repressive. Taking all the Yugoslav successor states, Slovenia is the hot favorite to develop a healthy political future with an active but controlled state interacting with society. This positive future is partly because Slovenia has a history of "order" and because it has few outside distractions and ambitions and few ethnic problems.

A strong state should not be confused with strongman leaders (still less with a strong-arm leader). Postcommunist Eastern Europe has had enough of these—and not just in the Balkans. Wałęsa was one in Poland. His electoral defeat in 1995 was a decisive step in the maturing of Polish democracy. Mečiár in Slovakia was certainly another. His electoral defeat in 1998 saved the hope of Slovak democracy. The Balkans have seen Berisha, Miloščvić, and Tudjman in charge. The common characteristic of all these strongmen was not only their nationalism, but their contempt for the law.

Bureaucrats and Politicians

An effective democratic state needs, not strongmen, but a competent and respected bureaucracy; sufficiently strong, sufficiently controlled military and police forces; governmental leadership; and a certain legislative vibrancy. Eastern Europe still lacked enough of any of these assets at the end of the twentieth century.

Much of the bureaucracy had to be carried over from the communist era. Many former communist bureaucrats were competent and ready, whatever the reasons, to serve the democratic state. But many others were mediocre placemen or women, narrow-minded, mean-spirited, and petulantly authoritarian. They would be pensioned off in time; large numbers of them were coming up to retirement. The problem would be in replacing them. Here lay a striking contrast with precommunist times. Then, many of the best and brightest went into the bureaucracy (see chapter 1), but now their postcommunist counterparts were flooding into business, commerce, and finance, and many were looking for opportunities to emigrate. This problem can at best be mitigated, not solved. The French pattern of high-standard training institutions, leading to posts with prestige and competitive pay, both to draw recruits and to discourage corruption, seems to be the best way to tackle the problem. Also to be emphasized is the importance of opportunities for women in the postcommunist order. Such opportunities had become restricted after 1989 for several reasons, the most pernicious being the resilience of Kinder, Kirche, Küche atavism.

As well as strongman leadership, some capable democratic leadership has come to the fore. The Slovene, Milan Kučan, has been outstanding; so was the Macedonian, Kiro Gligorov. Both of them are "carryover communists." Václav Havel has been a strong moral force, if sometimes politically inept. Václav Klaus, however perverse he became, has been undeniably able. President Árpád Göncz of Hungary won sincere international respect, but the restrictions of his largely ceremonial office helped to prevent him from being a decisive force. The former Hungarian premier, Gyula Horn, was a capable politician, just as President Aleksander Kwasniewski has been in Poland—two more carry-over communists. But however capable these former communists were, no matter how they abided by, even helped to further, democratic progress, their pasts tended to make them, if not vulnerable, then insecure. Where would the next revelation, true or false, come from? Had every skeleton been cleared from the cupboards?

But what of the new, "untainted" generation? Viktor Orbán in Hungary, winner of the parliamentary election in May 1998, is its most spectacular example. Peter Stoyanov, president of Bulgaria, who replaced the estimable Zhelu Zhelev, is another. New leaders like these will steadily appear. They are unburdened but as yet unproved. What is likely is a beneficial interaction between such leaders and a steadily improving democratic infrastructure. Better leaders must help mold that infrastructure. If they do, more good leaders will be produced.

The great thing about the new democratic legislatures is that their composition changes. Free elections are seeing to that. Otherwise, generalizations are difficult, and it would be invidious to compare the compositions and performances of the different legislatures throughout the region. Their defects and asininities make news, their achievements and common sense go unreported—just like those of Western legislatures. The knowledge of parliamentary procedures has certainly been improving. Western coaching has helped here. Some legislators, in fact, are a bit too proud of this talent. Style supersedes substance. Some legislators scorn the nitty-gritty and take themselves more seriously than they take their duties, let alone their constituents. Still, legislatures are getting stronger and more constructive—and more of a nuisance. The contrast with what they were before 1989 is breathtaking.

Changing the Complexion

Stable, working democracy is hostage to many contingencies. In Eastern Europe one of the most crucial is that the majority of politically active postcommunists evolve into genuine social democrats (or genuine democrats of any description). This change requires not just a transition but a conversion, not just a transfer of party cards but of political values. But this change can be, and is being, done. Just as many Stalinists became genuine reform communists, many reform communists are becoming genuine social democrats. ("Once a communist, always a communist, whatever the packaging" is plain nonsense.)

Many intellectuals also are changing. The victories of the democratic opposition in several parliamentary elections from 1996 through 1998 meant a return to influence of some intellectuals who had helped lead the anticommunist struggle before 1989 and played a leading role in the early democratic transition after it. It was essential therefore that they be more "democratically active" in government now than they previously were.

In a year-end article written for *Transition* in 1995, I criticized this first attempt at government by Eastern Europe's intellectuals:

Most of the democratic governments elected after 1989 were dominated by intellectuals. Some were capable, while others found that resisting communism was easier than picking up the pieces after it. Many, however, acted as if democracy were not so much a system of government as an exercise in enlightenment, with their own role more sacerdotal than practical. Getting down into the arena, soiling their hands with bargaining and . . . settling for second best, was not their idea of political leadership. Nor was getting down to the kind of detail that is often the very stuff of political life. "All politics are local," former U.S. House Speaker Tip O'Neill used to say. Some of Eastern Europe's new rulers should have taken him to heart. There is nothing ineffable or sublime about democracy; it is mundane and messy. And it is like that because the voters—remember them?—are not only made of flesh and blood but often have more savvy than the philosopher kings give them credit for.[38]

But the second time round, Eastern Europe's intellectuals have been improving. And one of the most important things they can do by their example and exertions, either in government or out, is to help induce their countrymen to think and act as individuals—civic individuals. A Danish novelist puts it pithily: "Most people secretly find it a relief to have the state divest them of the trouble of being an independent person."[39] This is true everywhere. But in Eastern Europe and the former Soviet Union the recent past has made it not so much an attitude as a culture. Intellectuals would seem admirably equipped to help break this culture down. By doing so they themselves would cease being a caste and become citizens.

Eastern Europe—all of it, not just parts—has one big thing in its favor: the rapidity with which the communist worldview has faded. Many East Europeans may wish to retain some aspects of communist rule. But their way of thinking never went down the tramlines that communist orthodoxy laid out. In Russia the thinking was always much straighter and more predictably ideological. In the Christmas 1994 issue of the *New York Review of Books,* Jamey Gambrell discussed the fate of the Soviet Exhibition of the Achievement of the People's Economy (VDNX), built in 1939 and still standing—if with considerable indignity—in the north of Moscow. (Large chunks of it have been privatized.) Toward the end of her article, Gambrell came to grips with the basic significance of VDNX. After dwelling on the touching absurdity of much of the exhibition, she writes:

> However, there were important ways in which the Exhibition never ceased to exert an ideological influence. Statistics on the achievements of socialism continued to articulate a world view in which nothing was left to chance. In this tightly constructed universe, no subject was too insignificant, no detail too trivial to warrant the parental concern of state and Party. . . . Every person and every event was connected to the fate of the collective and thus to the omnipresent, omnipotent state. When applied to, say, hog raising or the cotton crop, the results seem comic today. But a text on hog farming would be connected by the logic of its rhetorical tone to far more serious matters. For a person indoctrinated in this chain reaction thinking, an accolade to the cotton

crop can raise the specter of competition with America, and hence of Western plots to destabilize the Soviet Union and the threat of nuclear war. . . . This cast of mind is still very much evident in Russian social and political discourse today—as anyone who has listened to a session of the Russian parliament or to Vladimir Zhirinovsky knows.[40]

There is not much of that mentality in Eastern Europe. There never was much.

Country Profiles: Facing the Future

WE NOW LOOK AT THE individual East European states, not so much in terms of how the past has shaped their present, but how their present is likely to shape their future. In this chapter we will cover those aspects of each country's geopolitical, domestic political, and economic situations that will seriously affect its progress in the new century. These pages contain neither a stocktaking nor a balance sheet; instead, they report on a scouting trip, an assessment of potential. Points made in other chapters will be amplified. Some repetition may be unavoidable, but it will be kept to a minimum. Some countries inevitably get more space than others, but not necessarily more attention. In the twenty-first century the situation of some of the smaller countries in Eastern Europe will be critical; on their survival the peace of an entire international neighborhood might depend.

Bosnia-Hercegovina is not included because at the end of the twentieth century it had no real attributes of statehood and seemed unlikely to acquire any. It consists of the two "Entities" established by the Dayton peace agreements, intensely hostile to one another, with a central government neutered at birth. Bosnia-Hercegovina's future is discussed at length in chapter 6.

Serbia is obviously included and must take pride of place. What happened there in 2000 not only completed the East European transformation of 1989, it put Serbia itself back into international company.

Serbia 2000: The Road to Redemption

Winston Churchill, speaking straight after the Serbian coup d'état in March 1941 that overthrew the pro-Axis government in Belgrade, said that the

"Yugoslav nation" had "found its soul." Many people were saying pretty much the same thing in October 2000 when the Serbian people delivered the coup de grâce to Slobodan Milošević. Churchill did not at first truly understand what had happened in 1941 and those who described what the Serbs did in 2000 as a "revolution" were not quite right either. It was only a partial one at most. But both events did serve as inspirations; they were gales of fresh and cleansing air descending on scenes dominated by disappointment and even despair. Certainly in 2000, however complex and difficult the future might be, the cornerstone of tyranny was dislodged.*

The immediate pretext for the Serb uprising was Milošević's attempt the previous month to deny victory in the *Yugoslav* presidential elections (involving Serbia proper and, at least technically, Montenegro and Kosovo, too) to the leading opposition candidate, Vojislav Koštunica, who had won decisively. Milošević had fiddled, or "ensured," all previous elections, too. But this fraud went too far.

It went too far because it crystallized all the dissatisfaction that had been accumulating for several years. First of all, Serbia was a defeated nation. It had lost wars in Croatia, Bosnia, and Kosovo. Serbia had lost wars before in its history. In fact, out of its greatest defeat—at Kosovo in 1389—it had conjured up an inspiring legend (see chapter 7). But the defeats in the 1990s were considered shaming because they involved victories for nations that Serbs despised, nations that they were accustomed to lording it over—Croats, Muslims, Albanians.

In this context, a few words on the nature of Serb history are relevant. Serbia has always been a *Volksstaat,* never a *Rechtsstaat.* Under the Turkish yoke Serbs had looked back to the glorious days of Stefan Dušan and had embroidered the Kosovo myth. And when Serbia regained its independence during the nineteenth century, the ambition of its political elites was not to build a modern state but to recover a medieval empire. As for the overwhelmingly illiterate mass of the population, sheer survival was its main preoccupation. But its opium, too, was nationalism, and any politician, royal or bourgeois, could be sure of its potency. The Yugoslavia that emerged after World War I came close to achieving the Serb historical ambition, but the clash of Serb and Croat nationalisms helped kill the dream.

Tito sought, with his mixture of federalism, socialism, and "moderniza-

---

*Of the many articles I have read about Serbia's future none is better than that by Andres Wysling, Neue Chance für Serbien," *Neue Zürcher Zeitung* (Internationale Ausgabe), October 26, 2000 (no. 250).

tion," to make nationalism, particularly Serb nationalism, irrelevant. But he was basically a socialist-dogmatic. His modernization, after some initial success, was inept and his socialism a brake on political and economic progress rather than the motor for it. In Tito's Yugoslavia most Serbs began to feel victimized rather than fulfilled. In the early 1970s, when a new Serb political leadership wanted to lay *civic* foundations, Tito the Leninist purged it. When he died, nothing was left but nationalism, resurgent and vengeful. From nationalism to socialism and then back again—that was the Serbs' historical path.

This path led to the demoralizing defeats of the 1990s, defeats for which Milošević was held responsible. True, Serbia had not been invaded (except by Serb refugees from other parts of Yugoslavia), but it had felt every other repercussion of defeat. It had been severely bombed by NATO forces in the Kosovo conflict. It was diplomatically isolated; even its former supporters, Russia and China, distanced themselves. It suffered from the punishments of war and its government's incompetence. Its economy was in ruins, its infrastructure shattered, its finances bankrupt, and its commerce devastated.

But defeated nationalism and its consequences were not the only factors crystallizing Serb resentment. Milošević's domestic conduct widened and deepened this resentment. Serbs no longer considered him a leader but an insult. The semblances of democracy were whittled away—freedom of speech, of association, and of the media. Opposition parties, those still officially tolerated, were circumscribed, infiltrated, suborned, or terrorized. The numbers, powers, and perquisites of the police were enhanced, especially after demonstrations of youthful discontent. The judiciary was corrupted and its level of competence degraded. Many of the best and brightest Serbs, especially the younger ones left in disgust or despair.

But, more than anything, it was shame that overcame Serbs the most, shame at their own and their nation's debasement and shame at being governed by Milošević and his squalid *Camarilla*. Public life in Serbia, centered on Belgrade, had become a cesspool. Floating atop it was Eastern Europe's last surviving double-bed dictatorship, that of Slobodan Milošević and his fearsome spouse, Mirjana (Mira) Marković—professor of Marxism, socialist with an inhuman face, a grim reminder of Rudyard Kipling's dictum about the female of the species being more deadly than the male. Their son, Marko, repulsively recalled Nicu, the Ceaușescus' unspeakable offspring. Marko was a "businessman" (read "mobster"), hugely successful for obvious reasons. (When his father fell from power, Marko, with true filial solidarity, tried to decamp to China, which wanted no part of him.) In some East European countries the mafia came close to running the country, but Serbia was the only one where the ruling family ran the mafia.

One reason why Milošević lasted so long was that the political opposition to him was so divided, incompetent, and unworthy. But for the election in September 2000, the bulk of the opposition did settle on a leader whose background and integrity caught the voters' mood. Vojislav Koštunica had been the almost unknown leader of an almost unknown party, the Democratic Party. In the election his party was supported by a loose collection of groupings called the Democratic Opposition of Serbia (DOS).

Koštunica is something of an "old-fashioned" nationalist Serb. He admired the first Yugoslavia, which was Serb-dominated and in which his father was a military officer. He is also a devout son of the Serbian Orthodox Church and has always been a bitter anticommunist. An academic lawyer by profession, he is a man of honor and principle, serious in mien and intent, the heroic anti-hero.

The revolution he led was anything but a sharp break with the past. It simply opened the way to a democratic transition, with short-term and long-term aspects. The Milošević ruling machine could not be dismantled at once. The first task was to get rid of his puppet *Serbian* parliament, dominated by members of, or allies with, his Socialist Party. That could be done by free and fair elections. After that would come the "long march through the institutions"—purging the police, the praetorian guard in the army, the judiciary, and the *nomenklatura* in the bureaucracy and the economy. This dismantling would take time and would tax the patience of many Serbs. But Koštunica knows that quick law is no law. Democratic Serbia was to be under the rule of law.

His victory is a huge step forward. What is now needed most of all is a psychological change in the Serb nation, a realization (and an admission) that evil deeds have been done in its name, but a realization, too, that it can indeed become, and be accepted as, a *normal* nation. Perhaps Koštunica will not complete the task, perhaps he is not up to it. But others will be. These leaders may come from the young, for the young are least touched by the nationalist obsession.

MONTENEGRO

After the Serbian revolution, interest in, and about, Montenegro centered on its future relations with Serbia. This relationship is discussed in chapter 7. But two points need to be stressed here.

One is Montenegro's minuteness in terms of area and population. In 2000 its total population is less than 700,000, even after a considerable increase due to influxes from the wars in former Yugoslavia. About 20 percent of the total influx is Muslim. This tiny population makes Montenegro by far the smallest political unit anywhere in postcommunist Eastern Europe (its population is only a third that of Kosovo). On the point of size alone, therefore, full independence seems hardly a viable option.

The second point refers to the "creeping demoralization" of the population. Striking similarities can be drawn with Serbia itself. By the turn of the millennium Montenegro had become not only a sink of corruption but both a mafia center and a mafia haven—almost a small-scale Albania. The ports on its coastline (the only access *Serbia* had to the sea) almost rival Durrës as centers for the transfer to Italy of drugs, guns, cigarettes, women, and illegal emigrants. Several reasons can be given for this degradation: Montenegro has been part of a rump Yugoslavia, engulfed by war and bullied by Serbia, whose "Yugoslav" armies number conscripted Montenegrins; it has been afflicted by wartime shortages, Western embargoes, and the growth of a smuggling culture; Albania, Kosovo, and Italy are close neighbors.

Montenegro, therefore, is no longer the land of Peter Njegoš in the nineteenth century or even of Milovan Djilas in the twentieth. But the main questions now are how far, and how, its foreign and domestic policies, its very nature and existence, will be affected by a democratic Serbia. What form, if any, will the connection now take?

Poland

Poland today is in a better situation than at any time in its entire history. Many Poles might demur, pointing to the sixteenth century, when Poland was at its greatest, with possessions stretching from the Baltic Sea to the Black Sea. But greatness led to partition later. That greatness was deceptive. What was, in reality, the Polish "empire" totally disappeared, and its subject peoples shed few tears. But the Polish nation did not disappear. Nor did it merely survive; it resisted, and after World War I the Polish state reemerged. It was almost destroyed by the new Red (Russian) Army in 1920. But, by the "Miracle on the Vistula," the Poles saved not only their own new state from Soviet rule, but probably Germany as well. Then, less than twenty years later, Poland was indeed destroyed by Nazi Germany, which partitioned it with Soviet Russia. In that Nazi occupation the Polish nation came closer to destruction than it ever had before. But yet again, its spirit was indomitable.

After 1945, Poland did not regain its independence but became a satellite of the Soviet Union. For the Poles, this was a humiliation, but obviously it was preferable to the annihilation with which they had only recently been threatened. Poland, too, was now ethnically compact. All but a few thousand of its Jews had been lost in the Holocaust, most of its Germans were expelled, and all but a few hundred thousand of its former Ukrainians and White Russians had lived in territories that were now incorporated into the Soviet Union. Its new German territories acquired after 1945, up to the Oder-Neisse border, were infinitely preferable to those that it lost in the East. Still more important, acquiring them jerked Poland westward. And beyond the Oder-Neisse, Germany was divided. Poland now bordered on a small, "fraternal" slice of the old Germany: the GDR.

Under Soviet domination, the Polish independence of spirit lost none of its strength and resilience. It not only set an example for the rest of Eastern Europe, but it constantly reminded the West that Poland's will to freedom had to be taken into account. Eventually, Poland helped to set in train the actual destruction of communism and the Soviet Union itself. Let Poland be Poland! After 1989, it was Poland at last. It had taken practically the whole century for the German-Russian nutcracker to be split in half. Poland was free and its external security ensured.

Not only ensured but enhanced. Many Poles were initially alarmed over the reunification of Germany in 1990, but the new Germany finally recognized, unequivocally, the Oder-Neisse border; it also became a strong economic support and a staunch advocate of Polish entry into both NATO and the EU. To the east, the Soviet Union ceased to exist. Russia now bordered Poland only through its enclave at Kaliningrad. Lithuania, Ukraine, and Belarus, Soviet-successor states, were Poland's new neighbors, and the Russian threat to Polish independence was not likely to rise again. Poland at the beginning of the twenty-first century was comprehensively secure.

Poland and Poles also were more respected than they had ever been. World War II and then the refusal to be cowed or seduced by Soviet communism had built that reputation. So had the election of a Polish pope in 1978, a reminder to everyone that Poland was part of European history and civilization. The vibrancy of Polish culture helped, too, winning world recognition even during the communist era. Indeed, communism had to accommodate to the Poles more than the Poles would accommodate to it.

Politically and especially economically, Poland also had made a good postcommunist beginning. The anticommunist forces, based on Solidarity, were roundly criticized in 1989 for making too many concessions to the communist government (see chapter 4). In retrospect, though, this caution was beneficial. Former communists were included from the start in the new democratic process, and enough of them responded constructively to give that process a healthy start. Indeed, in 1993, they were voted back to power and proceeded with the broad and deep reform that brought big dividends for the Polish economy. Their political behavior, though far from impeccable, was also encouraging. And when defeated at the polls in 1997, they retired with procedural correctness. In 1995 a former communist, Aleksander Kwasniewski, was elected president. He was easily reelected in 2000. In that same election Lech Wałęsa, his famous predecessor, received 1 percent of the vote.

Some Polish cities give the impression of an economic miracle. And their glitter does not totally deceive. Western Poland is doing outstandingly well. The countryside, though, is still largely gray, grim, and meager; socially, the downward escalator (see chapter 4) is jammed. But enough vigorous young Poles and enough room on the upward escalator combine to maintain equilibrium, provide opportunity, and generate dynamism.[1] Gross national product was rising in the last years of the twentieth century, briskly but not headily; inflation was down to manageable proportions; and unemployment, though high, had not become socially precarious. Western investment, after a slow start, was beginning to rise, and by the year 2000 Poland was beginning to outstrip Hungary and the Czech Republic as that investment's No. 1 recipient. With Berlin only about forty miles from the Polish border, Poland also looked set to benefit from Berlin becoming the capital of Germany again in 1999. What would have been a disconcerting prospect in the past was now an attraction and an opportunity.

If melancholy was ever the Poles' main characteristic, as is often averred, they managed to do their best to dissemble at the end of the twentieth century. They were confident in themselves and their country. The craze, or yearning, for emigration, so characteristic of the early 1990s had abated to some degree. Many able young men and women seemed ready to stay and chance their luck (and talent) in a "Poland in Europe." Many "Volkswagen Germans"—Poles with, say, only one German grandmother—had migrated to West Germany in the 1970s and 1980s for economic reasons, but some were now drifting back. Traditionally, the Germans had an expression, *polnische Wirtschaft*, meaning a sloppy, disorganized way of doing things—a shambles. They do not use it much today, not only because they have become more polite, but because it no longer fits. As a young Pole, with a command of American idiom, put it to me in 1996: "Poland is on a roll."

But many Poles were also aware of present and future dangers. The economy was facing several weaknesses and risks. The most serious lay in the growing balance of payments deficit. The economy was steadily becoming susceptible to the manifold woes that befell the Czech economy in 1997. But one of Poland's not inconsiderable advantages was that Leszek Balcerowicz was for several years at its economic helm. Balcerowicz knew better than anyone that, while the macroeconomic transition had been successfully made, structural reform still remained. And this meant not just downsizing the heavy industries of the old state but also radically reforming the agricultural system. (In any case, this last was necessary for entry into the EU.) Balcerowicz showed no sign of shrinking from the necessary measures. His position was constantly threatened, but he was that rare bird in politics, East or West: a person who meant what he said.

The problem was that Balcerowicz's iron prescriptions, however necessary, were too much for many Polish politicians. Economic sanity would entail huge structural changes, "declassing" the former "proletarian aristocracy," and dislocating innumerable peasants (see chapter 3). They had led to growing strife within the governing coalition, with the dominant Solidarity grouping not willing to press the reforms till they hurt.[2] Many were already making Balcerowicz their main scapegoat, and he was forced out of office in mid-2000 along with other members of the Freedom Union, a liberal centrist party that represented a formidable concentration of political talent, breadth of view, Western orientation, and democratic instinct. The same could hardly be said of Solidarity Action, the biggest partner of the governing coalition, an unwieldy political conglomerate. Neither the ability nor the democratic convictions of several segments of this conglomerate were reassuring. In fact, they represented the distinctly undemocratic streak in Polish politics that had been evident since 1989, first in the antics of Lech Wałęsa as president and in those of some of his friends and enemies.[3] Indeed, it seemed that they, not many of the reform communists, needed lessons in democracy. Marian Krzaklewski, who led the Solidarity Action movement to victory in the 1997 elections, seemed openly to reject some Western notions of liberty and to be blissfully unaware of others.[4]

Some of the Freedom Union's leading members had shone in the struggle against communism and were now shining in the struggle to build democracy. They were the leaven of Polish politics, holding none of the prejudices of some of their colleagues and none of the suspect baggage of their postcommunist opponents. Over the longer run, what was needed to ensure, and then drive, Polish democracy was an alignment of democratic "post-comms" with democratic "anticomms." The former wanted it, the latter hesitated. But it was probably coming.

The "transition" to Polish democracy is incxtricably bound up with the future of the Roman Catholic Church. The church has become, through its past exertions and example, identified not only with the nation but with the nation's very survival. (Mary is "Queen of Poland"; Marian Krzaklewski once suggested making Jesus "King of Poland.") But the church is now on the defensive and, despite the enthusiasm and emotion of successive papal visits, on the decline. Most Poles have unavoidably become infected with Western materialism, free thinking, and what is denounced as "immorality" from the pulpit. Many are also becoming increasingly anticlerical. The church's wealth is contrasted with the poverty of most of its members. And Pope John Paul II, whatever his spiritual strength and inspiring dignity, is painfully frail. This sense of defensiveness and decline partly explains the assertiveness of "Christian nationalism." Instead of hope for a brighter future, fear of the past being gone forever has given the Catholic radio station, Radio Maryja, its stridency and its large, nervous audience. Many Catholic clergy are uneasy over the militancy, obscurantism, anti-Semitism, and chauvinistic crudeness that the station has generated. But the Polish Church has been badly led by Cardinal Józef Glemp, who basically shares much of Radio Maryja's ethos. When Pope John Paul II dies, the worldwide Catholic Church could be plunged into crisis, but most of all the Polish Church. However, it would still retain a strong influence provided it got a new leadership, became aware of what century it was in, knew its place in Polish society, and, above all, knew itself and its vulnerabilities.

Indeed, the Church could again lead the way for the nation if it did its own soul-searching. For Poles the heroic age is over; so is their own heroic view of themselves. There is no need now for the "life-sustaining lies," to use Karl Jaspers's term, that sustained them in the past. Then, those lies helped to inspire and survive. Now, they could mean danger—danger to the extraordinary potential Poland has.

The Czech Republic

In 1993 the Czechs, not uncharacteristically, settled into the quiet life. They were not consulted about the break with Slovakia and the demise of Czechoslovakia. (Neither were the Slovaks.) Premier Václav Klaus was the one who opted for those decisions. Probably no solution could have kept Czechoslovakia intact. National particularism was sweeping the former communist world. The Slovaks initially wanted to see their national *identity* fully expressed, but by the end of the twentieth century, in Czechoslovakia and elsewhere, this expression of identity apparently could be achieved only through independence. The dialogue of the deaf in which the Czechs engaged to try to accommodate Slovak aspirations was virtually bound to fail. And, after all, Czechs and Slovaks did part company peacefully. East Central Europe had had enough of conflict.

Still, the Czech Republic did come into being in an unusual way. As I wrote in *Hopes and Shadows:* "It was not the result of any popular, patriotic drive for independence. . . . It was essentially a by-product of the original Slovak demand for identity. It backed into the world rather than charging into it."[5] In short, not so much fulfillment as anticlimax.

Most Czechs probably would disagree with this assessment, arguing that their fulfillment lies in becoming irreversibly a part of the West, of Western Europe, where culturally they have always belonged. They were, therefore, coming home in 1993 after a long period of exile. History was being righted and was paying its debt to them. The year 1989 had seen the communists' departure; 1993 saw the Slovaks go. Now the Czechs could take their natural place in the Western community. And indeed, for several years after 1993, it seemed like plain sailing for them. With foreign favor, real democracy, political stability, a distinguished president of world renown, Václav Havel, and spectacular economic progress under Premier Václav Klaus, the Czechs were on their way.

But where to? The West, of course! But for the Czech Republic, the West is ineluctably Germany. Its leaders might publicly demur, but could they imagine the West meaning anything else? The real center of decision for the Czechs will not be Brussels, the European Union capital, but Berlin. The Czech Republic at the end of the twentieth century was already becoming an appendage of Germany, and it would become more of one into the twenty-first. In this respect it was becoming like Austria. (But the Austrians, or most of them, are after all German.) What the Czechs were doing was rejoining their history and assuming their customary place under German hegemony. That hegemony would now be less direct and more diluted than under the Habsburgs. From 1620 to 1918, Vienna ruled them directly, and the large German community pressed them into inferior status. Now, Berlin's authority, or seniority, would be subsumed under EU and NATO partnership. Association, not subordination, will be the official term. But this word will not hide the inequality of relationships in Central Europe. Czech dependence on Germany will become all the greater.[6]

Many Czechs already were becoming aware of the dangers behind their new, exclusively Western orientation. It is not just the massive German tourist invasion, but also the reality and implications of the evolving Czech-German relationship. Anti-German petulance markedly increased. What, in fact, was emerging was a familiar historical pattern: Czechs being dominated by Germans, accepting the inevitability of it, yet resenting it, too. No one embodied this ambivalence more than Klaus himself. He tried to combine free market economics with a defensive economic nationalism and a political nationalism as well, both of which were basically anti-German.

Many Czechs also supported Klaus in his eagerness to avoid the entanglements of Eastern Europe into which, as they argued, Slovakia would have ensnared them. The Czech Republic now borders on Austria, Germany, Poland, and Slovakia; Czechoslovakia had bordered on Hungary and Ukraine as well, and this southern and eastern pull certainly implied complications. The ripple effect of Ukrainians' relations with Russia could have been serious, and relations with Hungary could easily have soured over the Hungarian minority issue in Slovakia. The Slovaks, too, would inevitably have become more assertive, not less, and Slovak nationalists always would have resorted to the blackmail of threatening a break. President Edvard Beneš once fantasized about Czechoslovakia becoming the bridge between East and West. Many Czechs now wanted no talk of bridges, but rather of drawbridges, to be pulled up as firmly and as quickly as possible.

But Czechoslovakia (or Czecho-Slovakia or the Czech and Slovak Federative Republic, as it was called in its last days) could have played an important role in postcommunist Europe as a player and, if not as a leader, at least as a doer. A challenge was there waiting to be met. Nor would this role have been inconsistent with eventual NATO or EU membership. It would, in fact, have enhanced Czechoslovakia's value to both organizations. But the Czechs wanted neither the bother nor the risk—nor the novelty—of becoming internationally important. Safety certainly has its consolations, but too much safety can be dangerous.

Politically, the Czech Republic reverted easily to the democracy it had lost over a half-century earlier. But few were prepared for the economic downturn in the second half of the 1990s. And just as Klaus had deservedly taken credit for initial successes, so he deserved much of the blame for later failings. He epitomized the triumph of reborn liberal economic theory, not just in relation to socialist state planning, but over Keynesianism as well. In some Western quarters he became a near cult figure. In practice, though, Klaus was not as Friedmanite as he pretended to be. He refused to grasp the nettle of real structural reform.[7] And in the second half of 1996, things began to go wrong: lower economic growth, higher inflation and unemployment, a sharp currency devaluation, bank failures, the necessity of an austere budget, the failure of the vaunted voucher privatization scheme, and, perhaps most decisive of all, a high current account deficit. These setbacks seriously dimmed Klaus's halo of infallibility, but what damaged him most was the mounting evidence that his administration had become a sink of corruption.[8] It was a corruption compounded by Klaus's doctrinaire refusal to set up the necessary regulatory agencies, especially in the financial sector, and his parochial discouragement of foreign ownership in this realm. Transcending everything in the eyes of most people was Klaus's strong but totally unacceptable personality, his pathological arrogance, his inability to accept that he could have been wrong. He fell from his pedestal, was denounced publicly by Havel,[9] and lost his premiership. His Civic Democratic Party seemed certain to be put out in the cold in the general election of June 1998. The Social Democrats, led by Miloš Zeman, seemed set to take over.

What followed was worthy of the Czech satirical tradition. The Social Democrats won the election statistically, but really lost it. As one of them put it, "we suffered a victory." They then took office, but with a government that was not in control. Klaus's Civic Democratic Party came second in the vote, doing much better than expected, largely through Klaus's vigorous "red bogey" campaign and the basic Czech distrust of experimentation. Eventually, a stunning compromise was reached between Zeman and Klaus. The Social Democrats would form a minority government, the Civic Democratic Party would go into opposition, but for the coming legislative period the Civic Democrats would not try to bring the government down through a no-confidence motion. Zeman would be premier, but Klaus would be president of the parliament and have much to do with the political agenda. This compromise, not a coalition government but a "tolerance pact," as Klaus insisted, was extraordinary because of the personal and political enmity, the total lack of trust, between the two men and the obvious incompatibility between their two parties. How long would it last? No one knew. But one thing was sure. One of the results of this "tolerance pact" would be the lessening of Havel's influence as president. In any case, Havel's support in the Czech political milieu had begun to erode considerably. By the end of 1998, popular support was also waning. He appeared to have lost his political touch, and the unpopularity of his second marriage, especially the public's dislike of his second wife, only added to his difficulties.[10]

Both the election result and the ensuing compromise were also extraordinary in the way that they reflected Czech political history. The election result showed Czech moderation, a distrust of experiment and extremes. The ensuing compromise reflected the fix-it politics so characteristic of the First (interwar) Republic. In the twenty years of the First Republic, no change of *power* took place based on democratic decision; neither has any clear-cut political change taken place since 1989. Democratic politics, of course, mean compromise, but nothing of the democratic spirit infused the Zeman-Klaus compromise of 1998. The only things that the compromise served were short-term party and political interests. The Czech Republic could be moving toward a two-party system. If two parties contested power, that might be good for democracy, but not if they shared it. It was hardly surprising that the Czech Communist Party, unreformed and unapologetic, was climbing in the opinion polls. Another similarity to the First Republic!

The truth by 2000 was that, after an impressive start, the Czech Republic was looking seriously like a failure. Its politics had become petty, its leaders discredited, its economy suspect, its public life corrupt, and its foreign policy clumsy. What it needed was not excuses but inspiration and purpose, and a new democratic leadership that could provide both.

Slovakia

After September 1998, Eastern Europe seemed to have one fewer "strong man." Vladimír Mečiár lost the Slovak parliamentary elections, not by much—his party received the most votes—but by enough to put him out of office. In the last week before the elections, he had pulled off a stunt that excelled even his own Barnum & Bailey style. With the opinion polls nothing but doom-laden, he shipped in the celebrities Claudia Schiffer, Gérard Depardieu, and Claudia Cardinale to try to seduce the Slovak voters. Their motives for coming, other than pocket money, are unknown, since they had no links with Slovakia. For Mečiár, though, their appearances seem to have been his way of showing that, if Europe's politicians did not like him, then its beautiful people did. But the gambit did not work. For most Slovaks, Mečiár counted, not his beautiful friends.

Mečiár had made Slovakia the odd man out in East Central Europe. Although Slovakia was once a serious candidate for NATO's and the EU's first intake, Mečiár's and his government's behavior put Slovakia back among the also-rans. Distinct similarities could be drawn between Mečiár and Belarus's "strong man" Aleksander Lukashenka. But Mečiár was more calculating, more self-servingly predictable than Lukashenka. Mečiár was the classic demagogue, handling crowds superbly and pressing the flesh tirelessly. These talents, plus his native wit, political cunning, and skill in titillating the anti-Czech, anti-Gypsy, anti-Jewish, and especially anti-Hungarian prejudices of his compatriots made him a most effective and dangerous tribune.

Even more, Mečiár personified a small-state, "up-yours," truculence, not confined to Slovakia, but highly evident there. Claudio Magris sums it up:

> But a small people which has to shake off the disdain or indifference of the great—of those whose greatness may perhaps have only a little while to run—must also shake off its complex about being small, the feeling of having constantly to rectify or cancel this impression, or else totally reverse it, glorying in it as a sign of election. Those who have long been forced to put all their efforts into the determination and defence of their own identity tend to prolong this attitude even when it is no longer necessary. Turned inward on themselves, absorbed in the assertion of their own identity and intent on making sure that others give it due recognition, they run the risk of devoting all their energies to this defence, thereby shrinking the horizons of their experience, of lacking magnanimity in their dealings with the world.[11]

Mečiár, then, reflected Slovak political culture at its lowest. In Bratislava and in cities like Košice, a democratic, politically mature elite did exist. The former president, Mihal Kovac, whom Mečiár had incessantly hounded, and Rudolf Schuster, head of the Party for Civic Accord and now president, were outstanding examples of it. But they were not street fighters, and in Slovakia for most of the 1990s it was street fighting that counted in politics. Mečiár was a master at it.[12] He made political capital out of Europe's cold shoulder, for which he was mainly responsible. "If you don't take us, the Russians will." It was bluster, but it struck a chord.[13] Repressed by the Hungarians for ten centuries, then patronized by Czechs for one, eternally ignored by everybody else, the Slovaks are, as Magris says, inevitably touchy. They took their independence as a vindication rather than a fulfillment, with a grudge rather than with pride.

(In this and in other regards, the Slovaks strongly resemble the Croats. Both states have Slavic populations. Both are Roman Catholic. Both experienced long subjugation to Hungary. Both of them were geographically pitchforked into multilateral states after World War I, and both took distinct discomfort in those entities. Both states have had large ethnic minorities. Both of them were puppet clerical-fascist states during World War II. Both were subjected to communism after World War II. And both showed growing assertiveness toward independence—Croatia through war, Slovakia in peace.)

Mečiár's political record was dim and disgraceful. Most disgraceful was his frequent use of the security service in a manner that closely resembled the communist era at its darkest. Economically, his government apparently did better. For several years, Slovakia had a surprisingly buoyant economy. Immediately after 1989, Slovakia was expected to be hurt by economic change. The big state combines were vulnerable, and, since some of them were virtually the sole employer in certain districts, it was feared that their demise could lead to widespread unemployment. But a drop-off in jobs did not materialize to the extent that many expected.

First, some of these big Slovak factories were relatively modern; their technology, therefore, made them more competitive than some older Czech factories. Second, some Slovak industrial exports held up surprisingly well because of their ultracompetitive ("dumping") prices. Third, Slovak weapon exports did well. Fourth, structural reform, which involved breaking up the big combines, was as slow getting started in Slovakia as it was elsewhere in Eastern Europe. Hence, much human misery was temporarily staved off. When privatization did get started in 1995, some of the biggest Slovak enterprises were sold to government-favored insiders ("crony capitalism"), who amassed fortunes but were slow to begin the necessary root-and-branch reform.[14] They and their employees supported Mečiár along with the assortment of former communists and strident nationalists who had supported him from the beginning.

But from 1997, the good (or the not-so-bad) days were over. The Slovak economy began to face some of the same problems that were hitting the Czech. (About 30 percent of Slovak trade was with the Czech Republic.) Some indicators—GDP, industrial growth, inflation—were still satisfactory.

But the budget deficit was rising, and so was unemployment. The main worry, though, stemmed from the foreign sector. The trade deficit and the current account imbalance were growing, and foreign investment was low. Slovakia's foreign exchange reserves began to sink, and pressure on the Slovak koruna mounted. A currency crisis was in the offing. In one sector, though, nuclear energy, Slovakia with Western help has made reassuring progress in strengthening the safety of its nuclear power stations, which were long-considered a dangerous threat to both East and West.[15]

Mečiár's successors had a huge task. They were faced with four "musts." (1) put decency back in the governance of Slovakia; (2) mitigate the economic dangers; (3) impress the West with their good intentions; (4) help to promote a better regional atmosphere. But a fifth "must" soon became necessary: keeping a very close eye on Mečiár. He had announced his "complete retirement" after losing the parliamentary election. He seemed serious enough, but many were sure that his retirement was calculated or that, anyway, he could not resist the call of the wild. He was soon back. He stood as presidential candidate for his party, the Democratic Movement for Slovakia, in May 1999. In the end, he lost, but not resoundingly enough to throw him out of Slovak politics. He was back playing the anti-Hungarian card and capitalizing on growing economic discontent. Now and again he even preached civil disobedience. But, though he was topping the popularity polls, the odds still seemed against him. Too many Slovaks had got wise to him. The nation's maturity would be gauged by how long it needed to knock down this erstwhile boxer turned political brawler for a count of ten. Some Slovaks were deriving comfort from rumors in early 2000 that Mečiár was getting tired of politics. They were probably deceiving themselves. When Mečiár was tired of politics he would also be tired of life.

Hungary

Hungary was expected to buck the East European electoral trend in the second half of the 1990s. In 1996 and 1997, voters in Poland, Bulgaria, and Romania had turned out their postcommunists, but in the parliamentary elections of June 1998, Hungary was expected to keep its Socialist government, elected four years earlier. The voters did not do so. The postcommunists, led by Premier Gyula Horn, were defeated by FIDESZ (the Federation of Young Democrats) under its leader, Viktor Orbán, and its allies. (FIDESZ became FIDESZ—Hungarian Civic Party, or FIDESZ—MPP.)

The situation had been topsy-turvy. When they came to power in 1994, the Hungarian Socialists had seemed to promise an economic policy that would shield the unprotected sections of the populace from the rigors of the new capitalism. At first, they tried to do just that. At the beginning of 1995, the *Economist* flatly declared: "Hungary is heading for the rocks."[16] Then, governmental policy changed abruptly. By April 1995 the same *Economist* was suggesting that "after a rocky start, Hungary's Socialist-led government . . . may have come to its senses."[17] Less than two years later, the *Neue Zürcher Zeitung* was praising the effectiveness of Hungary's program of austerity. While Bulgaria, its report continued, had recently shown "what a shambles the wrong economic policy could lead a country into, Hungary during the same period had shown how a false direction could be corrected with thoroughly bold steps."[18] At the end of 1997, the *International Herald Tribune* was suggesting that Hungary was a "model for East Europe." What distinguished it from the Czech Republic and Poland and put it ahead of them was its combination of macro- and microeconomic reform—its progress in changing the old socialist structure of the economy. According to the *Tribune:*

> Hungary is on a real reforming track because its leaders not only have swallowed the standard medicine of macroeconomic adjustment, cutting government spending, credit, consumption and wages, but also have tackled the nuts and bolts of reform efforts and of using the government's muscle to give the economy a push at strategic points in the transformation process.
>
> What has been key and instrumental in getting Hungary to move has been rapid privatization and a strategy that has favored selling companies for cash to strategic investors who were putting real money into the companies and who were committed to them.[19]

Tackling the nuts and bolts, using government muscle where necessary, a sensible privatization scheme that encouraged both foreign and domestic investment—these were the distinguishing elements in Hungary's progress. To deal with all these issues took nerve as well as good economic management. And it helped to make Horn's former communists the darlings of the capitalist West.

There were other reasons for Hungary's good international reputation. Political democracy was working well, with the rule of law becoming established. The Socialist government had also pursued a moderate policy with its neighbors on the issue of minorities. The aggressiveness of the pre-1994 Hungarian Democratic Forum government, led by József Antall, was abandoned in favor of a conciliatory approach that led to state treaties being signed with Romania and Slovakia (see chapter 8). The issue of minorities was by no means solved, but some of its nationalist venom had been drawn, at least from the Hungarian side. The main motive for this shift in policy was Western approval—more specifically, helping to ease Hungary's acceptance by NATO and the EU—and that was what resulted. Hungary's reasonableness and maturity were respected and rewarded.

The West, therefore, generally wanted and expected a Socialist victory. It got a narrow but clear Socialist defeat. Why? For a number of reasons.

1. *Electoral technicalities.* Generally, the new electoral systems in the East European democracies need mathematicians to understand them. Hungary's is one of the most recondite. The Socialists' vote held up well compared with 1994, and, in terms of percentage of votes cast, they finished first. But they captured only 134 seats, a loss of 75. The vote for FIDESZ came to just over 28 percent, but it contrived to win 148 seats. Two things turned the election: (a) The disastrous showing of the Alliance of Free Democrats, the Socialists' junior partner in their coalition government, which dropped from about 17 percent of the vote to 7 percent and won only 24 seats; (b) The fact that the Smallholders' Party withdrew nearly half of its own candidates in favor of FIDESZ in the first phase of the election.

2. *Dissatisfaction.* (a) Not all Hungarians were as enthused about the Socialists' capitalism as the Western bankers were. Many were becoming worse off rather than better off. (b) Evidence of crime (common and big-time) and corruption, or spectacular cases of it, had been mounting in Hungary. Foreign and local mafias were active, not as deeply active as many believed, but pervasively enough for it to be serious and an electoral issue. On a more ordinary level, fewer citizens felt safe on the streets. (c) Different degrees of isolation, mistrust of foreigners, or xenophobia were most evident in the crime issue. Gypsies (Romanian or otherwise), Russians, and criminals from Third World nations figured prominently among the mafiosi and their hit men. And—keeping alive a familiar instinct—Jews were seen as being "at back" of much of the big-time skullduggery. At a different level, a sensitivity to Western "economic imperialism" persisted (the "family silver" syndrome), allowing Western buyers to "grab up" land, banks, and other parts of the patrimony. The traditional Hungarian fear of being exposed and vulnerable showed again in a new setting.

3. The Free Democrats, the "swing" factor in Hungarian politics for several years, now became a rump party. Many of the Free Democrats' original supporters had been disgusted with them for going in with the Socialists in 1994, and the performances of some of their ministers had hardly enhanced their reputation. (The party also had a considerable sprinkling of Jews.) Much support for the Free Democrats was transferred to FIDESZ.[20]

To some extent, the FIDESZ and the Free Democrats, which earlier had been regarded as the "father" organization of FIDESZ, changed places. The vote for FIDESZ had amounted to only about 7 percent in 1994. Now its percentage had jumped by 21 percent and it dominated the new government. Much of its success stemmed from its leader, the 34-year-old Viktor Orbán, the first charismatic leader produced by Hungary since 1989. He appeared set to be a dominant political figure for years to come.

But what of FIDESZ itself—its composition, its future? In *Hopes and Shadows,* I quoted Mária Kovács, writing in 1991, as saying that the Hungarian party system was structured "alongside the prominent divisions not in society but within the intelligentsia."[21] The "democratic" parties certainly were structured in that way. But now these divisions, and with them the political structure, were shifting. The Hungarian Democratic Forum, which dominated Hungary's first democratic government, was a rightist conglomeration that soon split, lost the 1998 election, and fell apart more severely. After the 1998 elections, it had seventeen seats in parliament and was supporting FIDESZ. The Alliance of Free Democrats, an intellectual conglomerate of left-inclined moderates, suffered disastrously in 1998. The sobering thought for FIDESZ is its own identity also as a conglomerate. Will it suffer the fate of the other two? Viktor Orbán has insisted that it will not, that it has evolved into a party of the middle class, and that it therefore represents a large (and growing) sectional interest in the new Hungary.

The Socialists remained the best-organized party with their sectional base still rooted in the working class. Like other East European postcommunist parties, they are likely to remain a coherent, united force. The Smallholders, a peasant party re-created from its precommunist forebear, had a strong electoral success, gaining 14 percent of the vote. This level of support partly resulted from the Smallholders' larger-than-life leader, József Torgyán, who represented a coherent rural constituency with articulated aspirations and fears. The Smallholders are hardly a model of democratic behavior, but their growing strength did reflect a steady move toward political structures based on sectional interests.

One thing was certain about the 1998 elections: Horn and his Socialists did not lose because they had been communists. Former communist leanings might still be seen as something of an issue in, say, Poland, but that view was much less important in Hungary. The fortieth anniversary of the Hungarian Revolution was marked in 1996. It was a particularly difficult time for Horn, who as a young man had been a member of a thuggish volunteer militia that helped to mop up the remnants of the Revolution. But this millstone was not enough to sink him in 1994, when he won the election, and it did not count for much in 1998.

The Revolution was a landmark in Hungarian and European history. It can rouse great emotion among older Hungarians. But its political impact was diminishing (and Horn's career was clear enough evidence of this fact). It was bound to fade, anyway, after forty years. But the thirty years of Kádár's "benevolence" played an important role in the fading of this historical memory, too. A poll of 1,854 respondents conducted in October 1996 to mark the Revolution's anniversary found that the majority of them "expressed no opinion" on what the Revolution really was or meant. Of the slightly less than 50 percent of respondents who did give an opinion, most had only a superficial knowledge of what the Revolution was about, and only 10 percent thought the anniversary of the uprising should be Hungary's most important national holiday. (Some 55 percent plumped for March 15, the anniversary of the failed 1848 revolution.)[22] It was not therefore a matter of forgiving and forgetting, but of fading awareness in the minds and emotions of the younger electorate.

At the end of the twentieth century, Hungary's domestic political future depended largely on three things:

1. The ability of FIDESZ to turn itself into a stable, centrist political force, representing a strong, new, "middle-class" interest, to counter the Socialists, who would develop into a social democratic party with its base in the working class. Hungary could then develop a two-party system, or at most a few-party system, in the framework of democracy and a market economy.

2. The continuation of economic reform measures, however painful and unfair they were to many. Hungary, having got so far, could not go back, and a deliberate slowing would be the same as going back.

3. Viktor Orbán himself and his orientation. Young, refreshing, charismatic, capable, Orbán was sometimes likened to Tony Blair—although probably neither would be flattered by the comparison. In the new century, Orbán could become a real statesman. But worried questions were asked at the beginning of his new administration and these questions later multi-

plied. He had obviously wanted the state presidency when Árpád Göncz retired in 2000, but this embarrassment was averted by some adroit maneuvering that led to a respected lawyer, Ferenc Madl, becoming president. But Torgyán was not finished. Perhaps the most disturbing thing about him was his crude nationalism, with bits of anti-Semitism mixed in. As for Orbán, though hardly anti-Semitic himself, he did little to discourage anti-Semitic attitudes either among the Smallholders or within his own party. He also occasionally played strongly on emotions over the issue of Hungarian minorities abroad. Moreover, the Hungarian Democratic Forum, a strongly nationalist group, as well as István Csurka's small nationalist group, now back in parliament, also supported the new government. (Csurka became increasingly assertive throughout 1999.) Hence, a more fundamental question about Orbán: how nationalist would he himself be? Or how strong would he be in coping with his nationalist allies? Some of his own early comments on Hungarian minorities abroad were far from reassuring and had understandably upset the Romanian and Slovak governments. They were also beginning to upset some Western investors in Hungary. Generally, FIDESZ was considered a "right-liberal" party. The Smallholders, the Hungarian Democratic Forum, and Csurka's followers reveled in the "conservative-national" designation. Thus, Orbán would be closely watched to see what and who he really was.

The first year of Orbán's administration was partly characterized by a concentration of power, a partisan and personal vindictiveness that, when it had happened under Horn's premiership, was condemned as typical communist behavior. What Orbán seemed to be threatening in the summer of 1999 was a wholesale settling of scores with his Socialist opponents. If he went on with it, he could hurt both himself and Hungary. An increasing political polarization was developing in Hungary and Orbán was mainly responsible for it.

Foreign developments were generally encouraging. The former Socialist foreign minister, Lászlo Kovács, who had won considerable respect in office, warned the incoming government in 1998 against taking too strong a national stand in its dealings with Europe; he further urged it to be "pragmatic" on the Hungarian minorities issue. It was wise advice from a man who realized how crucial foreign policy was to Hungary.

But NATO membership and EU application were not the only crucial foreign-policy issues. Regional policy was also vital for Hungary, which has about the same population as the Czech Republic of just over 10 million people. Other vital statistics are similar. Aside from the Roma, neither country has large ethnic minorities. Both are in NATO and will eventually be in the EU. Yet, while the Czech Republic has opted for international anonymity, Hungary is forced to show an international profile. Foreign relations and foreign impact are a necessity. Hungary borders Austria, Slovenia, Croatia, Serbia, Romania, Slovakia, and Ukraine. Four of those countries have large Hungarian minorities. Hungary, in fact, is pivotal to the region. Hungary is not Balkan. It would much prefer to be exclusively Central European. (Its culture unquestionably embodies that preference.) But Hungarian minorities in Serbia (Vojvodina) and Romania (Transylvania) ineluctably tug Hungary toward the Balkans. And the Hungarian minority in Ukraine, as well as the country's common border with Ukraine, jerk it slightly eastward. Its common border and historical links with Austria also are a conduit to Central Europe and beyond. And Slovenia, when it joins NATO and the EU, would provide it with a link with Italy and the Adriatic. Hungary could not, therefore, be provincial even if it wanted to be. But Hungarians have always been the least provincial of all the East European countries. They can respond to their international challenges and create opportunities out of them. They form a poised nation. Drops of the old aristocratic culture have trickled down; they could even be noticed in the nooks and crannies of communist rule. Now they are obvious: the occasional touch of class, hint of panache, sense of the occasion, feel for theater. Take one, by no means trivial, example: in Eastern Europe only Hungary has a Formula 1 auto grand prix event. Why not! It belongs here! Like Poland's, Hungary's future should be bright. It also should be safe. In a recent seriocomic novel about Hungary, the young antihero is admonished by a teacher: "You know our history. As a Hungarian you should be prepared for the odd cataclysm."[23] Not any more.

Romania

After the trauma of Ceaușescu and the revolution that toppled him, what Romania needed was stability. Ion Iliescu gave it stability of sorts and began a transition, if not toward democracy, then away from totalitarianism.[24] He lost the presidency in 1996 in a free and fair election. The very fact that such an election could be held after what Romania had been through for forty years was, in part, a testimony to his achievement. But he was now standing again for the presidency in the fall of 2000 with many tipping him to win. It would be a serious setback for his country if he did, not to mention his own reputation in history. Romania would take itself off the European road into a detour with virtually no way forward.

Iliescu's problem is his mind-set. The only ideal he has ever had in his life is communism. He was intelligent and human enough to realize fairly soon that this was indeed a god that had failed. But Iliescu could never cross the divide into democracy, in the way that, for example, Ivica Racan and Stipe Mesić in Croatia could. His language after 1989 was democratic enough, his intentions might even have been, but his mind-set remained authoritarian. What spurred him and his ruling clique was power—getting it, consolidating it, keeping it. This steadily drove him into demagogy and opportunism, hence, in the Romanian context, into nationalism. His "Party of Social Democracy in Romania," which he founded and then godfathered, had allied itself with the racist, ultranationalist parties to stay in power. He also deliberately played on the fears of peasants and many workers in opposing real economic reform.[25] Few expected principle from him, but they had a right to expect policy. All they got was the play for power, and power did corrupt. Material corruption, indeed, enveloped the government at every level. Perhaps Romania was "reverting to type," but this corruption was on an unprecedented scale. It has dominated Romanian democratic politics since 1989 and was the dominant feature of the election campaigns in 2000.

The new president in 1996, Emil Constantinescu, and the new coalition government led by Victor Ciorbea made a fresh start, promised much, and were welcomed in the West.[26] Ciorbea began his stay in office with apparent firmness. Price restrictions were lifted, and the currency was freed. An ambitious privatization plan was announced. Representatives of the Hungarian Democratic Federation in Romania, the Hungarian minority's political party, were taken into the government. It seemed a bold beginning, and the public seemed to respond in a positive way. But after only a year in office, the governing coalition's popularity had declined sharply; it was talking big and doing little. The public was getting restless, as was the international community. Most important, so was the International Monetary Fund.

Ciorbea himself was clearly one problem. He was proving a temporizer, not a man of action. His own party, the largest in the coalition, created another difficulty. It was now called the National Peasant Party—Christian Democratic, and it was turning out to be as unfocused as it sounded. Making matters worse was its biggest ally in the coalition, the Democratic

Party, led by Petre Roman, a former premier under Iliescu and a slick operator with whom no superior could ever feel safe. Roman looked as if he would be around for some time—guard up, elbows sharp, never cooperating, always jockeying. At the end of 1999 he did, in fact, become foreign minister. In early 1998 the Ciorbea government had fallen. An "old-new" government replaced it under Radu Vasile, and a new reform program was introduced. It seemed both déjà vu and déjà entendu.[27] Vasile's government lasted until the end of 1999 and was replaced by a more promising-looking one under a former head of the state bank, Mugur Isarescu. But most disturbing of all about the political situation was the increasing popularity of the Greater Romania Party, led by one of Ceauşescu's former lickspittle poets, Corneliu Vadim Tudor. The strengthening of this ultranationalist, openly anti-Semitic, Hungarian-hating, anti-Western party was both a measure of democratic failure and an urgent warning that improvements had to be made. Tudor was clearly aiming to capitalize on worker discontent, and by early 1999 he was having some success. Romania began the new millennium with bleak prospects. If Iliescu returned to the presidency, they would look even bleaker, at least in the long run.

But whoever won elections, whoever was "in" or "out," Romania's politicians continued to lack credibility. So did politics as a whole. Long before communist rule, during it, and now after it, political amorality has been the bane of Romanian public life. Policy, however forcefully, attractively, and sometimes sincerely presented, becomes an afterthought when power is gained. The same is true for political loyalties and the sense of public good. This is the Romanian political disease from which very few politicians have been immune. The public is aware of this deficiency and mostly resigned to it. But, to counter it, the people sometimes have looked to political outsiders for rescue—to generals and patriarchs, for example, in precommunist Romania. Now, since 1989, a call has gone out for "technicians." But the supremacy of technicians means democratic surrender. Romania needs help to avoid lapsing into this sinkhole. France, its traditional patron, could help show the way—whatever France's motives might be. Ultimately, though, help must come from Romanians themselves. Many of them, men and women of ability, are aware of that need. But they often find it more congenial carping from ringside than getting inside the ropes.

Monarchy and the question of its return are nothing more than political distractions in the Balkans. But it is a sizable distraction in Romania. Sentiment, the backward leapfrog to the precommunist era, a political gesture against the "communists," a sense of political failure since 1989, a deserved respect for King Michael and his family—these are some of the reasons that the subject arises. But basically it is like the technician solution—a cop-out, an avoidance of political responsibility. Besides, at a time when Romania's need is for healing, it is hard to imagine a more divisive issue than the monarchy's restoration.

Romania, a relatively large and potentially rich country, has been important in South Eastern Europe. Although Romania's cultural orientation has been emphatically westward, questions of security and national integrity often have made it look eastward toward Moldova, Ukraine, and Russia. Relations with Moldova were bound to be sensitive in view of Moldova's Romanian ethnic majority, its incorporation into Romania during the interwar period, and the hope of many Romanians that it might be reincorporated after the breakup of the Soviet Union. But more recently a growing disinterest is apparent in Romania itself for any eventual reunion. That lessened interest is best explained by three things. (1) Romanians realized that they had enough problems on their hands without adding Moldova. Considerable travel took place between the two countries, and for many Moldovans, Romania was the West. (This fact gives some idea of how bad things were in Moldova.) (2) Romanians and Moldovans had grown away from one another. Romanians complained about the Moldovans having become "Russified." This was hardly surprising in view of the province having been part of either Russia or the Soviet Union from 1812 to 1992, except for the twenty years between the two world wars. Moldovans, for their part, had no sense of homecoming when they visited Romania; they felt like strangers and were often treated like suspect outsiders. (3) On account of its involvement in the Dniester Republic, the small enclave in eastern Moldova, Russia would almost certainly regard any reunion of Moldova with Romania as provocative. The Romanians realized this possibility, and also grasped that their chances of membership in the EU and NATO would not be enhanced by frictional entanglements to the east.

On the other hand, the Romanians were aware that better relations with Ukraine would help their cause in the West. Ukraine was now Romania's principal eastern neighbor. Relations since 1992 had been complicated by Ukraine's possession of Northern Bukovina, which had been ceded to the Soviet Union under the secret Molotov-Ribbentrop pact of 1939. Romania would have liked the territory back or, at least, the secret pact condemned. But Ukraine refused to cooperate. For vociferous nationalists in both countries, Northern Bukovina became a rallying cry. But in 1997 a state treaty between the two countries was signed. The Molotov-Ribbentrop pact was not specifically condemned, but "unlawful acts of totalitarian regimes and military dictatorships" were. At the same time, both sides affirmed the 1975 Helsinki principle of the inviolability of borders and the Council of Europe's Recommendation 1201 about the protection of minorities (see chapter 8). Honors were considered even, and an encouraging bid toward advancing intraregional relations had been made.[28]

The treaty with Ukraine had taken three years to negotiate. The Romanian-Hungarian treaty took longer. It was eventually signed in September 1996, after interminable delays. The real bone of contention was the status of the Hungarian minority and Budapest's specific refusal to recognize the border between Hungary and Ukraine until that minority's status was "improved." But bilateral relations had definitely grown better, and both sides were anxious to get into the West's good graces. So a treaty was signed. Typically, though, at the core distrust still existed. Romania insisted on a caveat to the treaty, repudiating any notion that it might mean collective status for its Hungarian minority (see chapter 8). This signal declared that the historic dispute was not at an end, but it was entering a more conciliatory and, hopefully, healing phase.

As it had always done, Romania was looking better in diplomacy than in democracy. Its aplomb abroad, of course, had to be maintained. But Romania could do with more aplomb at home in the service of its patient population.

Bulgaria

Kyril Drezov in a brilliant essay on Bulgarian politics since the fall of Todor Zhivkov used the eyebrow-raising term "democratic communism" to describe political developments between 1989 and the electoral defeat of the socialist government in 1997: "As an ideal type construct, 'democratic communism' refers to *a society which combines 100% public ownership of the 'means of production'* (industry and land) with a *functioning multi-Party democracy* (free and fair multi-party elections and alternation of different parties/coalitions in power, free media, rule of law, constitutional separation of powers, and effective checks and balances between them)."[29] The definition is not exact, but, as Drezov says, Bulgaria is the one "empirical case that comes closest to democratic communism." He goes on:

If one imagines a continuum, on one side of which would be pure "democratic communism" (100% public ownership combined with full democracy), and on the other side would be a combination of a non-democratic polity with a fully developed market economy, then Iliescu's Romania would have to be positioned further away than Bulgaria from the pole of "democratic communism"—because of a more suspect democratic component and a more consistent approach to marketisation and privatisation. For similar reasons all other Balkan transition societies would have to be positioned further away from the pole of "democratic communism" than either Bulgaria or Romania.[30]

Communist Bulgaria had been characterized by dogmatism. But hardly *non movere* dogmatism. However eccentrically, Zhivkov was an innovator. But although some of his innovations aspired to be far-reaching, they had one thing in common: they allowed for neither spontaneity nor real initiative. Partly as a reaction against this restrictiveness, an explosion of political and personal freedom occurred after 1989. Sometimes the explosion was hardly democratic, savoring more of mob rule. But a refreshing atmosphere of freedom was generated that was not likely to be dispelled. Both postcommunist and anticommunist governments since 1989 deserve credit for this opening. But most credit should go to the Bulgarian public and its determination to hold on to freedoms long denied.

What was lacking until the end of the 1990s was meaningful economic change to buttress the political freedoms that had been gained. A few liberal macroeconomic measures had been begun, but very little structural reform had been initiated to break the statist mold, encourage foreign investment, and get the economy moving. Bulgaria, in fact, fell to the bottom of the transition league table, that is, it was now the slowest in Eastern Europe in moving toward the market. Until the Union of Democratic Forces (UDF) ousted the Socialists from power in 1997, no likelihood of change seemed in store. In fact, the Socialist government, elected with a strong majority in 1994, had become a do-nothing government, bringing the Bulgarian economy and most Bulgarians to the brink of destitution.

Three conditions caused this lack of movement: First, little real entrepreneurial tradition exists in Bulgaria. Today, a growing army of young capitalists is stirring, but a generation will be needed before the word "competition" acquires much meaning among Bulgarians in general.

Second is the collectivist mind-set. Probably more than anywhere else in

Eastern Europe, most members of Bulgaria's former communist party remained communist. Whether senior or junior, however chastened and reformist, they shared a pathological antipathy to all things "capitalist." A strong bolshevik tradition persisted in Bulgaria, as did a strong pro-Russian leaning. Where Poland, Hungary, and the Czech Republic were on one of the main European pathways and generally in touch with political and intellectual developments on the Continent as a whole, Bulgaria, tucked away in the southeast corner of the Balkans, was isolated. Still, hopeful signs could be detected. A few postcommunists *did* become social democrats, either remaining inside the Socialist Party (the former Communist Party) or leaving it to form their own political grouping. Bulgaria is no exception to the rule that a hardy democracy will depend on whether many communists can become social democrats and cooperate with center liberals.

Third, too little entrepreneurial and too much collectivist tradition cannot adequately explain the government's *immobilisme* from 1994 until 1997. Organized crime, "nomenklatura capitalism," must be taken into account. The Socialist government was influenced, intimidated, and corrupted by the gangster groups that were running large parts of Bulgarian life. This subject has been discussed at length in chapter 4. Here, it simply needs to be added that crime had already received a huge impetus in the 1960s when Bulgaria became part of the transit route for many hundreds of thousands of Turkish workers in Western Europe. By then, Sofia had become a European drug center. After 1989, the issue of privatization—preventing it, preempting it, perverting it—gave organized crime its decisive impetus.

The UDF government since 1997 has been addressing both crime and its economic inheritance. The government began the task at a great pace and has been much more impressive than the "reform" governments in neighboring Romania. But it is still plagued by corruption in its midst. It also must tackle the basic problem of upgrading the status of the country's large Turkish and Gypsy minorities, however (see chapter 7). And overarching everything else is Bulgaria's demographic problem. Bulgaria has the lowest birth rate in Europe. By the year 2000 its population is expected to drop to 8.1 million and by 2020 could be between 6.9 and 7.4 million. Every fourth Bulgarian will be a pensioner by that year. Between 1989 and 1996, about 650,000 mostly young people left Bulgaria.[31] Many more wanted to go. There were several reasons for this exodus, and the general issue of emigration is discussed in chapter 3. Emigration is the most tangible expression of the dolefulness and pessimism that pervade the whole country. The Bulgarian government could do more to dispel this pessimism. Bulgaria could become a rewarding, challenging crossroads in the twenty-first century if its democratic government survives and succeeds. To do that it needs credibility, a rare commodity indeed, not only in Bulgaria but throughout the Balkans. But Bulgaria is already in peril, and if its present government fails, Bulgaria will be in mortal danger. Its government is trying to do the right things, but the right things are often unpopular.

Albania

By the end of the twentieth century, Albania had become premodern, as some observers darkly called it. The state, the economy, social services, law and order, all had broken down. The same thing had happened in Bosnia-Hercegovina, but Albania was supposed to be at peace.

Historically, Albanians had a reputation for lawlessness—at least in the Western sense of the notion. Blood feuds were part of its lore, and King Zog's derring-do was classic High Albania. But the same King Zog also did much to bring about a semblance of order, a suggestion of unity, to his country—a mini-Atatürk, perhaps. Enver Hoxha was a modernizer in his own way. He introduced real reforms, most notably in education and social policy. He certainly imposed order and greatly strengthened the power of the state. His notion of "beleaguered Albania" also kindled a nationalism of sorts. But it was precisely Hoxha's terror-driven despotism that was the underlying cause of the barbarism that occurred with the riots of 1997. After communism's collapse, the country drifted back toward tribalism and gangsterism.

The immediate cause of the 1997 disaster was the collapse of several large "Pyramid" financial schemes. The "cheated," those people who had lost everything in the collapse, reacted violently. Then gangsterism took over. A rough-edged level of political culture and Kalashnikovs combined to produce anarchy.[32] Gunrunning already had become one of Albania's best-paying industries. So had drug running, which was even more profitable. In the early 1990s, Albania, most notably the port of Durrës, had become one of the main drug conduits to Western Europe. Traffic in young girls for prostitution and smuggling emigrants and tobacco also paid well. Durrës attracted not just local gangsters but the international set. Its proximity to Italy, so beneficial in some respects, facilitated a grisly, criminal link.

Drug running and other traffic were, of course, a form of free enterprise. But in Albania in the 1990s, more legitimate free enterprise was in play too.

This enterprise was classically rugged, "kiosk" or "hillbilly," capitalism. Thousands of small shops and booths sprang up; roadside fruit crates became emporia of trade. Banned under Hoxha, private automobiles now choked whatever roads were passable. The ages of those cars were questionable and their provenance suspicious. Obviously, however, the communist steamroller had not flattened the entrepreneurial spirit. Albania's new fame spread. Some in the West hailed it as a plucky little trailblazer at the new capitalist frontier.[33] But this "progress" simply collapsed, for three immediate reasons:

1. The president, Sali Berisha, who should have been leading and monitoring democratic development, was simply riding the crest of the wave. The West thought he was one of theirs. In fact, he was a Balkan demagogue—autocratic, energetic, opportunistic.

2. "Hillbilly capitalism" inevitably led to economic power becoming increasingly concentrated in gangster hands.

3. Impoverished by socialism, many Albanians, like many other South East Europeans, at first identified capitalism with bonanza. The Pyramid schemes that eventually betrayed them had at first appeared to be dazzling. When those schemes collapsed, the bonanza seekers responded with blind fury, the only way they knew how. Not all of them went to the streets; many tried to leave altogether, becoming Europe's boat people, risking their lives trying to get to Italy and beyond. For them the southern Italian coast was what the Florida coast was for Cubans.

In the mayhem that followed the Pyramid's collapse, many of the looters and murderers were undoubtedly former supporters of the communist regime and members of the old Sigurimi, its secret police. This fact led some Western observers, mainly supporters of Berisha, to back his own claim that the riots were a counterrevolution aimed at restoring communism.

But this explanation speciously simplified a complex situation. The only hope for Albania was to start afresh. The United States had backed Berisha politically, economically, and militarily. Now, it was time for the United States to reconsider its options, keeping in mind that the inherent volatility of the Albanian situation precluded its backing of a lone contender. The Socialists under Fatos Nano, a former communist leader, succeeded Berisha. They seemed to be ruling sensibly; the population was calm. The elections that returned Nano to power in 1997, despite expectations, were peaceful. Was all passion spent? For a while, it seemed so. At the height of the anti-Berisha furor in 1997, one citizen of Tirana was heard to say: "in six months' time they could be cheering their heads off for Berisha again." He might have been only slightly exaggerating. In September 1998 the mob was out in Tirana again, almost lynching the governing cabinet in revenge for the murder—perpetrators unknown—of an opposition politician. Premier Nano was soon forced to resign. The incident bore all the marks of an attempted coup by Berisha. The next parliamentary elections were due in 2001. Berisha would be at least a serious candidate.

There did seem to be one hope amid the encircling gloom. Political generations in Albania were changing as they were throughout Eastern Europe. The old communist "Party of Labor" evolved into the Socialist Party, led and typified by Fatos Nano, more socialist than democratic, mindful of change but not embracing it. These in turn could eventually give way to a younger group, genuinely social democratic and Western-oriented. Something similar was happening in the Democratic Party camp, where a younger element was asserting itself. One of the main differences between them and their older colleagues was that they were unencumbered, not only by the politics of the past but by the hatreds of the past, the injustices they considered they had suffered, and the perceived need to use their new power not for the good of the country but for their own revenge—a new variation on the old vendetta! Instead, the younger generation could concentrate on Albania's future.

In 1999, of course, came the Kosovo conflict. Albania was virtually transformed into one huge refugee camp (see chapter 7). The Albanian people took in their Kosovo brethren but they could not cope with the strain for long. The camps themselves became virtually dominated by the Kosovo Liberation Army (KLA), which for a short time took over much of the country—it and the gangster bands that robbed the refugees. But then came the NATO victory in Kosovo. The refugees went home. Albania had become even more destitute. But even with a reduced Western presence, economic and military, it could be heading for more security, stability, and economic well-being than it ever had. Albania has always been a client state; the Western powers might be its best patron yet.

Slovenia

Just as Slovakia and Croatia are comparable (see p. 117), so are Slovenia and the Czech Republic. Slovenia's population of some 2 million is only about one-fifth that of the Czech Republic. Otherwise, similarities are remarkable. The two countries' populations are overwhelmingly Slavic; they were ruled for centuries from Habsburg Vienna; they are considered the most Germanized of the Slavic nations; and except for the Gypsies in the Czech Republic, they have no sizable ethnic minorities. Both countries are largely Roman Catholic, but neither of them seems conspicuously dutiful or active in religious practice. Both countries are economically oriented. Bohemia was the workshop of the Habsburg empire, Slovenia the workshop of Yugoslavia. Their standards of living have always been relatively high. For much of the twentieth century, both countries also were parts of larger, multiethnic states.

Since the collapse of the communist system and the disintegration of both Yugoslavia and Czechoslovakia, some similarities between the Czechs and Slovenes have persisted. Both have been determined to escape from their former geopolitical space—Eastern Europe in the Czech Republic's case and the former Yugoslavia (the Balkans) in Slovenia's. Both countries want to be exclusively part of the West, and they have succeeded in making their point. Both countries have become known for their economies more than for their politics, and for several years after the fall of communism, both of them enjoyed outstanding economic success.

But while the Czech economy floundered badly in 1997, the Slovene economy continued its run of success. It enjoyed a rising GDP, although—and this fact puts it in an overall European perspective—its per capita GDP was still lower than even Greece's. Generally, Slovenia had also achieved impressive macroeconomic stability and enjoyed a solid international credit rating. Its foreign trade position also continued to be sound, no mean achievement for a country of which 70 percent of its trade had been with the former Yugoslavia. By 1997, Slovenia was exporting 65 percent of its production to the European Union.[34]

Still, nervousness persisted in both Brussels and Ljubljana that Slovenia might be resting on its economic laurels. (The Czechs had done precisely the same.) Some of the multiple problems of structural reform would remain until, as the *Neue Zürcher Zeitung* put it, "all the relics of self management socialism are swept away, new growth potential released and EU entry without competition-shock made possible."[35] One danger was the familiar postcommunist malaise of "crony capitalism" and the appropriation of state institutions, banks, companies, of whole regions, according to political orientations. Finally (yet another similarity with the Czech Republic), to gain EU membership Slovenia would have to open its doors much wider to foreign investment and ownership. It realized the danger of becoming a Western appendage, but, in opting for the Western club, it had to abide by the club's rules.

Slovene politics since independence have been largely dominated by two former communists, the president, Milan Kučan, and the Liberal Democrat left-of-center prime minister, Janez Drnovsek. Slovenia probably leads the field in genuine per capita conversions from communism to social democracy. Political stability has been maintained, but sometimes only through feverish maneuvering and some bewildering governmental coalitions. The Drnovsek government, formed in February 1997 after an indecisive election, had the Liberal Democrats allied with the conservative People's Party, a marriage of convenience for which many were predicting a rather nasty divorce. This came early in 2000. But President Kučan, no slouch at maneuvers himself, strove successfully to keep Drnovsek afloat, thus averting free Slovenia's most serious political crisis. Kučan is the most impressive Slovene leader since Monsignor Anton Korošec in the first Yugoslavia, the radically different ideological provenance of both men reflecting the realism and adaptability of their nation.

Slovenia borders on Hungary, Austria, Italy, and Croatia. It has good relations with Hungary and sees itself as an essential link, to be strengthened by NATO membership, between Hungary and Italy and the West beyond.[36] Its relations with Austria are now good, despite the sourness after both world wars over frontiers and ethnic minorities. With Italy, relations have been difficult. The right-wing nationalist Italian governments in the 1990s tried to revise old agreements—thus reopening old wounds—over Slovene confiscation of Italian property after World War II. But the Italian center and left have wanted good relations with Slovenia, both on principle and because economic partnership would benefit both sides, especially Italy's northeastern districts. Slovenia's main problem in foreign affairs will center on getting quick entry to the EU and on improving relations with Croatia. Economic, financial, and infrastructural problems have occasionally made those relations tense. Slovenia has not been blameless. But at the root of the tension has been Croatian resentment that the Slovenes have fewer problems and more friends. Still, Slovenia's Western prospects and Croatia's now democratic government with its own Western aspirations should ensure mutual restraint.

Croatia

Any profile of Croatia must begin with the late Franjo Tudjman. "Tudjman's last rally? Is Croatia's autocratic president at death's door?" The *Economist* was asking this question at the end of 1996.[37] But in Croatia's presidential election the following June, Tudjman cruised to another five-year term. Almost everyone had written him off, except for Tudjman himself.

Tudjman and Milošević have often been paired. They were the two principal villains in the Yugoslav tragedy. Both men saw the disintegration of Yugoslavia as an opportunity to fulfill their nation's expansionist dreams. Tudjman was the more complex political animal. He was more of a genuine patriot than Milošević. All too often he betrayed some of the less attractive aspects of Croat national culture. He made frequent outbursts expressing racism, fascism, and chauvinism. After 1991 he became Washington's man, gaining American support against Serbia, partly because the United States feared Milošević's becoming a protégé of Moscow, and partly because Serbia was the main aggressor. Hence, Tudjman occasionally had to preach, and sometimes even toe, the American line—a distasteful obligation for him. But he knew only too well that he shared a dependency with Washington. He was obviously dependent on the Americans, but they, having committed themselves to him, had to allow him some leeway. They knew about his war crimes and his massive corruption.

Tudjman was naturally authoritarian; hence, his curtailment of media freedoms, his chicanery in trying to silence opposition, and his paranoia over independent institutions, especially those with a "corrupting" Western connection. His was a simple formula: he who is not with me is against Croatia.[38] He assiduously courted the Croatian Roman Catholic Church, which probably became even more politically powerful than the church in Poland. The Vatican responded favorably. Tudjman remained popular in the country as a whole until about the middle of 1998 despite his difficulties with the sophisticated Zagreb electorate and the hostility of many democratic Croat intellectuals. But he seemed able to face down most opposition. The public show of protest that probably affected him the most was in early 1997 when Zagreb soccer fans objected to his changing the name of their team from Dinamo Zagreb to Croatia Zagreb. He fumed at this alleged evidence of "Yugo-nostalgia." In the summer of 1998 he was in his element over Croatia's remarkable progress in soccer's World Cup matches. That progress did indeed put Croatia on the world map, further fed Croatian nationalism, and was a shot in the arm for Tudjman.[39] He made the whole team "Knights of Croatia" for free! (He usually charged between five thousand and ten thousand U.S. dollars for the honor.)

The final return of East Slavonia to Croatia in January 1998—the crowning of Croatia's recovery from the war and its defeat of Serbia—gave him another boost. Croatia had not only regained what it had lost, but in a couple of years it had rid itself of most of its historic Serb minority. The involuntary exodus was completed in 1997 and reduced the Serbs from 12 percent of Croatia's population to about 5 percent.[40] Was this now enough for national fulfillment? It may not have been for Tudjman. Ideally he would have liked to spread Croatia into Bosnia-Hercegovina. But his physical frailty finally caught up with him and he died in December 1999.

In the parliamentary and presidential elections that followed his death, his party, the Croatian Democratic Community, was routed and the democratic opposition triumphed. Perhaps ironically, the two most powerful politicians now in the country, the newly elected president, Stipe Mesić, and the new premier, Ivica Racan, were both former communists (as, of course, Tudjman himself once was). Mesić was actually the last state president of Tito's Yugoslavia. But both had crossed the ideological divide and they lost no time in putting Croatia back on the democratic road.

In general, Tudjman's death and the democratic succession secured the ascendancy of the *civic* over the *ethnic* factor in Croatian politics (Croatia Zagreb did, incidentally, again become Dinamo Zagreb—small wonder, said the rightists, with those "reds" back in power!). It also resulted in a more conciliatory and cooperative attitude in Balkan politics, especially over Bosnia-Hercegovina. (It remained to be seen, however, whether the new government in Zagreb would or could keep its promises about the return of Serb refugees. See chapter 6.) Finally the gates of Europe were now opened, too. Croatia was becoming more democratic, less corrupt, and more businesslike. It would be a long time before it became liberal, honest, and prosperous. Unreconstructed nationalism was still strong. But at least the will was there and so was the dynamic.

Macedonia

Macedonia's modern history has been picturesquely summed up by Adam Wandruszka, who tells the story of a Mr. Omerić: "Omerić, who was so-called under the Yugoslav monarchy, became Omerov during the Bulgarian occupation in the Second World War and then Omerski for the republic of Macedonia—part of the Yugoslav Federation. His original name, Omer, was Turkish."[41] Now he is Mr. Omerski again, an independent Mr. Omerski. How long he stays that way could decide the fate of the entire South Balkan region.

Mr. Omerski's independence has been closely identified with the leadership of Kiro Gligorov. In November 1999, Gligorov, once a Titoist and now a "democratic socialist" (renamed but not entirely recycled), constitutionally and even graciously handed over the presidency of Macedonia to Boris Trajkovski, the right-wing candidate who had just won the presidential elections. Gligorov, more than eighty years old in 1999 and obviously weakened by the unsuccessful attempt on his life five years earlier, did not contest the election. Though disappointed by its result, Gligorov could rightly consider his replacement by a political opponent as a milestone on the democratic path that his new state had followed since 1991. Macedonia was the only republic of the former Yugoslavia to break away into independence without bloodshed. In its first few years it encountered outright hostility or only grudging acceptance by its neighbors. Gligorov must take the major credit for his country's evolution.

But his leadership was not entirely beneficial. Though observing the democratic rituals, his experience and inclinations were authoritarian. He gave Macedonia a stability of sorts. His critics argued that it was not *democratic* stability, but *undemocratic* continuity. Many members of his post-communist party—the Party of Democratic Transformation—were simply unreconstructed placemen. The economy contained too much residue from the old Titoist self-management approach. Privatization was on an "old comrade" basis; corruption and organized crime were rampant; and the media were still under the influence and control of the state. And though elections were free, they sometimes were not fair. Still, warts and all, most Macedonians agreed that Gligorov was the right man at the right time.

In international affairs, Gligorov was eminently successful, not only patiently neutralizing regional hostility, but also showing himself aware of the broader aspects of Macedonia's situation. He realized that, just as Western (i.e., American) assistance had been necessary to help Yugoslavia survive after 1948, so Macedonia would need similar help to preserve its independence after 1991. This help was symbolized by UNPREDEP (the United Nations Preventive Deployment Force), originally a force of some 1,300 soldiers, including an American contingent of about 500. Not specifically designed to protect Macedonia, UNPREDEP with its presence and especially its American element had a remarkably reassuring effect on Macedonia's sense of security and self-confidence.

Later, a large NATO force was stationed in Macedonia to monitor the situation in Kosovo. Then the conflict in Kosovo itself saw the increase of the NATO presence and the situation became complicated because of the "Albanian problem" inside Macedonia itself (see chapter 7). Public opinion among Slavic Macedonians then turned against the United States and the NATO powers. This turnabout stemmed from U.S. and NATO actions in Kosovo itself and, by extension, against Serbia. Slavic Macedonians held NATO responsible for the massive Albanian exodus into Macedonia, thereby endangering its delicate "ethnic balance."

The regional implications of the strong Albanian presence in Macedonia will be further analyzed (see chapter 7). This presence constitutes the biggest threat to the country's survival itself. The birth of independent Macedonia coincided with the "Albanian emergence." Both events were historically unexpected, and both will need new international approaches if they are not to lead to disaster (see chapter 7). Elisabeth Barker, writing of Macedonia a half-century ago, said that "rivers of blood" had been shed for it. "The only saving solution," she argued, was an "integral, free, and independent Macedonia. Only then can it cease to be an apple of discord and become a healthy unifying link between all the Balkan peoples."[42] Barker was right, except that she ignored the Albanians. Everybody ignored the Albanians back then.

Nobody can ignore them now. And in the future, even less so. Macedonia's present prime minister, Lupčo Georgievski, is leader of IMRO–DPMNE—the Internal Macedonian Revolutionary Organization–Democratic Party for Macedonian National Unity. The legendary IMRO, having modified its policy under Georgievski, had now modified its name as well. It won the parliamentary elections in 1998 and formed a governmental alliance with the more "extreme" Albanian nationalist party under Arben Xhaferi. Their collaboration was a surprising combination which prompted many observers to think that both parties and both leaders had "mellowed" (see chapter 7). The newly elected president, Trajkovski, was an attractive man, partly educated and partly molded in America. But his election only seemed to produce new tensions. Trajkovski got a heavy vote in Albanian districts, in some of which were strong suspicions of fraud. Allegations of fraud now aroused many members of the defeated left. Because they lost, they were convinced of electoral hocus-pocus, and they feared that the presidency as well as the government could be susceptible to stronger Albanian influence. The ethnic factor was simply all pervasive and seemed to be further eroding not only Macedonia's stability but ultimately its integrity, too.

6

The First Yugoslav War:
Serbs, Bosnians, Croats

TWO WORLD WARS OCCURRED in the first half of the twentieth century. Within them, regional or local wars were waged in the Balkans. Sometimes the world and local wars overlapped; sometimes they remained distinct. The world wars may have been ignited by the local wars, but they did not provide the context for them. These regional conflicts had their own contexts, their own aims, alliances, and alignments. The world wars and the local wars often ran parallel.

The Balkan Wars of 1912 and 1913 preceded the start of World War I, which broke out in the Balkans after the assassination at Sarajevo. But the Great War, as it once was called, was not *caused* by developments in the Balkans; had it not started there, it would have started somewhere else. The war began in the Balkans because the international situation that enabled the "balance of power" to operate had broken down, and the two Balkan conflicts were a symptom of this breakdown. The Congress of Berlin, the Indian summer of the balance of power, ostensibly brought order to a volatile Balkan situation. But the power balance could not control or contain this volatile Balkan situation. Turkey was too weak to sustain the balance. Austria, smarting under its losses in Italy and its defeat by Prussia in 1866, was looking for new fields to conquer. Russia saw its Balkan opportunities opening up with the Ottoman decline. Reunited Germany, soon with Wilhelm II and without Bismarck, was impatiently pawing the ground.

The Congress of Berlin made two huge errors that had disastrous consequences. For one, it assigned Bosnia-Hercegovina to Austrian "administration," when Austria had no intention of ever giving the region up and in 1908 formally annexed the territory. Just six years later, the assassination of

Franz Ferdinand at Sarajevo led to World War I. Second, the Congress of Berlin gave Macedonia back to Turkey, which was totally incapable of governing it. This act led to the "Macedonian Question" and the Balkan Wars of 1912 and 1913, wars that continued during both world wars.

The situation after World War II, however, was much different than that following World War I. The historic conflicts in Western and Central Europe were settled, and reconciliation took place. But in the Balkans, these conflicts were largely frozen in an ice age of communist dominion. When the ice melted, they simply thawed out, ready not to be settled but to be resumed.

The antagonists, too, were much the same parties, with one notable exception. Bulgaria began behaving circumspectly. Its regional policy since 1989, whether conducted by postcommunists or anticommunists, has been exemplary. The Bulgarian communists' policy of not recognizing a separate Macedonian nation or language was continued, but in early 1999 this too was being modified. The new Bulgaria was the first Balkan state to recognize the independent Macedonia that emerged from the collapse of Yugoslavia. This action may have been the result of a certain "inverted proprietarism," and some Macedonians maintained that the Bulgarian leopard had not changed its spots. But the truth was that the Bulgarians, like the Hungarians, had learned things the hard way during the twentieth century. They may not have become reconciled to their losses; many people are still bitter about them, but most of them are resigned to the fact of their loss. The big question now is whether the Serbs, too, will soon reach the same realistic judgment.

The War, the Peace, and After

Already the literature is enormous that has accumulated on the agony and death of Yugoslavia. It need not be added to here, but a few reflections can be offered on the reasons for Yugoslavia's collapse, the background to the wars that followed it, the Western role in those conflicts, and the Dayton agreements.

Yugoslavia was unviable. It was cobbled together in the ethos of Wilsonianism and in the romantic belief that nations ethnically and linguistically similar could cohabit, coalesce, and integrate. But the first Yugoslavia was on the verge of collapse before World War II. Tito's Yugoslavia, held together by authoritarianism, guile, and ultimately by force, collapsed rapidly after his death.[1]

Early on in Tito's Yugoslavia, nationalism began to prove much stronger than communism. Unofficially, it became the principal ideology, one driven by mutual antipathy or disdain. The antipathy spun out of control when Tito died, and it became active hatred when Yugoslavia crumbled. This hatred partly explains the cruelty of the wars that have followed. Unspeakable acts of cruelty and destruction were committed by all sides, though more often by the Serbs than by any other group. But the Serb attitude to the Bosnian Muslims was also driven by contempt. Historically, the Bosnian Muslims were mostly Serb "renegades" to Islam, "Turks," traitorous opportunists who had lorded it over the Serbs during the centuries of Turkish occupation. And when the racist venom, spewed over Belgrade radio and television, took effect, many Serbs began considering their Muslim enemies as lower than human. The same was to happen in 1999 with regard to the Albanian Muslims in Kosovo. Such a murderous coarsening of attitudes was by no means new. Many Germans, for example, had experienced it sixty years earlier, especially in their attitude to East Europeans, Jew or Gentile. In communist labor camps the guards, thuggish to begin with, were conditioned to think of their prisoners as less than human.[2] At the beginning of the twentieth century in the Balkan Wars, such attitudes were apparent on every side. The 1913 Carnegie Endowment Inquiry into the Balkan Wars published two photographs of Greek anti-Bulgarian war posters. One showed a soldier of ferocious countenance apparently biting at the face of an enemy soldier. The other showed a soldier in the heat of battle gouging out an enemy's eye. The posters were not aimed at showing up *Bulgarian* cruelty. The two soldiers committing these atrocities were Greek, not Bulgarian. The Bulgarians were the victims. The allusion was to Emperor Basil II, the "Bulgar slayer," who, having routed the Bulgarians in 1014, blinded 15,000 prisoners, leaving one man in a hundred with a single eye to guide them all back to their own king. "You've done it once, now do it again" was obviously the message.[3] The "Bulgar slayer" as role model!

The Carnegie Endowment Inquiry described scenes of almost unbelievable cruelty. Such ghastliness was overshadowed by the Holocaust and the horrors of World War II. But these scenes were also a prelude to the atrocities of the Yugoslav wars of the 1990s, the atrocities in Bosnia, and those in Kosovo. The similarities are striking. So is the fact that much of the malevolence in former Yugoslavia was directed against Muslims.

SIGNPOSTS OF MISUNDERSTANDING

Armchair hindsight should be made a criminal offense. I am guilty of it with the following few points about the attitudes, inhibitions, and misunderstandings that characterized the course of the war in former Yugoslavia. Hopefully, brevity will count as a mitigant, if not an exoneration.

THE UNITED NATIONS

1. Its leadership, if not "bored" by Yugoslavia, was bored—even irritated— by the constant Western clamor about it. For Secretary-General Boutros Boutros-Ghali, this din was a sign of Eurocentrism. Worse things were happening elsewhere.[4]

2. The UN officials in former Yugoslavia were a mixed bunch. Some were outstanding, others should have been denied entry.

THE EUROPEAN UNION AND NATO

The EU has had no effective foreign or defense policy. Despite constant efforts it still has none. The "hour of Europe" had to wait. Policy differences between France, Germany, and Great Britain—palpable impotence, obsolete concepts, personal dislikes, cynicism, and intrigues—led to months of fiasco. Led by the United States, NATO eventually entered the Bosnian war, but only after a delay that could have been fatal for its reputation and even for its future. The near-disaster of NATO in Bosnia partly explained its determination over Kosovo. It knew that its credibility could be permanently lost.

THE UNITED STATES

For too long, U.S. policy was enervated by Vietnam and by White House priorities. They, in turn, inhibited NATO action.

U.S. prestige, therefore, dipped in former Yugoslavia at the beginning of the conflict because of Washington's laborious pondering. But when President Bill Clinton, partly as a result of Serbian excess, finally galvanized NATO into action, the end was inevitable. Serb military weaknesses were exposed, and peace imposed at Dayton, Ohio, in 1995. U.S. prestige then took off again. The United States was seen as having power and being prepared (after some nudging) to use it. The United States also has the advantage of being historically new in the Balkans, without selfish intentions. France, Britain, Germany, and Russia had been around for a long time and were seen as anything but disinterested.

The West Europeans came to count for little. This outcome was unfair in several ways. Certainly, since the cease of the war at the end of 1995, the EU has been bearing the burden of Bosnia's reconstruction. Many West Europeans have certainly been toiling away there, counting neither cost nor encumbrance. But translating this manifold help into respect and influence is difficult, especially in an environment where military strength has recently dominated and could easily do so again. During the war, the paradox was that the Americans eventually benefited by *not* being there on the ground in Bosnia. The French, British, and others *were* there, doing their best as peacekeepers. But their political orders often made them look like fools rather than soldiers, eliciting local contempt for themselves and their governments.

BALKAN ATTITUDES

Some Western negotiators mistakenly assumed that the Croats, Serbs, and Muslims meant what they said—or signed. However many agreements may have been signed by the warring parties in Balkan history, these parties had no intention of keeping them unless the agreements turned out to their advantage. In the hoary jargon of international legalistics, *pacta sunt servanda,* by all means, but *rebus sic stantibus.* In an expansive rendering, that translates: Keep treaties as long as the situation in which they were signed does not change to our disadvantage. If (when) the situation does change, so much for the treaties. And who decides whether the situation has changed? We do.[5] This had been standard operating procedure elsewhere, of course. But in Western Europe, its use was becoming fatigued. In the Balkans, it was still fresh and instinctive.

"Conspiracy culture" also must be mentioned. It is found throughout the Balkans, often in its more grotesquely infantile form. Some of the fanciful interpretations of the West's policy (and) ineptitude in former Yugoslavia provide jolting examples. It is often difficult to convince even the more broad-minded South East Europeans to accept that things are indeed sometimes as they seem to be, and that in international relations the only thing worse than naive belief in everything is the inverted naïveté of believing in nothing.

Balkan provincialism also became a key factor during the turmoil of the 1990s—a contradictory fixation that the Balkans were peripheral to the West's *concerns,* yet at the same time at the center of the West's *machinations.* Combined with this notion was the conviction (not just a suspicion) that the West (especially the United States) might sometimes have an impressive knowledge of developments in the region, but only the most superficial understanding of their implications and dangers. Natives everywhere have this conviction about foreigners, but in the Balkans it seems to be essential to self-affirmation. On the evidence of the collapse of Yugoslavia as a whole and of the disasters in Bosnia-Hercegovina in particular, such a conviction, of course, might have some validity. But this conviction was based not so much on recent experience as on ingrained instinct. And, just as the West tends to look down on Balkan volatility, so the Balkan nations, almost by reflex, tend to blame the "self-seeking" Western powers for their situation.

Then there is the Balkan attitude to compromise. What is regarded in the West, particularly in the English-speaking countries, as essential to democratic government still tends to be regarded in the Balkans as a sign either of weakness or insincerity. (In Russia this attitude is also common.) The reactions to compromise proposals often consist of hitting still harder at perceived weaknesses or doubting the opponent's integrity and being doubly wary of him. (If he really believed what he said, he would not be prepared to dilute it!)

The degree of corruption on all sides in former Yugoslavia both during and after the war disgusted many Westerners. Gunrunning rackets that involved both allies and enemies existed in profusion.[6] Western money and supplies of food, medicines, and items for reconstruction, amounting to billions of dollars, were stolen or siphoned off to other purposes. Drugs, hard and soft, wended their way between the fighting lines, distinguishing between neither friend nor foe. The divided city of Mostar was pulled together by crime; the Croat statelet of Herceg Bosna in western Hercegovina maintained itself through murderous racketeering. Some Bosnian Muslim leaders (*not* including Alija Izetbegović) seemed to vie for the title of "Mr. Eight Percent"; Radovan Karadzić's tiny Serb stronghold in Pale was also a gangster center. Scores of examples can be cited. What is staggering about former Yugoslavia has been the sheer volume, the ingenuity, and the cynicism of the criminalization and corruption taking place there, its pervasiveness not only appearing in high places, but further down the social scale, too. And this was true not only in countries directly affected by war. "Corruption has become part of the mental make-up of the majority of people in Montenegrin society," one observer wrote.[7]

One aspect of Balkan diplomacy, though as old as the Eastern Question itself, seemed to especially surprise Western participants in the Yugoslav wrangles of the 1990s. This approach can be called bazaar bargaining in its crudest form, based on a twisted notion of reciprocity—the "you-owe-me-one" principle. If I agreed to do something that you wanted done and I did not, then you must let me get away with something that I want and you do not. Not only Milošević but Tudjman as well (much more "Balkan" than he pretended) were dedicated to this principle. Milošević, "the man who made Dayton possible," proceeded to assume that he now had a free hand in Kosovo. Franjo Tudjman enjoyed the distinction of being "Washington's man" in the Balkans (see chapter 5). The main U.S. aim was to contain and defeat Serbia. That goal was met. Tudjman's reward was U.S. connivance at the offensive against the Krajina Serbs in 1996. But Tudjman went further. He forced most of the Serbs out of Croatia and then stonewalled on allowing them to return. The United States, whatever its protestations, took part in this chicanery.

Ethnic Cleansing—Balkan Style

"Ethnic cleansing" is nothing new in Europe—West, Central, or Eastern. In the Balkans, which came relatively late to nationalism, the most massive example of it was the international transfer of Greeks from the new Turkey and of Turks from Greece in the 1920s. This exchange led to indescribable hardships, but it helped solve a problem and was relatively peaceful. Had it not occurred, then the bloodiest ethnic cleansing of the early twentieth century would likely have been perpetrated by each nation against the other. In Eastern Europe, huge migrations or expulsions of people took place toward the end of World War II and immediately thereafter. Once that communist rule became entrenched in 1948 and the problems of nationalism were officially being solved, such acts were dismissed as ghastly memories of a bygone age. But ethnic cleansing did not totally become a thing of the past. Early in the communist period and then toward its demise, Bulgaria had recourse to a form of cleansing—albeit mainly without bloodshed. "Macedonians" vanished from Bulgaria's national population censuses after the break with Tito in 1948. "Statistical genocide"! Then, in the 1980s, the Zhivkov regime sought to "Bulgarize," or "re-Bulgarize," the large Turkish minority. Subsequently, the Zhivkov tack changed, and many Turks were induced to leave for Turkey (see chapter 8). With the disintegration of Yugoslavia, ethnic cleansing became not only a means of war, but a postwar strategy. The Serbs committed it most savagely and on the largest scale. Their atrocities, in fact, led to worldwide revulsion against them and pressure for intervention, and essentially to the establishment of the International War Crimes Tribunal at The Hague.[8] The Serbs' aim was to obliterate the Muslim presence in Bosnia. The Croats did it, too—against Muslims in Bosnia and, on a large scale, though with little carnage, against the Serb community in Croatia. Likewise, the Bosnian Muslims tried to wipe away Serbs and Croats—barbarically in places—but on a much smaller scale. Then came Kosovo. In a province plagued by "mutual" ethnic cleansing throughout the century, Milošević massively increased it in 1998 and 1999 with now-familiar Serb intensity. In retaliation, the Kosovars unleashed efforts to exterminate some of Kosovo's defeated Serbs (see chapter 7).

Dayton: Future Peace?

It was appropriate that the peace talks should be held in the United States; appropriate, too, that they should be held at a U.S. Air Force base. Agreements reached in Dayton, Ohio, stopped the fighting. Troops from the UN were placed in Bosnia-Hercegovina. Of these, the Americans symbolically and politically were the most important. After some hesitation, the United States also decided that some of its troops should stay. This decision kept other UN contingents in place. Had the Americans pulled out, the whole operation would have collapsed, causing the concept of international order to be irretrievably damaged.

Dayton, then, brought the fighting to a standstill. But it did not secure the peace. It may even have made the peace eventually harder to secure. In a way, Dayton relived the Paris treaties after World War I. Just as U.S. President Woodrow Wilson misjudged European realities then, so President Bill Clinton misjudged Balkan realities now. The essential difference was that Clinton agreed that U.S. troops should stay—and stay involved. This stance, not Dayton itself, could prevent a new war.

The Dayton agreements themselves had three practical flaws or inconsistencies.[9]

1. The republic of Bosnia *and* Hercegovina (note the new official title) has no central defense capacity. Its central government is responsible for foreign policy but not for overall security. Defense is vested in the two mutually hostile Entities: Republika Srpska and the Muslim-Croat Federation.

2. The Muslim-Croat (or Bosnian-Croat) Federation, "upon which the

new Bosnian edifice depends,"[10] is a ramshackle construction that looks distinctly *un*dependable. The "marriage of convenience," as President Izetbegović described it several times, is really a marriage of incompatibles, with each side hating, distrusting, or despising the other. It worked well in the later stages of the war in Bosnia, its allied troops becoming clearly superior to the overstretched Serbs. But can anyone see this Muslim-Croat Entity withstanding the strains of peace and cooperation? Tudjman's real views about Muslims, which he made little attempt to hide, give the answer:

> The Muslims want to establish an Islamic fundamentalist state. They plan to do this by flooding Bosnia with 500,000 Turks. Izetbegović has also launched a demographic threat. He has a secret policy to reward large families so that in a few years the Muslims will be a majority in Bosnia [at that time they were 44 percent]. The influence of an Islamic Bosnia will then spread through the Sandzak and Kosovo [Muslim areas of Serbia] to Turkey and Libya. Izetbegović is just a fundamentalist front man for Turkey; together they're conspiring to create a Greater Bosnia. Catholics and Orthodox alike will be eradicated.[11]

Obviously, Tudjman's death and the relative liberalism of his successor (see chapter 5) might go some way toward vindicating the negotiators at Dayton. The mood for reconciliation also began to improve in Sarajevo itself. But it is difficult to see the Muslim-Croat Federation as being anything but a fiction.

3. The two Entities were given the right to establish "special parallel relations with neighboring states consistent with the sovereignty and territorial integrity of Bosnia and Hercegovina." These neighboring states, of course, are Croatia and Serbia. This concession was what was left of the "confederation" notion to which the Americans and West Europeans had earlier been drawn and which would virtually have meant the incorporation of the Muslim-Croat Federation into Croatia and of Republika Srpska into Serbia.

The confederation notion, therefore, had to be watered down. But, even as it stands, this article in the Dayton accords can create future difficulties. What is "consistent with the sovereignty and territorial integrity of Bosnia and Hercegovina"? Tudjman obviously had his own ideas. His successors, however well-intentioned, may find it hard to be as "international" as the West would like them to be. Tudjman's proposals for special parallel relations with the Muslim-Croat Federation as early as November 1997 virtually amounted to an economic takeover bid. Izetbegović indignantly rejected them, seeing in them "a flagrant contradiction" of Dayton.[12] Two years later, Tudjman was going much further. Speaking to foreign journalists in Zagreb, he called for Bosnia-Hercegovina to be divided into *three* Entities. Only then could it survive.[13] Many Croats later were thinking the same.

Apart from these three practical flaws, any one of which could prove destructive, Dayton contained one flaw that was, above all, moral. It put the Muslims, who had suffered by far the most in the war and whose plight had been taken up by the whole Western world, into an Entity that, even with a less nationalist government in Zagreb, would be under the shadow of Croatia. True, Muslims easily dominate numerically in the Muslim-Croat Federation, but that could make it more, not less, liable to interference from Zagreb. When serious differences between Muslims and Croats occur within the Federation, most Croats will look to Zagreb. Local conflicts could occur between members of the two nations within the Federation. Then Croatia might be justified in wanting to intervene. Practical disasters could stem from this moral wrong inflicted on the Muslims.

Why, then, not give the Muslims their own state, however small?[14] Arguably, such a state would be unviable. But access to the Adriatic could have been provided to it from parts of Croatian Dalmatia. Western Hercegovina (Herceg Bosna) could have gone to Croatia as compensation. Western troops would have been needed to guarantee the Muslim state's independence, but they would be needed under any dispensation. A Croat minority obviously would remain in the new Muslim state. Some might want to leave; others could try their luck as an internationally protected minority. Why, then, no Muslim state? Because of two fears: the fear of precedent; the fear of Muslims.

A genuine fear persisted in South Eastern Europe that granting statehood or the right of succession to minorities would create a dangerous precedent. (This was to become even more evident over Kosovo; see chapter 7.) Bulgaria, Turkey, Romania, Serbia, even Greece had their fears. The list is virtually complete! But there also was genuine fear of new Muslim ("Islamic") states in the Balkans. (And a Muslim Bosnia might not be the only one, as speculation about Kosovo and a Greater Albania subsequently increased; see chapter 7.)

But how "Islamic" would these Muslim states be? Bosnian Muslims once were almost ostentatiously secular. Tolerant, too. "Ilija till noon, Alija after noon." Not much of that spirit remains. The question now is, "What is more likely to increase or decrease the chances of Muslim Bosnia becoming Mujaheddin Bosnia?" Although speculation is difficult, it seems as if an independent, Muslim Bosnia, Western-guaranteed and assisted, would be unlikely to succumb to Islamic extremism. There is no doubt that signs of a "Muslim presence" have considerably increased in parts of Bosnia since the conflict there. But these signs are more expressions of Muslim *nationality* than of *religious* adherence. Several Islamic groups or sects also are inspired, and financially supported, by extreme Islamic movements in the Middle East. Taliban influence is seen here and there. Obviously, conspiracy theorists thrive on the presence of such groups, but the number of Bosnian Muslims influenced by them is tiny and is likely to remain so.

More to the point, the West (Western Europe, in particular) needs to become more realistic and less neurotic about the Muslim presence. The Muslims are now a major player in practically all of Europe—politically, culturally, economically, socially, and internationally. The Ottoman remnants, despised for a century, are becoming more assertive in South Eastern Europe. Millions of Muslims now live in Western Europe, the vast majority of them wanting to stay there in a dignified rather than a demeaning existence. Islam is very much part of Europe. Whether it is a constructive force or a destructive problem largely depends on how calmly and fairly Muslims are treated. The "Muslim Problem," like other ethnic problems, is mostly the making of others.

In South Eastern Europe it is difficult to categorize Muslims. Secular, moderate, militant, or fundamentalist? Generally, though, among Muslim political elites, the national and ethnic dimension has been much stronger than the religious. But now a notion is growing of competition between the "Muslim-national-secular" conviction and a vague universalist Islamic concept. The parallels with both Christian and communist history are suggestive. In the case of both Christianity and communism, the national concept prevailed over the ultramontane and the international. In the case of Islam, despite its apparent universalist strength, the same probably will happen. Islam has no authoritative center the way that Christianity (Rome) and communism (Moscow) did. Established Muslim states caught up in the manifold tasks of governance are likely to become more secular and particularist. But despised Muslim minorities and frustrated national movements could become religiously zealous and universalist—inclined to identify with extremism, not moderation. This possibility should be kept in mind when considering Bosnia's future—and eventually the future of the Albanian nation, too.

In the meantime, even before the war in Kosovo, Balkan devotees of the conspiratorial and the apocalyptic were already contemplating the coming great Christian (Orthodox)-Muslim confrontation. They saw the two protagonists as describing two arcs. The Christian (Orthodox) arc began in Moscow, extended through Ukraine, Romania, Bulgaria, Greece, Slavic Macedonia, and then into Serbia. The Muslim arc, also dashingly known as the "Green Transversal," started in Turkey (or even farther east), went through the Turkish areas of Bulgaria, took in Greek Thrace, proceeded northward into the Albanian areas of Macedonia, then into Albania itself— Kosovo, Sandjak, Gorazde—and ended in Sarajevo. The sweep of both these putative arcs is awesome, and they inevitably, if not too accurately, bring to mind the theories now associated with Samuel Huntington.[15] Whether they form a realistic concept is open to question. But even if they do, the best way for the two eventually to coexist is for Balkan Christians (the practicing few and the nominal majority) to accept two realities: (1) Balkan Muslims must exist as equals; (2) any danger of a return to Muslim domination, to life "under the Yoke," exists only in primitive imaginations, fed by fanatics or opportunists. Broader education might help.[16]

Bosnia: Fixations and Facts

The restoration of Bosnia-Hercegovina became a Western fixation explained not only by the "Muslim threat," but by considerations like the two below:

First, partitioning Bosnia-Hercegovina would have set the precedent of changing national borders and broken one of the tenets of international relations since World War II. That was one reason why the Kosovo issue, despite Albanian expectations, was not covered in the Dayton negotiations. That and the desire not to press the "obliging" Milošević too hard. But many now agree that it would have been better to have grasped the nettle at Dayton. The Kosovo catastrophe might have been preempted, wholly or in part, by Western pressure there. It would certainly have reduced the level of Kosovar frustration and sense of betrayal. Besides—and this is the basic and broader issue—the "international community" will keep running into brick walls if it dogmatically sticks to its no-border-change principle. Kosovo has surely demonstrated that much. The Western community should start considering whether "each case on its merits" is not a fairer and more effective approach. A weary, wary, gray-haired caution has pervaded Western thinking about the Balkan future. It is certainly not wisdom. A bit of boldness, based on current and coming realities, might help everybody concerned. (See also chapter 7 on Kosovo's future.)

The West has also held a rosy view of multiethnic or multicultured "harmony" in the former Bosnia-Hercegovina, with a Pollyanna confidence that it could be restored.

Three points about the history of Bosnia-Hercegovina need mentioning in relation to once-and-future ethnic "harmony."

At the best of times, little more than peaceful coexistence, rather than ethnic harmony, was the norm there. This condition was forced on Bosnia-Hercegovina from above rather than evolving from below. Behind the compulsion to coexist could be found latent tension, much suspicion, and little trust. Domination—Ottoman, Habsburg, Titoist—tended to obscure this tension, but everyday life could not. The historical pattern was simple: when domination ended, trouble started. Trouble in one place led to trouble in others, and the divisions invariably traced ethnic lines. Multiethnic or multicultural living could survive anything but freedom. The Dayton agreements were an ill-thought-out, breakneck set of documents, made possible by the tiredness of the antagonists, and pushed through primarily to stop the war.

Ivo Andrić's description of Turkish power in Bosnia as vanishing "like an apparition" has been quoted. Andrić goes on to put part of the Serbs' historic resentments against the Muslims into the mouth of a young Serb: "you are the only nobles in this land, or at least you were; for centuries you have enlarged and defended your privileges by sword and pen, legally, religiously, and by force of arms."[17] Stoyan Protić, the first Yugoslav prime minister in 1919, is worth quoting yet again. When asked what was in store for the Bosnian Muslims with the establishment of Yugoslavia, he replied: "As soon as our army crosses the Drina, it will give the Turks twenty four . . . perhaps forty-eight hours to return to the faith of their forefathers [i.e., Orthodoxy] and then slay those who refuse, as we did in Serbia in the past."[18]

The Austrian Habsburg prime minister, Baron Max Hussarek, in a speech in October 1918, just days before the empire fell, described Bosnia-Hercegovina as "ein staatsrechtlichundefinierbares Neutrum"[19] ("a non-

descript creation which cannot be defined in terms of political science.")
Hussarek was right and has remained so.

Some public and journalistic optimism arose in the West in 1998 about the course of events in Bosnia. More alleged war criminals, though not the most notorious ones, were being captured and whisked off to The Hague. A political moderate (genuine or opportunistic), Milorad Dodik, stepped forward to become prime minister of Republika Srpska, whose president, Bilyana Plavšić, was now clearly worsting Radovan Karadzić in the local power struggle. (This was the same Biljana Plavšić who, only a few years earlier, had been one of the fieriest of Serb nationalists. During the war, her likeness was painted on some Serb tanks, apparently not so much to frighten the enemy as to identify with her brave Serb "boys.") In addition, the capital of Republika Srpska was removed from Pale, the extremist hotbed, to the less provincial, more moderate Banja Luka. The central government in Sarajevo also was beginning to take on some of the trappings and symbols of authority.

This was progress, undoubtedly, but it had been forced through by Western civil authorities and by 35,000 foreign troops. Bosnia-Hercegovina, in fact, had become a virtual protectorate of the West by early 1998, probably the first of several Balkan states to come under that umbrella (see chapter 7).[20] But the crucial question remained of the return of the refugees to their *original homes*. This, after all, was the essence and the imperative of Dayton. It has become, however, Dayton's most obvious failure. A few figures underline the problem and the failure to solve it. The war in Bosnia-Hercegovina created 2.3 million refugees or expellees. Early in 1998—more than two years after Dayton—there had been 35,000 so-called "minority returns," i.e., returnees to an area now controlled by another ethnic group. Of the three ethnic groups wanting to return to their original homes, 79 percent were the Muslims; 61 percent, Croats; and 22 percent, Serbs.[21] In the early months of 2000 a larger number of applications for return were being made, but they were still depressingly small. The main reason for the failure to achieve this modest goal of refugee return was fear, and it was difficult to see how any number of UN troops, armed with the best weaponry and the broadest authority, could enforce a genuine, permanent return. Whatever official statistical successes may be claimed, the locals on the ground will make or break the refugees' right of return. And the locals have appeared determined to prevent it from taking place. The devices and stratagems being used to ease the return are a distraction from the problem, not a solution. By the end of 1998 it was claimed that about 600,000 refugees had returned to Bosnia and that many more intended to do so. But the overwhelming majority were going to areas dominated by their own ethnic groups. This, then, was cementing ethnic divisions, not breaking them down.

The Serbs were not the only ones to blame. Croats and Muslims were equally determined to defy Western illusions about Dayton. In Croatia itself, the authorities have made it indirectly but abundantly clear that returning Serbs were not welcome. In April 1998 a Swiss correspondent visited Krajina in Croatia. He spoke to a Croatian woman who had suffered through several phases of the war. She put it simply: "I was never a nationalist before. But, after all we have gone through, I want no part of the Serbs, nothing to do with them. In this small town they killed 50 or 60 people and destroyed everything. Living together now is out of the question. There's no trust anymore."[22] What is true for this small town in Krajina is true throughout former Yugoslavia. Croats, Serbs, and Muslims think the same about each other. And the Serbs, surely, can hardly have made themselves less unsavory anywhere by their behavior in Kosovo.

In June 1998 the Croatian parliament, clearly bowing to international pressure, passed a law that removed several official impediments to returning Serbs.[23] In international circles diplomats hoped that this law would set the "return carousel" in motion and have a similar effect in Republika Srpska in Bosnia. If refugee Serbs living there returned to Croatia, the homes they had been occupying would be made free for returning Bosnian Muslims and Croats to move back in. But there was more cynicism than sincerity in Zagreb over this move. The new government after Tudjman's death was obviously better intentioned, but the real decisions would always be made at the local level, where there was no inclination whatsoever to take back Serb refugees. Many of these refugees were so miserable and unwanted in Serbia itself that they were of a mind to return to Croatia. But they knew the implacability that awaited them, and they could imagine the physical danger as well.

The Muslims, too, preferred the Serbs to be out of both sight and mind. The population of Sarajevo used to be about 50 percent Muslim, 27 percent Serb, and 7 percent Croat. In 1998 it was 87 percent Muslim, and Izetbegović meant to keep it going that way.[24] As for Republika Srpska, a few Muslims lived there, and the number was slowly increasing. But this Entity would remain predominantly Serb, whatever "moderation" the West might force its leaders into. Milorad Dodik, Republika Srpska's moderate, Western-favored prime minister, made what sounded like rash promises on the subject, putting his political credibility and his political future on the line.[25]

One other important aspect, crucial in the long run, should be noted. The schools in Bosnia-Hercegovina were separate; they taught different subjects in different ways. Their history books, especially, were instilling ethnic hatred.[26]

The great exception to this ethnic frigidity in Bosnia-Hercegovina, and a phenomenon worth explaining at some length, is Brcko, originally a small town on the Sava river situated in the narrow connecting corridor between the eastern and western parts of the Republika Srpska Entity. Brcko had been largely Muslim before the war, but after ethnic cleansing it had become predominantly Serb and was considered strategically vital by the Serbs. Muslims also considered it a crucial north-south link with the outside world and they desperately wanted it back. Brcko was too hot a potato for the Dayton peacemakers to handle and attempts at a solution were constantly being delayed. It was finally decreed a self-governing district, part of neither the Muslim-Croat Federation nor Republika Srpska. From then on the Brcko problem solved itself. The town became a cosmopolitan district with a government and a police force made up of Muslims, Serbs, and Croats. Refugees were confidently returning; prosperity burgeoned because of trade, especially smuggling, and because of economics both fair and foul. Now at a vital Balkan crossroads, Brcko developed from a tumbledown emporium of junk and contraband ("Arizona Market") into a well-organized multiethnic multimarket. The mafia were steadily pushed out by the international agencies and military muscle established at Dayton and the new Brcko, an ethnic, political, and economic miracle, emerged. A model, then, for the rest of Bosnia? Hardly: Brcko was sui generis, almost the exception that proves the rule.

Despite Brcko, therefore, the only realistic course in Bosnia was to accept and institutionalize ethnic partition and then work to mitigate it. Borrowing two cold war German expressions, a new policy should aim to forget about *miteinander* and concentrate on *nebeneinander*. The former Yugoslavia left part of an integrated economic system that once crossed republic borders and now crosses national borders. However badly battered, this system could still be partly restored. In Bosnia-Hercegovina the former economy was integrated on a republican basis and had extensive economic links with Croatia and Serbia. With Western guidance and conditional economic aid, some of these links could be restored. That restoration, in fact, has been one goal. But only when ethnic borders are recognized can any economic integrational effort be successful. If successful, it could "soften" the partitions.

There should be no doubt that these partitions were still not softening at the turn of the millennium. Local elections in Bosnia-Hercegovina in the spring of 2000 essentially confirmed this. Obvious and sometimes massive interference occurred during these elections by the Western "protectorate" representatives backed by a strong Western military presence. Some hard-line nationalist candidates were prevented from standing; the Serbian Radical Party was kept out of the election altogether. Refugees and displaced persons were allowed to vote. This Western pressure was mainly responsible for some successes by relatively moderate national candidates. But four years after the Dayton accords, and with four years of the Western presence, these elections were in no way a breakthrough for moderation. A clear majority of Bosnians still thought, voted, acted, and reacted on national lines, and such behavior was not likely to change.

In June 1999, influenced no doubt by the frustrations in Bosnia and by the impact of the Kosovo conflict, the Western powers, at the initiative of the European Union, announced their "Stability Pact for South Eastern Europe." President Clinton himself spoke in Sarajevo at the launching of the project. Its aim was to accelerate political reform and economic improvement on a regionwide basis, thus leading, it was hoped, to permanent stability and pacification. The basis of this effort was the "preservation" of the multi-national and multi-ethnic diversity of the countries of the region and the protection of minorities.[27]

The motives for the "Stability Pact" were admirable. But the West's insistence on "preserving" or "restoring" multiethnic diversity seemed to fly in the face of reality. In fact, practical steps were already being taken that recognized the real situation. For example, refugees were given the right to sell their old homes in areas to which they feared to return and to buy new homes elsewhere. Although "minority returns" remained the official policy, such steps, extremely difficult though they might be in practice, indicated that new, more realistic thinking might be coming into play.

One Balkan expert summed up the situation perfectly:

A restoration of the former ethnic map of Bosnia-Hercegovina seems impossible. No one can expect refugees, for the sake of some lofty political goals set by foreigners, to return to places where they don·t feel wanted and where they see no future for themselves. This all points to the fact that the multi-ethnic and multi-cultural society of Bosnia, which diplomats and fantasy-weavers were wont to rave about, cannot be revived in its old form—if in actual fact it ever existed and was not just wishful thinking.[28]

No "Stability Pact," however well-intentioned, can bring real peace to the Balkans if it ignores the wisdom of warnings like this.

7

Kosovo:
The Clash of Two Nationalisms

THE SERBS HAVE ALWAYS HAD a strong national sense, much stronger than, for example, the Russians. Historically, it has centered on Kosovo.[1]

Kosovo is the Serbs' historic heartland, the "cradle" of their nation. It was the center of the Serb Orthodox Church and Serb medieval civilization. Until it was abolished in 1766, the Serbian Patriarchate was at Peć. About four hundred churches and monasteries—many surviving, many ruined—attest to the Serb tradition in Kosovo.[2]

Kosovo Polje is the site of the famous battle in 1389 that caused the downfall of the Serbian medieval kingdom and helped consolidate Ottoman power in the Western Balkans. The Battle of Kosovo remained in the collective Serb memory as both a major trauma and a major inspiration. It generated a large volume of epic poetry, passed on orally in many Serb households during and after the Ottoman dominance. The Kosovo legend has left an indelible mark on the Serb psyche. The Balkan region is studded with historic national symbols that still have enormous influence, and no symbol is more powerful than Kosovo Polje. Kosovo, as many Serbs intone, is their Jerusalem.

The Kosovo legend has been subjected to much tampering, embroidering, and beautifying. In the nineteenth century, with the great Serb reawakening, it was turned into a hugely effective instrument of nationalist propaganda, some of it, like most legends, so spurious as hardly to survive an hour's objective research.[3] But that is hardly the point. What counts is not the legend's credibility but the Serbs' credulity. Every nation has its life-sustaining lies. Kosovo has been that for the Serbs, and, in a situation where nothing else seemed to remain, they stuck to it all the more tenaciously. Their view of themselves has been one of self-adulation, self-deception, and self-pity. They need scapegoats and excuses. Not surprisingly, Kosovo Polje has its Judas theme. (It needs to be added at this point that the manufacturing of tradition or the fashioning of symbols has not by any means been a Serb monopoly in the Balkans. Milovan Djilas used to recall in conversation how, under Tito's orders, he spent many hours after World War II working up a national culture, legend, and literature for his native Montenegro, shortly to become a constituent federal republic. After independence, Macedonia reviewed its efforts to create a history for itself, infuriating the Greeks but only boring the Bulgarians, who could claim that they were used to it. But early in 2000 there was a renewed bout of traditional "symbol mongering" between Bulgaria and Macedonia. The Bulgarian Constitutional Court outlawed a two-men-and-a-boy political party in Pirin that seemed to be advocating the accession of Pirin to Macedonia itself. This decision did not say much for the Bulgarian courts sense of perspective. But the new president of Macedonia, Boris Trajkovski, only compounded the absurdity by formally protesting to the Bulgarian government. Absurdity? Yes! for everyone except the Bulgarians and Macedonians. For them such things are still no laughing matter.)

In Kosovo, the Serb legend has been overshadowed for centuries by the growing Albanian presence. Certainly by the beginning of the twentieth century the Albanians clearly outnumbered the Serbs, and the gap grew inexorably wider. This discrepancy made little difference in terms of power in the first Yugoslavia, when Serb control in Kosovo was total, or even in the first years of Tito's rule. But in the 1960s a change began in the governance of Yugoslavia that involved the erosion of Serb power. This diminishment took place under the rubric of decentralization, and it immediately raised Serb tempers over Kosovo. In 1968, Dobrica Ćosić, the famous writer and later president (briefly) of Serbia, protested against decentralization, increasing Albanian nationalism (serious rioting occurred in the province), and continuing Serb outmigration. In 1971, with further measures of decentralization, other Serb intellectuals came forward with much stronger criticism. Opposition spread throughout the Serb intellectual milieu and among Serbs generally. The depth of Serb humiliation can be understood only if their racist contempt for Albanians is also realized. Remembered humiliation added an extra dimension to their frustration and their fury.

The last straw snapped with the 1974 Yugoslav constitution that gave Kosovo (as well as Vojvodina, the other autonomous province of Serbia), with its large Hungarian minority, practically the same rights at the Yugoslav federal level as were enjoyed by the Republic of Serbia itself. At the same time, Serb outmigration was increasing, caused partly by Albanian intimidation. (This intimidation was crudely exaggerated by the Serbian media, but it nonetheless existed.) Tito died in 1980, and within a year serious ethnic rioting broke out in Kosovo. From then on, discontent was transformed into a Serb crusade against the alleged attempts to humiliate their nation. The crusade was preached by intellectuals and propagated most forcefully in a memorandum of the Serbian Academy of Sciences leaked to the press in 1986. A strongly nationalist document, shot through with resentment, it set the Serb agenda for the next ten years. What the crusade needed now was a standard-bearer, a leader. He appeared in the unlikely person of Slobodan Milošević.

Milošević

Veljko Vujačić has written perceptively about Milošević's motives and tactics:

Analysis of the Milošević phenomenon which insist on only one dimension of his appeal (typically nationalism), are bound to miss the point. On the contrary, it was precisely the combination of simultaneous appeals to different constituencies which helps explain Milošević's success. Yugoslavia, unity, and Titoism for the party orthodox and army officers, Serbia for the nationalists, reform and rehabilitation for the intellectuals, protection for the Kosovo Serbs, social justice for the workers, and pensions—this was the Serbian leader's equivalent of Lenin's "bread, peace, and land." Nevertheless, there was one, but highly significant, difference between Vladimir Ilich and his Serbian pupil, which reflected the new "dialectical" turn in mature orthodox communism: Through a peculiar process of Hegelian transcendence, the "left" was becoming "right" in a striking confirmation of the old French wisdom—*Les extremes se touchent.*[4]

Vujačić's point is worth repeating. Milošević was a man on the make, a pragmatist, an opportunist. He was not consumed by nationalism in the way that many of his fellow Serbs were. Serb nationalism was seeking a Milošević, not the other way round. He was looking for a constituency and an issue. To see him as the great manipulator, the man who led his unwitting nation into catastrophe and ignominy, is totally false.

The nationalist constituency had five groupings in Serbia proper: the academics, the writers, the church, the party, the people. That roster included practically everybody. The role of the academics has been touched on; it became notorious. The role of the writers was scarcely less so. Before the 1980s, Serbian writers, generally through the Serbian Writers' Association, had been a liberal force. But Dobrica Ćosić, the most prominent of them, had taken up the nationalist cudgels early on. Others followed, and the Academy of Sciences memorandum in 1986 had a strong influence on many of them. As Gordana Igrić stated: "Torn between yearning for freedom and the desire for nationalist expansion, some members [of the Writers' Association] coined and embraced the term 'democratic nationalism,' which allegedly reconciled universal interests with specific Serbian aims."[5]

Some writers became not "democratic nationalists" but sycophants of a nationalist crusade. In a transport of adulation, one went so far as to describe Milošević as "the young, handsome orator who with sunshine gilds his hair."[6] But much more dangerous was the whimpering sentimentality of some of the literature shoveled onto the market bemoaning Serbia's destiny, tragedy, and "misused innocence."

The Orthodox Church was playing much the same game. It not only rode the nationalist waves, but helped to make them. Ostensibly for peace, the church stirred the emotions of war. It supported Milošević when he was winning, ditched him when he was losing, and excoriated him when he "surrendered" at Dayton. Then it found a new hero: Radovan Karadzíc, nationalist, anticommunist, demonstratively Orthodox, fully devoted to the clergy, and accused war criminal. The truth was that the church backed nationalist winners. When those winners became losers, it threw the Book at them.

Many Serbian communists, their ideological fervor running dry, easily rediscovered their nationalist heritage. Tito had purged the Serbian party of its liberal leadership in the 1970s, replacing it with "Leninists," with whom he always felt safer. Nationalist sentiment undoubtedly grew in the party after his death and was susceptible to the new, fashionable intellectual current. But the leadership had remained Titoist and relatively moderate on the nationalist issue. That is, until Milošević outmaneuvered and replaced his mentor, Ivan Stambolíc, as party leader in 1986. Soon after that, the same process gripped the Serbian party as had been assumed by the Romanian communist party in the 1970s and 1980s. *Les extremes se touchent.*

Most Serbs, communist or not, were ready for war in Bosnia; full of contempt for their adversaries, they expected quick victory. But—and here was the great inconsistency—how many of them would fight it? Many did, and many others were ready. But many young Serbs would not take part, and they either dodged the draft at home or emigrated. Accurate numbers of emigrants are impossible to determine, but they were certainly in the tens of thousands. (Many Croats and Muslims also emigrated; Albanians and Vojvodina Hungarians emigrated, too, unwilling to fight Serbia's battles.) Indeed, along with the dead and the displaced, one of the most serious results of the wars in former Yugoslavia was the number of fit, able, young people who left during the fighting.[7] Many of them would never return. The apathetic, almost nihilistic, mood of some young Serbs as the wars dragged on is best described by the novels written about it. Vladimir Arsenijević's *In the Hold* is a good example.[8]

In the Hold centers on young Serbs who avoided the Bosnian war. But a few Serbs of all ages protested against it openly: journalists on the Belgrade *Vreme*, for example; workers on anti-Milošević radio and television stations, who, despite oppression, chicanery, and even government terrorism, would not stop; scholars and writers who remained true to their consciences; even the few politicians who risked oblivion by demonstrating their courage. Upholding Serbia's honor at the beginning of the twenty-first century was extraordinarily difficult, but those who were trying to do it knew that one day they would be vindicated. How long, though, would it take for the honor of the Serb nation to be redeemed after the savagery of Bosnia and Kosovo? Yet most Serbs right up to, during, and even after the war with NATO in 1999 remained convinced that they were fighting a war of defense—even survival. Their expulsion from Croatia, the "denial of justice" in Bosnia, then the threat of losing Kosovo, above all the NATO bombing in the spring of 1999, all pointed to a world conspiracy against them led by the United States. This conspiracy, they averred, was the only lesson to be drawn from the successive Yugoslav wars of the 1990s. As for alleged Serb atrocities, many Serbs claimed that such acts were grossly and deliberately exaggerated. And those atrocities that did occur could be excused; in Kosovo, for example, the Kosovo Liberation Army was basically to blame. There are, in fact, two apparently basic Serb attitudes that have played a tragic role in Yugoslavia and still do: their refusal to live as minorities in other countries and their refusal to admit guilt for the wrongs they have done.

Albanians Emerging

"We have always been losers," said an Albanian-American to me in 1994, referring presumably to his nation of origin rather than his adopted land. But now, he added, "we are players. Soon we will be winners."

The Albanians had not always been losers. The vast majority of them converted to Islam under the Turks, and, as Muslims, they enjoyed the rights and privileges of the Ottoman dispensation. The Ottoman empire gave them some status and security. They were in no hurry to plunge into the shark-infested waters of national independence. Growing Turkish weakness, however, virtually forced them to take the chance. A sovereign Albania was finally proclaimed in 1912 during the first Balkan War. But the Albanians were immediately cheated. In four Balkan *vilayets* of the Ottoman empire—Kosovo Scutari, Monastir, and Janina—they had composed a numerical majority. But only half of the Albanian nation was included in the new independent Albania that the Great Powers agreed to. One reason for their being given an independent state at all was to check the growth of Serb power. And after World War I it was mainly through American insistence that even this rump Albania survived.

An inauspicious beginning. Almost by definition, Albania was a client state, economically too weak to be viable, militarily too weak to be secure. Yet, situated at the mouth of the Adriatic, forty miles across from Italy, it had obvious strategic importance. It fell increasingly under Italian domination and was occupied by Mussolini's troops in 1939. Many Albanians adapted well enough to Axis occupation during World War II. Italians and even Germans were preferable to Serbs, Montenegrins, and Greeks. What further appeased the Albanians was the merging of most of Kosovo and parts of Macedonia with Albania proper, which also obtained a sort of independence as Greater Albania. (The Albanians felt what many Croats and Slovaks felt at that time: fulfillment, whatever the auspices and the crimes that had brought it about.)

Immediately after World War II, communist Albania became dependent on communist Yugoslavia. But Albanian nationalism had increased during the war, which was reflected in the Hoxha regime in Tirana. Albania's resentment at Yugoslav domination was the carryover from traditional Albanian hatred and fear of Serbs and Montenegrins. Thus, when Stalin expelled Yugoslavia from the Cominform in 1948, Hoxha repudiated Belgrade's direct domination in favor of Moscow's more indirect control. Later, toward the end of the 1950s, when Khrushchev and Tito were making their edgy rapprochement, the Albanians became fearful of Yugoslavia again and took advantage of the emerging Sino-Soviet schism to switch their allegiance to China. Then, after nearly twenty years of distant patronage, Albania broke with the Chinese, allegedly because the Chinese communists were becoming soft on capitalism. China's real sin, however, was in becoming soft on the Yugoslavs, more specifically the Serbs.

HOW MANY ALBANIANS AND WHERE?

With the Albanians' share of the population steadily increasing, the following figures show how many there are today and where they live and work.[9]

> *Total number of ethnic Albanians (approximate):* Albania, 3 million; Kosovo, 1,800,000; Macedonia, 500,000; Montenegro, 60,000; Italy, 100,000; and Greece, 50,000.
>
> *Migrant Albanian workers (official):* Germany, 125,000; Switzerland, 110,000; Italy, 100,000; Greece, 300,000.
>
> *Birth rate:* For many years Kosovo's birth rate was the highest in Europe, followed by that of Albania itself. Early in the 1960s it was 29.2 per 1,000 people, and by 1988 it had dropped to 23.2. It will continue to fall, but all projections point to its continuing at a very high rate.
>
> *Emigration:* From 1991 through 1995 more than 300,000 left Kosovo, while 400,000 left Albania. Many Albanians entered West European countries illegally; since 1995, though, many of them have been obliged to return.

ALBANIANS IN MACEDONIA

After the serious disturbances in Kosovo in 1981, many Kosovo Albanians fled to or through Macedonia. Many Kosovars continued to do so, helping to swell the large number of Albanians already there. Their numbers varied according to who was taking the census. The 1994 census in Macedonia put the officially registered Albanian population at 22.9 percent, or just under 500,000. This figure was generally considered not too unreliable, although some experts thought 30 percent was closer to the mark. Some 150,000 "unregistered" Albanians also should be added. The overwhelming majority of the unregistered originally came from Kosovo, and the Macedonian government consistently refused to officially recognize their existence. Historically, the Albanians have lived mainly in western Macedonia, but many

Albanians also reside in Skopje, where ethnic relations have often been tense—so tense, in fact, that many Albanians have feared that Skopje could become another Mostar.

The situation of the Albanians in Macedonia always has been much less difficult than that of the Kosovars. Though the Slavic Macedonian "majoritarian nation" has refused to grant what even the most politically moderate Albanians demanded—"constituent-nation status," i.e., self-administration—the government in Skopje slowly increased its recruitment of Albanians into the police force, the civil service, the army officer corps, and other public bodies. The Albanians have their own schools, although their attempt in 1994 to set up their own officially recognized university in Tetovo was forcibly suppressed.[10] Television and radio programs in Albanian increased, and a sizable Albanian press emerged. Most striking of all was the fact that the Albanians not only had their own political parties, but that two of them have been represented in parliament and have had ministers in ruling coalition governments. All in all, much more interaction has always occurred between Albanian and Macedonian elites than between Kosovo Albanian and Serbian elites. Much more flexibility also was present on both sides. But despite this willingness to bend, a basic, irreconcilable, difference prevailed between what Albanians demanded and what Macedonian authorities were prepared to give. The Albanian concept has implied eventual collective status; the Macedonian, integration.

For those Macedonian Albanians who resisted integration, three main escape hatches were available. One was emigration—to Greece, Western Europe, almost anywhere. Another was economic advancement. The most visible evidence of advancement could be found in some of the towns of western Macedonia—perhaps most notably in Gostivar. Capitalism was making some Macedonian Albanians rich. This made many Slavic Macedonians jealous. Puzzled, too. Wealth did not fit the Macedonians' view of what Albanians were, could be, or should be. The third Albanian escape hatch was Islam. The mosque sublimated the frustration and reinforced the dignity of a small but increasing number of Albanians. And the Islam they were turning to was militant. Some Muslim Albanians in Macedonia were already deciding that patience was getting them nowhere. As their ethnic alienation grew, so did their religious zeal.

The coalition formed after the Macedonian election in November 1998 included the Democratic Party of Albanians, hitherto regarded as the most nationalist of the larger minority groupings; this gesture led to some optimism about Macedonian-Albanian reconciliation. The creeping Kosovo disaster seemed to be forcing antagonists together. But Arben Xhaferi, the Albanian party leader, almost immediately gave the government an ultimatum. He wanted not only constituent status for the Albanian minority as a whole, but also more openings for Albanians in the public service as well as recognition for the University of Tetovo—that is, *official* recognition, not just the nod-and-wink sufferance of recent years. If the government balked, Xhaferi threatened to leave the coalition, making the ethnic rift even wider.

Still, Xhaferi was asking for the best of both worlds: collective status and more integration. These contradictory demands reflected either the tactics of moderation or of indecision. But after the Kosovo war in 1999, the demands for integration seemed to become nothing but a delaying tactic. Macedonia's Albanian problem became more inextricably linked to Kosovo. Even before the catastrophe in Kosovo in 1999, developments in one region had repercussions in the other. After the catastrophe, the link with Kosovo went beyond region to acquire an international significance.

Prelude to the Kosovo Conflict

The first organized exodus from Kosovo was that of allegedly more than 300,000 Serbs in 1690 under the legendary patriarch Arsenije III Črnojević. A partial exodus, it was caused by fear of Ottoman revenge after the withdrawal northward of Habsburg forces, which had advanced far enough south following the Turks' failure to take Vienna in 1683. The migrants settled mainly in what is now Vojvodina.

During the nineteenth century, with their gradual emancipation from Ottoman rule and the flowering of the Serb renaissance, the Serbs looked to recover Kosovo, which fell to them in 1912 and was incorporated into the new Yugoslavia after World War I. The problem now was the Albanian presence there, which in 1921 amounted to nearly two-thirds of the region's total population. The Serbs attempted to solve this problem by Serb and Montenegrin colonization and by wholesale persecution of the Albanians, which Belgrade hoped would lead to mass emigration.

It is worth looking at the development of the Albanian ethnic percentage in Kosovo after World War I: 1921 (65.8 percent), 1939 (54.4 percent), 1961 (67.2 percent), 1971 (73.7 percent), 1981 (77.4 percent), 1991 (91 percent).[11] (The drop in the interwar years shows the effect—meager in terms of hopes—of Belgrade's colonization policy that increased the combined Serb-Montenegrin total from 21 to 33 percent. In the context of Serb persecution, by 1930 not a single Albanian language school or Albanian language newspaper remained.)

Still, Kosovo Albanians would not leave in sufficient numbers to suit Serb tastes. It was then that plans for their mass expulsion began being laid. The best-known scheme was that of Vaša Čubrilović, a prominent historian and an adviser to the Yugoslav government. This plan called for the resettlement of the entire Albanian population of Kosovo to Albania and Turkey.[12] World War II intervened, and the Čubrilović plan was shelved. But it was not forgotten. It became the inspiration for Slobodan Milošević's Operation Horseshoe in 1999. Thus, Milošević's policy of expulsions had a well-known precedent, and, as an OSCE publication in December 1999 convincingly showed, his expulsions were carefully planned well before the NATO intervention began.[13]

With World War II came the creation of Greater Albania under Axis auspices and the mass persecution of Serbs there. But after 1945 and the return of Serb domination, the boot had very much changed feet. That boot now belonged to Alexander Ranković, a nationalist Serb, Belgrade "centralizer," minister of the interior, chief of what became the UDBA (the new Yugoslavia's secret police), and a man to whom repression came naturally. Mass persecution by Serbs (and Montenegrins) returned on a massive scale.

However, a historical shift in Albanian attitudes was occurring. Many Kosovars no longer were intimidated by this new cycle of Serb repression. They began to realize what their numerical superiority could mean in terms of power; they had experienced the fulfillment of having their own enlarged state; most important of all, a new, younger elite was forming, conscious and proud of its ethnicity and no longer ready to kow-tow to Serbs or anyone else. In 1965, Ranković was comprehensively purged in Belgrade, swept away by the tide of political and economic reform and of ethnic devolution. Sensing that they had gained something but could gain more, Kosovars—many of them students—took to the streets in the capital, Priština. The Albanian University of Priština, founded by Tito in 1970 as an ethnic "safety valve," soon became a hotbed of ethnic nationalism.

The new Yugoslav constitution of 1974, seen as an insult by the Serbs (see pp. 163–64), was viewed by the Kosovars as another big step toward freedom. But freedom alone did not satisfy them; it simply spurred them on.

They had come to regard Tito as their best bet against the Serbs, and after he died in 1980 the massive rioting in Kosovo was the expression of regret, anger, uncertainty, fear, and a determination not just to keep what they already had gained, but to expand it. The steady disintegration and then the collapse of Tito's Yugoslavia, however, left the Kosovars at the mercy of Serbia's military superiority. The boot had once again switched feet—and now it belonged to Milošević.

Serb repression and persecution began in 1989. The high points of Kosovar resistance are outlined in table 1.

One of the most remarkable aspects of Kosovar passive resistance was the steady building of the Albanian parallel (or shadow) state. It began to be erected soon after Kosovo's fully autonomous status was abolished in 1989, and it came to include a presidency, a government, a legislature, a health care system, a comprehensive education system from primary to university levels, several newspapers, and a proliferating second economy manned in many cases by sacked public employees. The parallel state, sometimes called "the world's most successful NGO," was financed by collections within Kosovo itself and by remittances from Kosovo Albanians abroad. (Some of these remittances included drug-running and gun-running proceeds, though clearly not as much as the Serbs claimed.) Obviously, such illegal activities could not have operated without some blind-eye connivance by Serb authorities. The Serbs did not collect taxes

Table 1. Kosovar Resistance and Serb Repression, 1989–1992

1989	Milošević abrogated 1974 Yugoslav constitution and Kosovo's status under it.
1990–92	More than 100,000 Albanian officeholders, professional people, and workers were dismissed. "Serbification" began (or was resumed). Albanian educational facilities were severely restricted.
September 1990	The "underground" Kosovo parliament declared Kosovo an "independent Yugoslav republic."
September 1991	Parliament declared *total* independence of Kosovo.
October 1991	Establishment of Kosovo government-in-exile, under premier Bujar Bukoshi.
May 1992	"Underground" parliamentary and presidential elections gave huge majority to the Democratic League of Kosovo. Its leader, Ibrahim Rugova, was elected president.

rigorously and did not draft Kosovars into the armed forces. They issued drivers' licenses, identity cards, and other necessary documentation. They even issued passports (the more Albanians that departed, the better). The Albanians did not ask for welfare and social benefits, nor did they try to usurp Serb police control of the streets or Serb governmental control of television. However, no one should imagine that this connivance implied any cosiness between Serbs and Kosovars or dulled the mutual hatred that existed in Kosovo. The *need* for this connivance, if anything, aggravated the tension, causing both sides to wonder how long the whole arrangement could continue.

The Albanian parallel state had three important spinoffs: (1) It did something to raise Albanian self-respect in Kosovo and something more to increase international respect for the Kosovars, even if no foreign country (including Albania itself) recognized the parallel government. (2) The parallel state helped develop at least a rudimentary civil society in Kosovo. (3) The second economy released an entrepreneurial instinct, which, properly guided and buttressed by remittances from abroad, could lay the basis for a better economic future.

The Albanians in Kosovo had hoped (and were convinced that they had been led to believe by the Western powers) that their case would be considered at Dayton in 1995. When it was not, many of them felt despair and betrayal. But not defeat. Their resistance moved into a new and more dangerous phase—from organic work to armed resistance. The Kosovo Liberation Army (KLA or UCK—Ushtria Çlirimtare e Kosovës), which began about 1994 as a minuscule, scattered terrorist organization picking off Serb policemen and Albanian "collaborators," became a real underground army and acquired a large arsenal, largely from Albania itself after the Pyramid rioting and looting there. The KLA quickly took over Kosovar resistance. Its goal was independence, and its means was armed struggle. Its numbers increased as more Albanians came back from the West and as Serb repression massively intensified. Many Kosovars, mainly young men, turned to the KLA because they wanted action and because the Dayton agreements, which they had hoped would regulate their situation, simply ignored Kosovo. The KLA's policy was "the worse the better." This credo strengthened the hard-liners in Belgrade and weakened the established resistance politicians in Priština. Although the KLA now saw its main job as killing Serbs, it was not above intimidating Kosovars to follow its line. A classic liberation struggle was on, with terror as its principal weapon.[14]

By the end of 1998, not only Rugova but the whole Kosovar political elite had begun to seem irrelevant. Nonetheless, it is worth recording what the elite activists had stood for—and still did. Their views and their differences mirrored those of repressed elites everywhere. Thus, whatever subsequent disappointments occurred, their role in their nation's history was secure.

The aim of Ibrahim Rugova and his Democratic League of Kosovo was full independence for Kosovo, but only peaceful means were advocated to achieve it. (Rugova's opponents dismissed this stance as "Gandhi-like"). At first, Rugova's strategy was dominant, but soon it began to be challenged by growing numbers of intellectuals and politicians who claimed that it was getting nowhere.

These opponents first proposed negotiations with Belgrade on a sovereign status for Kosovo (beyond the status of the 1974 constitution) inside a revamped Yugoslav federation. (The name "Balkania" was suggested.) They put forward their proposal mainly on grounds of "realism"; Belgrade might eventually negotiate even about far-reaching autonomy, but never about independence.[15] Advocating autonomy might also circumvent the West's refusal to countenance independence. As for means, the dissident politicians and intellectuals advocated active but still unarmed resistance— boycotts and street demonstrations. (Intifada also was mentioned, although how far such forms of resistance could go without the use of arms remained open to question.) This approach therefore was doubly opposed to Rugova's. It would settle, at least in the interim, for something less than independence, but it would use methods much riskier and vigorous than Rugova's. Adem Demaci, once dubbed Kosovo's Nelson Mandela, was its best-known advocate, an able, charismatic, man who spent nearly thirty years in Tito's prisons.[16] By 1998, though—and this changeover reflects the intensification of the struggle—Kosovo's "Mandela" had became the KLA's main political adviser. Demaci strongly resisted the Western "deal" at the Rambouillet negotiations in early 1999, which he refused to attend.

Militarily, the KLA was soundly beaten by superior Serb forces in 1998 in a massive, brutal, scorched-earth campaign that caused the exodus of scores of thousands of Kosovar refugees into Albania and huge dislocations of population within Kosovo itself. By early 1999, considerably more than 400,000 people had lost their homes. But the Serbs, and the West, were deceiving themselves if they thought this defeat was the end. The KLA came back menacingly as more Kosovars flocked to join it, all of them fully convinced now that the KLA was their only means of salvation. Subsequently, the Serbs were to excuse their own barbarities by pointing to the KLA's strength, menace, and methods.

EARLY SERB REACTIONS TO KOSOVO

Broadly speaking, before 1998 there had been three different Serb approaches on Kosovo: rejectionist, concessionist, and pragmatic.

For the rejectionists, Kosovo was Serb—and purely a Serb internal matter. Foreign interference of any kind was rejected. So were meaningful concessions to the Albanians. The rejectionists insisted that the Kosovars did have a certain autonomy, even after 1989, with which they should be satisfied. This approach was the one advocated all along by ultranationalists like Vojislav Šešelj as well as by Milošević. But in the eyes of the die-hard rejectionists, even Milošević was not a true keeper of the flame. He had compromised over Krajina, East Slavonia, and Bosnia, and they initially feared he might do the same over Kosovo. The die-hards were just itching to reach a final solution for Kosovo. They looked to Russia for support. But other rejectionists hesitated from going that far, predicting that this all-out approach would provoke another war that Serbia would lose, and that Serbia would suffer incomparably worse than before. The rejectionist front was divided, therefore, and not as strong as it looked from a distance. But the Serb offensive in 1998, and the official stand taken by the Serbs toward the peace talks at Rambouillet and Paris (see below) showed that this threat was more than strong enough.

Some of the milder rejectionists could have found common ground with the concessionists, who hoped that wide-ranging Kosovar autonomy and a willingness to compromise on other issues might restore stability and maintain Serb rule. The concessionists drew comfort from the West's refusal to support total independence for Kosovo.

The pragmatists were few but not insignificant. They were resigned to the Serb position in Kosovo eventually becoming untenable (say, by 2050), mainly because of demographics—the rapid Albanian birth rate. Serb policy, they argued, must be based on this assumption. Pillars of the establishment like Ćosić and the Academy of Sciences president, Alexander Despić, publicly urged acceptance of the inevitable. They advocated partition, with part of Kosovo being let go. The part they would retain, however, would not only contain some of the main Serb historic sites, but also most of Kosovo's industrial wealth—that is, not just the monasteries, but the mines, too.[17]

The Western nations—the United States in the lead—at first tended to pride themselves on their alertness over Kosovo. They might have dozed over Bosnia, but they would not be caught napping over Kosovo!

They certainly were not caught napping. But they were caught fiddling. Innumerable meetings at ascending levels were held by the UN, NATO, and the EU, as well as among worried states. Several military exercises also convinced everybody, especially Milošević, that the West meant business. The emphasis, however, was on consensus, usually a sure route to impotence. But this time, there *was* a tangible impediment to meaningful action. The Western powers stuck resolutely to the post-World War II axiom on the inviolability of international borders. They therefore supported a solution of greatly enhanced autonomy for Kosovo within "Yugoslavia" (i.e., Serbia), but not independence. They hoped to pressure Milošević into concessions toward this demand. This action certainly became a dilemma for him, but when the KLA began its widespread guerrilla war in Kosovo in 1998, it tactically played into Milošević's hands. As its own name implied, the KLA's struggle was for "liberation." The Serbs waged a scorched-earth war against it and against any civilians who stood remotely in their way. This began the great refugee dislocation—at first within Kosovo itself. The Serbs temporarily regained military control of Kosovo.

Against this background, the NATO powers and Milošević struck their deal in October 1998. This deal, like Dayton, was shallow and misleading from the start. But, unlike Dayton, it even failed to stop the fighting.

Although the West had been threatening Milošević with air strikes, the October 1998 agreement left him with the impression yet again of having considerable leeway. He still emerged, as he had after Dayton, as the guardian of the inviolability of international borders, the West's negotiating partner, and a "guarantor of stability" in Kosovo. The Kosovars were put in a position where renewed resistance could lead to their being blamed for disturbing the peace, for not being mature, patient, reasonable, and for failing to play the international game. Milošević banked on Western inactivity: much diplomatic posturing, but no military action. He realized that both he and the West ultimately agreed on one thing: no independence for Kosovo. Within the framework of this collusion, therefore, the KLA was their common enemy. Their chief tactic: grind down the KLA, and a stability of sorts would follow. Although the West would not like much of what was being done, its actions would not threaten ultimate Serb rule.

Serb troops and police, ostensibly rooting out the KLA, waged savage war on the whole Kosovar population, and it was this savagery, together with Kosovar resilience, that upset Milošević's calculations. The massacre of more than forty Albanian civilians at Rajak in January 1999 was an act nowhere near on the scale of Šrebenica and other Serb atrocities in Bosnia, or of other atrocities in Kosovo itself, but it was a spectacular example of the incorrigibility of Serb mass cruelty. It became a catalyst—simply one massacre too many. Western intervention became both necessary and justified. It seemed, in fact, that, whatever reservations existed about intervention as a principle and a policy, much suffering in former Yugoslavia as a whole would have been avoided had meaningful intervention occurred only a few years earlier.

RAMBOUILLET: ATTITUDES AND IMPLICATIONS

What followed were the unsuccessful negotiations at Rambouillet and, finally, in Paris. To call these negotiations one-sided would understate how much the Serbs were put under duress. Rambouillet was, indeed, a diktat. The Serbs and others were quick to allege its similarities with Hitler's diktat to Romania in 1940 and to Yugoslavia itself in 1941. But the attitude of the Western powers can be explained by two things. First, Milošević's deception, his lack of good faith, and his prevarication, all of which were plainly evident in the Serb delegation's behavior at Rambouillet, too. Second, the enormity of recent Serb atrocities, first in Croatia; then, especially, in Bosnia; and now in Kosovo itself. The fact that these atrocities were not incidental or spontaneous accompaniments to the brutality of war, but aspects of a carefully planned policy with obvious historical precedents, made the West's high-handed exasperation simply more understandable and defensible.

But an important "power" consideration was involved as well. The Western powers' earlier delay in dealing firmly with Milošević had put them in a position where not acting decisively at Rambouillet, or after it, would have meant a serious loss of credibility for the United States and for NATO. Indeed, for NATO, its perceived impotence would simply have confirmed the widespread opinion that, essential though it may have been during the simplicities of the cold war, it had become redundant for the multipolar complexities of the twenty-first century.

The details of the Rambouillet negotiations need not be recounted here. But these were the more important points rising from them:

The status of Kosovo. Kosovo should remain within the borders of the Federal Republic of Yugoslavia. But it should be quasi-independent, with its own president, executive, legislature, and judicial system; it should be the "furthest possible removed" from the control of Yugoslavia. At the same time, however, it would become, in effect, a Western protectorate with a peacekeeping force of 30,000, composed mainly of American, British, and French troops.

Independence? Obviously, Serb control over Kosovo was to be ended in all but name. The fiction, or fig leaf, of sovereignty was to be preserved—de jure sovereignty only. But the Western proposals stipulated that the situation be reviewed in three years and "further steps" decided on at that time. A referendum on *independence* after three years was neither specifically proposed or rejected. But many groups—Kosovars, Serbs, and outsiders—assumed that such a referendum was implicit, and this assumption persuaded KLA representatives to attend, in spite of the call for "irregular forces," i.e., the KLA, to be disbanded.[18] It was a makeshift plan—or the diplomacy of delay—putting aside an immediate problem and hoping that something would turn up. The West was learning that containment rather than solution was the only answer.

Serb unity. The unity among the Serbs during the negotiations was impressive. Whatever initial differences existed in Belgrade over a response to the West were soon papered (or cemented) over. Milošević was anxious to exploit the West's reluctance to give Kosovo full independence. He also seemed convinced that Western unity would crack, especially over how intense and sustained NATO "aggression" against Serbia should become. As always, he was keeping his nerve.

Albanian divisions. The known divisions among the Kosovars again became evident at Rambouillet. The KLA was dedicated to independence through armed struggle. The "moderates," still nominally led by Rugova, had independence as their ultimate goal, but their aim was to achieve that result by stages, through peaceful means, and with Western assistance. No sympathy whatever existed between the West and the KLA, but a mutual dependence developed between the West and the moderates. Rugova was "the West's man." The moderates, though fairly united at Rambouillet, contained serious divisions that certainly would resurface and deepen in the future. The KLA also was known to be divided, not only over military tactics, but over political principles, methods, and Albanian unity. Serious personal rivalries and generational tensions played a part, too.

The War Erupts

When the Belgrade leadership rejected the Western terms for settlement at Rambouillet, the conflict began. Planes from NATO bombed Serbia and the Serb presence in Kosovo, while the Serbs set about destroying the Albanian presence in Kosovo. Leaders of NATO seemed confident enough. But they made three major miscalculations.

1. They overestimated the effectiveness of their air offensive on which they planned to exclusively rely. Misled by the Bosnian precedent, they expected the Serbs to buckle in a few days, which the Serbs manifestly did not do. (Postconflict Western reviews of the air offensive, especially over Kosovo itself, showed how ineffective it actually was.)

2. The NATO leaders apparently were unprepared (in spite of Bosnia) for the degree and depths of Serb savagery in Kosovo. This raised the question of reconciling the morality of the West's motives with the fate of the people it was committed to save, but whose suffering it seemed to be aggravating.

3. Western leaders rejected the idea of a ground invasion of Kosovo. Especially in the United States, an invasion was judged to be both militarily and politically unfeasible. Bombing, therefore, was not just the preferred military option; it was the only one.

Western politicians and publics generally supported the moral reasons for the war and initially supported the conduct of it. But as the war continued, this unity began to erode. Opinion seemed to divide sharply between those demanding a more energetic prosecution of the war through a ground offensive and those prepared for negotiation and therefore compromise. And, since negotiating directly with Milošević was out of the question, any compromise would have to be directly reached with Russia, Milošević's protector.

DIPLOMACY—WITH RUSSIA "ON BOARD"

As the Kosovo crisis developed, some Western illusions existed about full Russian cooperation. But these expectations were dispelled as soon as the conflict started. Moscow stood four-square behind Belgrade, and Russian public opinion was outraged by the bombing of Serbia. At first, Russian outrage was discounted. The Russians would huff, puff, and bluff, but they could not divert NATO from its course.[19]

Just a few weeks into the war, however, with the bombing apparently getting nowhere, a ground offensive ruled out, and NATO unity cracking, Russia stopped being considered peripheral and became a central player, even an indispensable one, the only suitable "mediator" in the conflict. In fact, the irresolution of some NATO members, notably, Germany, France, and Italy, was allowing the conflict to become internationalized, to slip out of NATO's grasp and into that of the United Nations, which could be manipulated by the Russians and Chinese. Happenstance played some role in this development. The bombing of the Chinese embassy in Belgrade in May 1999 brought China bellowing onto the stage. Even before that calamity, President Clinton was hinting that Milošević might stay in office and was talking about Kosovo's future "autonomy," apparently with no account taken of what the Serbs had since done in Kosovo. Only Britain's Gladstonian prime minister, Tony Blair, still seemed to believe in the moral mission.

The Western signs of indecision meant that the Kosovars themselves were being pushed to the sideline. Ostensibly, the West's concern was still to get them back to their homes, or at least, back into Kosovo. But the internationalization of the conflict meant that the Kosovars' cause was up for bargaining. Moving the matter toward the UN meant that the issue was becoming overladen with diplomatic procedures, even chicanery. And if the UN were to decide the composition of any peacekeeping force in Kosovo, the "core" NATO contingent would be too small and the Russian and Chinese contingents too large to induce the Kosovars to return home with any degree of confidence.

In the event, most fears were allayed. The bombing of Serbia had a greater impact than the West had begun to believe, and Russia apparently saw no gain in the conflict continuing. Milošević therefore gave in. For NATO, the victory turned out to be real, but it had been a close thing. Had Milošević held out, say for two weeks longer, the disunity becoming evident in the West might have enabled him to get better terms than he did, despite his having just been indicted by the International War Crimes Tribunal. The serious Western disunity on which he had calculated could have been imminent, as Western leaders have since confirmed.[20] That disunity, then, nearly led to the Western disaster that many observers had predicted.

SERBIA AT WAR

Five interacting elements help explain Serb behavior in the 1990s, especially in regard to the Kosovo conflict. Some of them have been touched on, but they are worth bringing together here.

1. *The Kosovo mystique* (see chapter 6) True, few Serbs ever visited Kosovo to pay homage at their shrines, and Belgrade's attempts to settle Krajina refugees in Kosovo were an embarrassing failure because so few wanted to go, still fewer to stay. The official Serb recolonization policy between the world wars also had failed. But Kosovo had kept its hold on the Serb psyche, and it was now in danger—again from Muslims. The situation easily fitted into the *Serbia contra mundum* image that their history, and especially their historians, had conjured up.

2. *Sense of Solidarity:* "Samo Sloga Srbina Spasava!" (Only solidarity saves the Serb!) This slogan (see chapter 1) also was rooted in the Serb national consciousness. It partly explains Serb fortitude in the face of NATO bombing. It befits a heroic nation. But it also sprouts ugly offshoots—the inability, for example, to entertain any notion of guilt—present or past. The Serbs painted the initials of this slogan on the ruined walls of many houses that they destroyed in Kosovo.

3. *Ethnic contempt* This is another integral part of blinkered nationalism. Serbs, generally, have regarded Albanians as a lower order of human beings. The Kosovars were "criminal interlopers" on their "sacred hearth." In his letter to the foreign ministers of France and British rejecting the Rambouillet terms, Milošević referred to the Serb nation as protecting its "historical dignity against vermin who know nothing about history or dignity."[21]

4. *Milošević at bay* His basic opportunism, or pragmatism, was shown in his earlier career and later at Dayton (see chapter 6). But his rejection of Rambouillet and his resistance to NATO bombing seemed inconsistent with both of those characteristics. As mentioned, he was counting on NATO disunity and Russian diplomatic and military assistance. He also may have seen his future as a clear-cut choice between power in Belgrade and condemnation at the International Court at The Hague. But did he also think about his role in Serbia's history and the ignominy involved if he tamely let Kosovo go? His future reputation was best summed up by Dobrica Ćosić as early as 1993: "Today Milošević is an anachronistic phenomenon. I fear that his mission will end tragically both for himself and his nation."[22]

KOSOVO: THE KLA AND OTHERS

Stupefaction and suspicion greeted television clips early in April 1999 that showed Milošević and Ibrahim Rugova sitting together in Belgrade. The two leaders were described as discussing the Kosovo situation. Many explanations were offered for what was obviously a Serb propaganda coup. Some Serb mischief might indeed have been afoot. On the other hand, it might have reflected differences within the Kosovar leadership, with Rugova incensed at KLA "extremism" as well as seeing his own leadership steadily undermined. Possibly, it marked a futile effort by him to stop the widening conflict.

Whatever the explanation, most Albanians everywhere were outraged at Rugova. He seemed to have become "yesterday's man" in Kosovo (discredited no matter how much Western leaders still liked him). Later, though (and this was a step toward some moderation in Kosovar politics), he returned to public preeminence. But in the meantime Serb savagery was only reinforcing the KLA's position among all Albanians, not just those in Kosovo. The Western powers simply had to get used to it. Actually, the KLA was getting Western arms early in the conflict, and NATO considered its resistance struggle against the Serb forces invaluable. In fact, NATO and the KLA now became wartime allies.

But the West continued to be nervous about the KLA for a half-dozen reasons.

1. The KLA was for Kosovar independence *now*. Nor did it take easily to compromise.
2. Its financing was becoming increasingly suspect—drugs, prostitution, plain extortion, etc.
3. It was undemocratic. The political views of some KLA leaders and its rank and file ranged from Titoist to anarchist, Stalinist, or Maoist. Jeffersonian liberals were few. Brigands pure and simple were many.
4. When victory was won, the KLA could well dissolve into opposing, even warring, factions.
5. The KLA had a particularly strong following among Albanians in Macedonia. In fact, Albanians everywhere were becoming KLA.
6. It was not likely to be merciful to Kosovo Serbs, however innocent some were of the crimes committed there.

Serb propaganda did its best to demonize the KLA. Many Western opponents of NATO's action did virtually the same. Clearly, the KLA would be a headache for everybody. But the KLA must be put in some kind of historical perspective. In its terror, ruthlessness, and intransigence, it was no different from most freedom movements the world over. Certainly, Balkan history is full of "KLAS," and these are now idealized and romanticized by the nations for which they fought.

The KLA leadership after the war also knew that its organization was under intense Western pressure to behave and was aware of the importance of acquiring international respectability. It would certainly not be the first liberation organization to be transformed by the mask it was forced to adopt. How long it would take to do so remained to be seen. No question that, immediately after the departure of the Serb military and the massive return of the Albanian refugees, many sickening acts of retribution, revenge, and sheer barbarism occurred, not only against Serbs, but against Roma (most of whom had supported the Serbs before and during the war), Slavic Muslims, even some Turks, and a few Roman Catholic Kosovars.[23] But the worst excesses of this frenzy passed with the arrival of KFOR, the NATO soldiery, and the UN authority of Kosovo (UNMIK), despite periodic spasms of violent excess. Many Kosovars, while not actively persecuting the remaining Serbs, were unmoved by the stories of discrimination, expulsion, or even atrocities against them. "It's their turn" was the general reaction.[24] As for living, even coexisting, with Serbs in the future, Kosovars simply could not entertain the idea. Croatia, Bosnia, now Kosovo—hopes of restoring multiethnic society had become dangerous illusions. The number of Serbs in Kosovo would steadily decrease and this decrease could be punctuated by eruptions of violence. But the Serbs had no future in Kosovo, certainly not in terms of political power. A small number might eventually return, but the Serbs who did would simply have to get used to the fact (and show by their behavior) that they were a minority in a foreign land.[25]

What had occurred in the second half of 1999 was a massive spasm of fury. The fury slackened, although Kosovo would remain a lawless place, especially if the planned UN police force did not materialize in sufficient numbers. But a different kind of violence would reappear if the West (or the "international community") eventually rejected independence for Kosovo—guerrilla warfare, directed by a revived KLA. What was used in the 1990s against the Serbs would be used now against the West, against KFOR, against the UN and its minions. And not only in Kosovo. In the Albanian areas of Macedonia, even in the capital Skopje, serious unrest would occur. In coming to terms with the "Albanian emergence," the West will have to decide not what is best, but what is least worst.

The continuing violence perpetrated by the liberated Kosovars against Serbs and others in Kosovo was seen by those who had opposed NATO action against Serbia as a vindication of their entire position.[26] Some who had supported the intervention on moral grounds were now so sickened by what they saw that they reappraised their position on the grounds of "moral equivalence." There was, they alleged or implied, a "balance of guilt" that made neither side worth supporting.

Taking the twentieth century as a whole, there had, indeed, been a depressing see-saw of cruelty and oppression in Kosovo. Under the Ottomans the Albanians, as Muslims, were part of the ruling caste; in the first Yugoslavia the Serbs and Montenegrins had repressed the Kosovars; in wartime Greater Albania it was the Kosovars' turn; immediately after World War II the Serbs showed no mercy; in the 1970s and 1980s many Kosovars tended to flaunt their new powers, rights, and freedoms in Titoist Yugoslavia; throughout the 1990s the Serbs replied with a vengeance; now it was Kosovar's hour of bloody revenge. To many, therefore, "moral equivalence" was the only possible judgment, with the Kosovars disqualifying themselves from the sympathy they might once have enjoyed.

When the first anniversary of the conflict came around in 2000, "those against" the entire war were on the offensive, loudly and sometimes oversimply so. But however much one agreed that, just as the war was botched, the peace was being botched, too, two basic points remained on which there could be little *valid* argument. Two eminent journalists put them very convincingly.

First, Flora Lewis on the rightness of the war itself:

> The war with Serbia to stop tyranny and ethnic cleansing in Kosovo was a milestone. Wise or unwise, well or poorly conducted, it was the first war that was not for conquest, or defence or imposition of political power, but to establish standards of behaviour.[27]

Second, on postwar Kosovo, Jonathan Steele of the *Guardian* deplored the growing tendency morally to "equate" Serb and Kosovo crimes against each other:

> The notion of "balance" makes little distinction between a state-machine whose security forces use arson, artillery, and cold-blooded murder on a mass scale against people still in their homes, and the

revenge-seeking of bereaved people returning to destroyed villages and burning the houses of their Serbian neighbours. . . .

Now we have moved to a second post-war stage, where crime in Kosovo is random, opportunistic, urban and largely carried out by professional criminals who want to make money. It is the inevitable consequence of a law and order vacuum, for which the international community is mainly to blame for failing to provide the police it.[28]

The truth is that Kosovars deserve more credit than most outsiders are prepared to give them. Amid the squalor there is quality; amid the crime there is decency; amid the despair there is spirit. Given a chance, these are the virtues that will show.

But these virtues will show only if the peace stops being botched, a task primarily up to the Western powers:

1. *Administratively,* they must fashion more decisive and coordinated military, civil, and humanitarian organizations.

2. *Financially,* all the international organizations which have pledged must *deliver.* The record of most of them, especially the EU, is depressing.

3. *Strategically,* the Western alliance must decide on a policy for Kosovo that combines reality, vision and courage. On issues like independence and eventual Albanian unity this must involve overturning conventional wisdom, discarding shibboleths, discovering boldness, and showing determination.[29]

THE KOŠTUNICA FACTOR

The fall of Milošević and his replacement by Vojislav Koštunica (see chapter 5) was bound to have some impact on Serb policy and attitudes to Kosovo. There was some apprehension about him when he assumed power. He was on record during the conflict over Kosovo for not only opposing the NATO bombing but calling NATO's leaders "worse than the Nazis." The war crimes tribunal at The Hague he described as a "monstrous institution" to which Milošević should on no account be committed. As a conservative, nationalist, Christian Serb he was bound to insist on Serbia's right to Kosovo. And his early comment about the future of Montenegro, that "Yugoslavia" should now be officially entitled "Serbia-Montenegro," seemed to indicate that he had no time for the old "Balkania" idea, with Kosovo as an equal part of a triangular Serb-Montenegrin-Kosovar federation.

But in a very short time there was apparently some moderation of Koštunica's original hard line. Some of his closer associates and some Westerners were now putting him in the "pragmatists" camp regarding Kosovo. No one, though, could be quite certain. On the one hand, Koštunica knew that a more diplomatic line on Kosovo would go down well in the West, which would play a key role in Serbia's future. He also presumably thought that the milder the manner the better the deal he might be offered on Kosovo itself. On the other hand, he had to be very careful about Serb public opinion and the opportunities for mischief that a "surrender" on Kosovo would give to his numerous domestic enemies.

As for the Kosovars, they remained suspicious of anything in, or coming out of, Belgrade. Their attitude was well put by Bajram Rexhepi, mayor of the Albanian half of Mitrovica. Speaking to the London *Times* on September 13, 2000, he had this to say:

> Milošević is a cancer for the Balkans and I would like to see him go, but I don't see any other figure in Serbia who has taken a different stand to his on Kosovo. The international community knows that Milošević is a bad man. But an opposition victor, who shares the same attitude towards the Albanians as Milošević, could end up receiving support from the international community.

The truth remained that every Albanian, whether in Kosovo or anywhere else, wanted independence for Kosovo, and virtually every Serb was not only against it but insisted that, at a minimum, the link with Serbia should be kept. Still, the impasse was not as final as it looked. Belgrade had become a more civilized place since Milošević's fall; so had Priština, since the astonishing return to political preeminence of Ibrahim Rugova. He and Koštunica had similar values and standards. They would not solve the Kosovo problem but they might contain it, quieten it, "cool" it. If they could, it would be the most heartening sign of Balkan maturity ever.

KOSOVO AND BOSNIA: A COMPARISON

"Speed in Kosovo, standstill in Bosnia." This was the heading of a perceptive article in early August 1999 that contrasted the speed of recovery in Kosovo with the lack of it in Bosnia.[30] No amount of Western self-congratulatory propaganda about progress in Bosnia could hide the contrast.

The simple fact was that the Kosovars were working harder and better than the Bosnians (whether Muslim, Croat, or Serb). And this effort did not result from their getting more international help than the Bosnians. (International help, in fact, was only just beginning to flow into Kosovo.) Nor did it stem from any differences in character, religion, or history. Practically all Kosovars were Muslim, and Bosnian Muslims outnumbered any other groups. Both Kosovars and Bosnians had spent much of their history under the Ottoman empire (though as Muslims, not as subjects under the Ottoman Yoke). Four reasons combine to explain the difference.

1. Ethnic unity prevailed among the Kosovars while ethnic disunity and mutual hatred characterized the Bosnians as a whole.

2. Less material damage was done in Kosovo than in Bosnia. The war in Kosovo lasted about eighteen months; in Bosnia it lasted more than three years. One army spread destruction in Kosovo—that of the Serbs; in Bosnia, three armies—Serbs, Muslims, and Croats—did their damage.

3. In Kosovo, the masses of Kosovar refugees returned to their own houses and property. These dwellings and places may have been destroyed, but they were indisputably theirs. In Bosnia, few of the mass of refugees were able to return to their former homes.

4. In Bosnia, the greater parts of the economy were still in official government hands—that is, the hands of national nomenclatures. The emphasis still was placed on "big industry"—large factories, state-owned and state-(mis)managed. In Kosovo, Milošević freed many Kosovars from the state ownership mentality. Thousands were dismissed from their jobs and went into the "parallel economy," which was full of small, competitive firms. Many also went abroad, learned skills, and acquired a market mentality. Some of them were now coming back.

There was more free enterprise in Kosovo, therefore, than in Bosnia. Still, the contrast should not be pushed too far. Kosovo, in fact, was in danger of losing its initial advantages for three reasons: (1) The old concept of the omnipotent state was dying hard. Kosovo had its own behemoth (see chapter 3); it was still breathing and it was hard to move. (2) Practically no one knew who owned, or was entitled to, what. The old social ownership system was almost impossible to untangle. Laws of property were virtually nonexistent. Besides, so much relevant legal documentation had been lost in the conflict. (3) The Kosovar elites were set on *state building*. Thus, especially as heirs to the socialist dogma, they were anxious that the new state should own, or at least control, as much of the "family silver" as possible. Therefore, an ongoing struggle was taking place—ideological, cultural, political, and economic. The future of Kosovo would depend on its outcome.

Albanian Unity and the Future of Macedonia

Albanian *survival* had once seemed the most important question. Then it became the Albanian *emergence*. Now it is Albanian *unity*. Until recent years, unity had never been a pressing question. In fact, much disunity had prevailed always in the Albanian community. Kosovars thought Albanians were backward; Albanians thought Kosovars were arrogant. Neither Kosovars nor Macedonian Albanians had strong links with Albania proper. But they always had strong links with each other and these are now even stronger. They constitute a key regional factor.

Most Albanians knew that scant support existed for Albanian unity in the West. They also were aware of the dreadful condition of Albania itself. When Albanians were in the company of Westerners, therefore, they tended to play down unity, sometimes pointing to how the ethnically Germanic nation is spread out over Germany, Austria, and Switzerland. Some Albanians went no further in public than to envisage a "loose confederation," or those "special relations" that Dayton allowed among the two Bosnian Entities and Serbia and Croatia.

These reassurances about limited aims do not entirely convince. Rugova once told a Western journalist: "Over the longer term, it is the declared aim of the Kosovo Democratic Union to seek union with the Motherland."[31] Six years later, in May 1998, another distinguished Albanian, Fatos Lubonja, scion of a brave family and himself a noted writer in Tirana, told a French correspondent in May 1998: "The national idea began to ferment after independence in 1912. Communism after the war in Yugoslavia froze that evolution. The events in Kosovo have brought the subject back to center stage.[32] True, but the stage and the actors now seemed rather different.

Three facts about the Albanian nation were becoming clear and they could have a profound effect on the future of the southern Balkans. (1) The condition of Albania itself precluded it from taking an active role in a unifying process; (2) in Kosovo, despite all it had been through, some vibrancy still remained and a credible initiative for unity might arise; (3) a meaningful sense of inter-Albanian cooperation and mutual sympathy, even mutual identity, existed now between Kosovars and Macedonian Albanians. Albania, "Motherland" though it might be, was neither an example nor an ideal. Therein, of course, lay the danger to the future of Macedonia and of Balkan stability.

The impact of this potential Kosovar emergence on Macedonia was causing worry in the West and among the Slavic Macedonian majority. Many Macedonian Albanians wanted to be part of it, and such a development could destroy the Macedonian state. This danger could already turn Macedonia into the third international "protectorate" in the Balkans, after Bosnia and Kosovo. At the same time, the Western powers were pressing the Macedonian government to itself do more to defuse the danger—by a program of concessions and safety valves: by improving the economic conditions of the Albanian minority; by encouraging Albanian small businesses; by introducing more "affirmative action" in the public sector; by allowing an official University of Tetovo; and by promoting, rather than trying to forbid, cross-border contacts with Kosovo.

All of these options were sensible and well-intentioned. But they are probably too late. The Albanians in Macedonia were now increasingly seeing themselves as part of the larger Albanian family, certainly not as loyal citizens of a Slav-dominated Macedonia. Integration appeared to be very passé, which was making "affirmative action" pointless. Few Albanians would be prepared to "compromise" their nationality for the sake of a job at the Skopje central post office, except, of course, to equip themselves for future service in some kind of Albanian administration—the "organic work" syndrome. It is again worth remembering Tito's miscalculation about the University of Priština.

An unofficial international "protectorate" status for Macedonia would bring temporary stability, security, and prosperity. But for how long? Nobody, of course, knew. Macedonia was another of those Balkan problems that could probably never be solved, at best only contained, managed, or finessed. A touch of *alert* "Micawberism"—waiting for something to "turn up"—might be an element not of whimsy but of wisdom in this part of the world.

Montenegro's Balancing Act

By the end of 1999 the only control that "Yugoslavia" had over Montenegro was through the federal army. As Fabian Schmidt pointed out, "similar to 1990, on the eve of the dissolution of socialist Yugoslavia, today the only remaining functioning institution of federal Yugoslavia is the army."[33] Montenegro had the German Mark as a currency, controlled its own border crossings, disregarded Yugoslav visa laws, and pursued its own foreign policy with a growing number of (unofficial) diplomatic missions in Western capitals. At the same time its head of state, President Milo Djukanović, was waging an offensive and defensive war of words with Belgrade. He was continually threatening a referendum on independence.

By the middle of 2000 it seemed that Montenegro's future was very much in the balance. One more political or constitutional move by Djukanović and his supporters could mean either de facto Montenegrin independence, civil war, or the use of force by Belgrade to prevent Montenegro "slipping away." In any event it would cause another international crisis. The NATO powers sympathized with Djukanović and were giving him considerable financial aid. But, realizing the dangers and probably the unviability of Montenegrin independence, they would not support any overt move toward it. Helping Montenegro would pose military difficulties; such aid might well provoke Western disunity; and a new bombing campaign against Serbia would be hard to defend. Worst of all, the NATO powers would be blundering into a civil war.

Montenegro is quite different from Kosovo. Up to half its population, well over half in its northern part, supported Serbia against Djukanović and certainly rejected separation. This split reflected the traditional disunion in Montenegro between the westward-looking coastal regions and the eastward-looking hinterland. The whole country was proud of its historical independence, but not all were eager to return to it. The Yugoslav army, twenty thousand strong in Montenegro and with many Montenegrin soldiers in its ranks, could probably roll up overt opposition in a few days. In Serbia many citizens, including some who hated Milošević, would strongly resent Djukanović's "desertion." Many Serbs, too, had close family ties with Montenegro. For Serbia, Montenegro, tiny as it was, also had strategic and potential economic advantages. It had a coastline, which Serbia did not.

The real danger lay in Djukanović and his independence supporters growing nervous and impatient. By midyear 2000 Milošević seemed set on provoking him. An amendment to the federal Yugoslav constitution (see chapter 5) deliberately lowered Montenegro's status in relation to Serbia; in effect it made Montenegro a part of Serbia. Take it or leave it was the message. Then came the Serb uprising and the fall of Milošević. Would Djukanović now try to break away or wait to see what the new Serbia would offer? If he were wise, he would wait.

Before leaving Montenegro, though, it should be noted that it *could* play a key part in deciding Kosovo's future. Any successful declaration of Montenegrin independence would obviously mean the disintegration of rump

Yugoslavia. Thus, the state that had signed the June 1999 agreement with NATO ending the Kosovo conflict would no longer exist. Legally, therefore, the road to independence for Kosovo would be open.[34] On the other hand, if Montenegro remained inside Yugoslavia and Serbia were to democratize itself and become acceptable, pressure for the old idea of a loose federation of Serbia, Montenegro, and Albania would grow. Kosovars, therefore, wanted Montenegrin independence. But virtually nobody else did.

Russia's Balkan Role

Russia's role and prospects in the Balkans are worth closer examination. Four points need to be made.

First, Russia obviously missed a historic opportunity to gain leverage and prestige by helping to induce Milošević to accept peace when he did, virtually on Western terms. The timing was crucial. Another two weeks and the West's unity might well have been broken, NATO and the United States seriously discredited, Milošević reprieved, and Russian prestige elevated. One may assume that the Russians did not pass up this opportunity out of any sense of international responsibility or a compassionate urge to prevent further suffering. More likely, plain confusion prevailed in Moscow—too many cooks in the foreign policy kitchen.

Second, Russia's illusions of both influence and power were, in the end, painfully exposed. The bluff was impressive. The seizure of Priština airport in June 1999 was a real coup de théâtre (and it incidentally provoked serious differences in NATO's military high command). Then came the announcement that Russia was sending ten thousand troops to Kosovo, insisting that its troops have their own command structure and their own sector. However, the Russians then must have realized that they had bitten off too much. So came the quiet but obvious backing off. Then in October 2000 Moscow could not help Milošević in his ultimate moment of need. Russian diplomacy looked and sounded important but it could promise nothing and it achieved nothing.

Third, what now? The twentieth century has been unkind to Russian power in the Balkans. That power was at its peak in 1945, but in less than twenty years it suffered a series of unprecedented reversals. Now practically nothing is left. But the instinctive conviction remains—not confined to virulent nationalists—that Russia is being denied its birthright. After loudly espousing its cause, Serbia's defeat in Kosovo was an obvious humiliation, which was woundingly reflected in the decision by both Romania and

Bulgaria to deny Russian troop carriers airspace to get to Kosovo during one of Moscow's brushes with NATO in June 1999 after Serbia's defeat. This decision was aimed specifically *against* Russia and specifically *for* the United States, victor in the cold war and Balkan interloper.

Fourth, would Russia ever return? The West should not be too complacent about that unlikely possibility. Never say never! At the turn of the millennium, Russia, after all, did have troops in Bosnia and Kosovo. True, only a relatively few troops were in place, but they formed a presence. The real danger from Russia, however, could come if it deliberately began to play on national and ethnic fears; by stirring Macedonian and Bulgarian fears of "Islamic secession"; by insisting on national sovereignty at all costs; and by championing the Slavic-Orthodox cause against the Muslim "danger," which, as Chechnya showed, increasingly threatened Russia's own national sovereignty, too. In short, Russia could see itself as heading an anti-Muslim alliance of mutual self-interest—a new dimension to the Christian-Muslim confrontation! What the West cannot afford is to be, or seem to be, grossly insensitive to Balkan popular sensibilities. The West also must stand by its promises to reward and recompense those governments that stood by it over Kosovo. The Balkans are democratic now. Pro-Western governments can be turned out on an emotional issue. And at this juncture, new governments could be less friendly to the West and more friendly to Russia.

The Region and the Crisis

The Balkan countries briefly reviewed in this coverage of regional reaction to the Kosovo conflict are Albania, Macedonia, Hungary, Romania, Bosnia-Hercegovina, Croatia, Greece, Turkey, and Montenegro. Some of them border Kosovo; the others are near enough to have been seriously affected, or concerned, by the conflict there and in Serbia.[35]

Bosnia-Hercegovina was a tale of two Entities. Republika Srpska, "ethnically cleansed" and effectively Serb-controlled, was solid in support of Serbia. Kosovo, after all, meant as much to Bosnian Serbs as it did to all other Serbs. But this support could not be fully expressed because of the international presence. Also, many Bosnian Serbs, distrustful of Milošević since Dayton, identified with Kosovo, but not with him.

The Muslim-Croat Federation. The Federation was a totally different matter. In a rare show of unity, Muslims and Croats were pro-Kosovar and anti-Serb. Bosnian Muslims were ready to take increasing numbers of Kosovar refugees. They made little secret of their sympathy with the KLA, and also were proclaiming their solidarity with the Muslims of Sandjak in Serbia. And if the Serbs were allowed to defeat the Kosovars, then peace in Bosnia-Hercegovina could not be guaranteed. Dayton, they feared, would become a dead letter.

As for the Bosnian Croats, their view of the Kosovars, and Albanians in general, was one of contempt and distrust. But the enemy of their enemy was their friend—at least for now.

Croatia. "Remember Vukovar!" Other, older scores were there to settle too, but Vukovar seemed to symbolize everything. No Croat could forget it. It was only seven years since the Yugoslav army had totally destroyed Vukovar in East Slavonia, one of the most beautiful small cities in Europe. Vukovar was the symbol of all the horrors that the Serbs had inflicted. Now it was the Croats' turn. This stance put them fully on the side of NATO. The Croats had no tears to shed. Besides, it was another chance, after a longish period of disapproval, to get back into the West's good books again. Croatia's economy, especially its tourist industry, suffered. But its *Schadenfreude* burgeoned.

Montenegro. Montenegro took in many thousands of Kosovo refugees during the conflict, augmenting its own Albanian minority of about 80,000. It was the smallest country in the region, its population (about 600,000) only a third of Kosovo's original population, a fifth of Albania's. Most of its citizens, especially in the northern and eastern parts of the country, had instinctive pro-Serb sympathies and were instinctively anti-Albanian. In the western parts, the citizens understood the Kosovar desire to get out of Serbia, and they hoped that the Kosovar victory might mean their eventual success, too. But all Montenegrins resented their country being a target for Western bombing. Obviously, life and limb were the prime consideration, but many Montenegrins who were for independence did not like NATO, in effect, treating them like Serbs.

Albania. Albania's sympathy with the Kosovars' cause endured the costs, sacrifices, and dislocations caused by the war and the tidal wave of refugees. (Many refugees, however, especially those robbed by Albanian gangs, were less than enthusiastic about Albania's hospitality.) This burden weighed down on a country already devastated by misrule—communist and post-communist. But many Albanians saw a silver lining in the form of Western protection, support, and economic patronage. This silver lining soon faded but it could still, to some extent, become reality.

Macedonia. The nightmare became reality for Macedonia—for *all* of its citizens, if in different ways. For Macedonia's Albanians, anger and despair simmered over the fate of their ethnic kin in Kosovo. They cared for many more refugees than they were capable of handling, and they often were frustrated over how little they could do. The conflict brought these two branches of the Albanian family still closer, and Kosovars, perhaps unfairly, compared the succor they received in Macedonia favorably with what they received in Albania. The Macedonian government, however, was virtually overwhelmed by the reception and organizational problems presented by the refugees. This inadequacy, though, was not its biggest concern. What alarmed all Slavic Macedonians was what they publicly called the "ethnic balance" (see chapter 5); any permanent augmentation of the Albanian minority increased the threat to its own dominance. This possibility would lead not only to destabilization, but possibly to the destruction of Macedonia itself. The Skopje government therefore was not just unable, but also not too willing, to cope, and its attitude led to much adverse criticism in the Western media. The majority of the Slavic population, once strongly pro-American and pro-Western, now turned anti-NATO. The Macedonian economy and living standards also were hit by the blockade of Serbia. But fear of Albanians affected them most, and the West was seen as fully on the Albanian side.

Hungary. "Twelve days in NATO and we're already at war." This started as a rueful joke in Budapest, a bit of *Galgenhumor*. Most Hungarians initially backed the Orbán government's strong pro-NATO stand in the conflict. Hungary, after all, was a new boy on the NATO block, anxious to prove itself. The Hungarians also had a historic dislike of Serbs and a common revulsion at Serb behavior in Kosovo. But after a month into the conflict, alarm came to the fore, and support for NATO bombing turned into opposition. This change was reflected in the shifting position of the Socialist Party, which had supported the government's decision to make both Hungarian airspace and airfields available to NATO. Now, the Socialists wished to prevent NATO from using Hungarian airfields for air attacks on Serbia.

Hungarians were becoming more fearful of getting directly involved in the conflict.[36] Their fears were stoked by speculation in the West that Hungary might be suitable as a platform for a ground invasion of Serbia. Only a hundred miles from Belgrade across flat open terrain! Concern also was felt for the Hungarian minority of more than 300,000 people in Vojvodina, just over the border. They could become Milošević's hostages, possibly even victims of Serb ethnic cleansing and mass murder. This fear began to dominate Hungarian thinking and was a growing constraint on the government's freedom of action. Toward the end of April 1999, the government was flatly rejecting any notion that Hungary would be used as the launching pad for an invasion of Serbia. And that was that—NATO membership or not! Generally, though, the Orbán government stood firmly by NATO, especially when NATO discounted the launching-pad speculation.

Romania and Bulgaria. Two totally different neighboring countries! But they both bordered on Serbia, and their governments strongly supported NATO. This support mainly resulted from their "Western" aspirations. Both governments put their airspace and their airfields at NATO's disposal. But public opinion in both countries was largely against the war, and that opinion became more hostile to it as the weeks went by. Romanians and Bulgarians realized that this conflict was more serious than they had expected. And the more serious it got, the less they wanted to get involved. Irritation was felt in both countries over NATO's wanting to see them involved, but without giving any firm promise of NATO or EU membership. This lack of sensitivity by NATO also was seen in its not suspending the bombing of Serbia throughout the entire calendar of Orthodox Easter in 1999. Nor were Bulgarians amused when a stray NATO missile landed on a house in Sofia itself. In addition, the conflict was causing a severe economic squeeze. Both governments were getting worried, not just for now, but for when the next elections came along.

But deeper historical reasons were behind the public disquiet. Neither nation liked the Serbs, but they—especially the Bulgarians—liked Albanians less. More than simply foreign, the Albanians were Muslim. Not only had the Albanians not suffered under the Turkish yoke, but they were part of it. They were generally despised, and feared too. The Serbs, after all, were Orthodox Christians like themselves, who also had been oppressed by the Turks.[37] Both countries, too, had long-standing ethnic problems of their own, which they wanted to solve *their* way. They strongly opposed the notion that a country's sovereignty and integrity could be violated. What neither country wanted was outside interference, whatever the reason and from whatever source. Therefore, however much they might abhor the Serbs' methods, they understood their predicament.

Many Bulgarians and Romanians, along with many Macedonians, were also highly suspicious of NATO's motives, refusing to believe that the attack on Serbia had anything to do with "morality." Instead, they saw it as a way to consolidate American supremacy in the Balkans and to humiliate Russia further. The suspicions, often amounting to paranoia, were such that some Bulgarians and Romanians were persuaded that the bombing of the Chinese embassy in Belgrade was deliberate, aimed at "testing China's patience" (see also chapters 6 and 9).

Greece and Turkey. Two enemies within the same NATO alliance; two nations having intimate links with the Balkans, on the edge of the region but now being drawn back into it; two countries that see Balkan problems through the prism of their relations with each other. Their contrasting approaches to Kosovo came as no surprise. Greeks and Serbs always had had close links. They both had successfully fought Turkish domination, and they shared the Orthodox religion. In the early 1990s, Milošević's links with Athens were considered excellent. More recently, though, the Simitis government had been trying to reorient Greek policy westward. It supported the NATO action against Serbia, but only with serious and obvious misgivings. The Greek population, egged on by their Orthodox clergy, were strongly pro-Serb and anti-Albanian. At least 300,000 Albanians, and probably many more, were living legally or illegally in Greece. They reduced Greek wages and increased crime. They were not *Untermenschen* in the same way that Serbs saw them, but they clearly belonged to a lower order of civilization.

Some Greeks, too, were worried about their own Greek Muslims (Turks) in Thrace. Finally, the instinctive anti-Americanism of many Greeks, symbolized so stridently by the late Andreas Papandreou, caught fire again. The war against Serbia was yet another case of "American interference." This interference, it was alleged, had begun in 1947, saving the rightists and royalists and then propping them up for two decades. Then came the military coup in 1967, obviously American-inspired, according to many Greeks. Seven years later came the Cyprus debacle, with American "connivance."

Turkey's line was almost diametrically the opposite. It had close relations with Tirana, strongly supported the Kosovars, and was urging its fellow NATO members to even stronger measures against Serbia. Turks generally regarded Albanians, if not as brothers, then as coreligionist cousins. The remarkable showing of the nationalist forces in the Turkish general elections of April 1999, together with continuing support for the overtly Muslim political grouping in Turkey, were likely to further harden the Turkish attitude on Kosovo. Some early speculation posited that the Turkish government, perhaps embarrassed over the Kurdish question and seeing its similarities with the "Kosovar question," might keep a low profile. But such analysis and self-questioning were limited. Ethnic, religious, and historical ties put the Turks firmly behind the Kosovars. This support is likely to continue. For example, Ankara is expected to support independence for Kosovo. Indeed, many Turks would have braved straining relations with the European Union to delay or even jeopardize Turkey's chances of joining, rather than desert their "historic brethren."[38]

Well into 1999 it seemed, therefore, that Greece and Turkey would continue to be potential belligerents—belligerents everywhere, including the Balkans. Then came the earthquakes both countries suffered in the summer of 1999 and the humanitarianism they both showed in helping each other. The skeptics (including myself) thought that this was just a temporary interval in the continuum of enmity. But the interval extended and the hope was that it would now be the beginning of a *new* continuum, one of cooperation if not of harmony.[39]

January 2000 saw the first official visit of a Greek foreign diplomat to Turkey since 1962. The personal rapport was good, and the good intentions, backed by a series of confidence-building measures, were clear. (And this was only four years after the two countries almost came to blows over a wretched, rocky, deserted island off the Turkish coastline.) The new initiative was mainly that of Greece, the latest in a number of courageous efforts by the Simitis government to improve its relations with the West by improving its relations with its neighbors. This initiative not only supported NATO over Kosovo in the face of massive domestic opposition, it improved relations with both Albania and Macedonia. Then came Greek support for Turkish entry into the European Union. It was a sea change from the xenophobic populism of Andreas Papandreou, with every step of it dogged by domestic nationalist uproar.

Such efforts were not made, of course, without wider motives. Greece, an EU member since 1981, now keenly wanted to join the European Monetary Union, to join the Euro, by 2001. Keeping on the right side of both Brussels and Washington would do no harm. Turkey responded. At last seeing some prospect of eventual European acceptance, it agreed with Greece to refer territorial disputes to the International Court of Justice at The Hague.

But serious disputes still remained, the most serious of which was Cyprus. A dispute could also develop over the question of Kosovo's independence. Jealousies and suspicions sometimes burst out. But the venom had, for the moment, been extracted from mutual relations and hopes arose that the distorted prism through which each had viewed developments in the Balkans would be corrected.

The Economic Costs and Needs

Finally, a note should be added on the economic costs of the Kosovo conflict to the South East European region. Such a note may seem anticlimactic after the derring-do analyzed in the previous pages, but the region's economic present, and its economic prospects, could be at least as important as any other factor in determining its future.[40]

The costs can be placed in three main categories:

1. *Foreign trade in goods and services.* Only Macedonia and Republika Srpska in Bosnia-Hercegovina did much direct trade with Yugoslavia (Serbia and Montenegro). But for Macedonia and Bulgaria, Serbia was part of the direct transit route to important trade partners in Central Europe. The difficulties along this route were now magnified by the destruction of bridges on the Danube. This damage seriously affected Romania as well. Added to the UN trade embargo against Yugoslavia, such destruction brought freight transit virtually to a halt. The tourist trade also was hit. Croatia was the main victim here; its tourist industry was only just recovering from the war in the early 1990s.

2. *Investment losses.* Direct foreign investment was seriously damaged. Credit also became more expensive. These increased credit costs and drying up of foreign investment particularly jeopardized the hopes of Croatia, Romania, and Bulgaria to get financing for their privatization projects.

3. *Extra direct budget costs.* These costs went for internal and external security and for refugees. Macedonia and Albania were by far the most seriously affected countries.

Such damage would have come as a serious jolt to better-managed and prosperous economies. But here it affected small countries that had recently emerged fully independent and were suffering from economic disasters inherited or self-inflicted since independence. Take, for example, the war in Croatia, the war in Bosnia and Hercegovina, the Albanian Pyramid crisis, or the Bulgarian financial crisis. Or take high unemployment throughout the region, the severe balance of payments situation, and the budget deficits. Virtually every country needed substantial help, and since Western pressure had helped keep the Balkan governments in line, those countries now expected the West to deliver.

A World Bank official with responsibilities for South Eastern Europe asserted in early July 1999 that the economic losses in Kosovo caused by the war must not be separated from those of the neighboring countries. An overall concept needed to be worked out, which was explicit in the West's Stability Pact for the Balkans agreed in 1999. Western officials estimated that over the course of 1999, the average economic growth loss for Albania, Bulgaria, Romania, Macedonia, Bosnia-Hercegovina, and Croatia would be between 3 and 4 percent. The overall balance of payments loss would be about $1 billion, which the countries affected could cover only partly by their own efforts. External help amounting to about $450 million would be needed.[41]

The European Union's Stability Pact, just referred to, is astonishing in its comprehensiveness, covering subjects from educational training to agriculture to industry. The basic aim is to create the necessary infrastructure throughout the region in order to facilitate lasting economic progress. Albania, for example, by far the most impoverished country, is planned to have a thoroughly modern road and railroad system by about 2015 or 2200. If ever a vision has been well conceived, this Stability Plan has! But the money—colossal sums—must be found, not just promised, and it must be administered honestly. The political will must be sustained and the region must be kept free of serious conflict.

Most important of all, the Stability Pact must be seen by the beneficiaries in the Balkans as enabling them to get on their own feet, to stay on them, and to move forward. One basic principle must be accepted: largess is no good. It hurts, not helps. It will solidify dependency culture and perpetuate crony-mafia economies. It will do nothing to foster the market economies that the region needs. Of vital importance to the region are help in creating small businesses and an environment that encourages foreign and internal private investment, one that frees the entrepreneurial skills which these nations, often to their surprise, have discovered they have in abundance. If the West directs and regulates its economic support in this way, it might establish the firmest platform for prosperity and peace that the Balkans could have.

8

Key Minorities and Key Questions

Eastern europe still abounds in minorities. Despite genocide, ethnic cleansing, massacres, assimilation, integration, submergence, or creeping extinction, the ethnic mix remains one of the region's most fascinating and saddest features.[1] But some of its historically large minorities did not survive the destructive rigors of the twentieth century. The Jews, the Germans, and the Ukrainians largely disappeared—the Jews in the Holocaust, the Germans and Ukrainians largely through map-changing, resettlement, and ethnic cleansing during or after World War II. Their removal has left Eastern Europe as a whole with three key minorities—key in the sense that they could seriously affect local, national, and international relations during the new century.[2] (The Albanians are more an emerging new nation than a minority; see chapter 7.) These key minorities are the Hungarians (Magyars), the Bulgarian Turks, and the Roma (Gypsies).

Vanished Supremacies

The Hungarian and Turkish minorities are the remnants of vanished imperial supremacies, recalling an epoch when Hungary and Turkey were dominant in large parts of Eastern Europe. By the end of the twentieth century, there were about 1.7 million Hungarians in Romania, 580,000 in Slovakia, 160,000 in Ukraine, and probably more than 300,000 in former Yugoslavia, most of them in the Serb province of Vojvodina.[3] The Hungarian irredentism of the interwar years, the deceptive quiet of the communist period, and then the nationalist exuberance of the immediate post-1989 period have been discussed. But a period of calm descended from 1994 through 1998 during the Socialist government's period of power in Budapest. Irredentism, and the nationalism that encompassed it, became negligible in Hungarian politics, a favorite election gambit perhaps, nostalgic and emotional, but discarded as an instrument of government policy. Several reasons can be cited for this change.

1. Hungary had largely learned the lesson of the twentieth century. Its period of "greatness," of being a major power, was over. It learned the hard way; the sudden shock of loss took many years and lives to get used to. (See also chapter 5.)

2. With irredentism largely banished, and a foreign sovereignty recognized over those "lost" Hungarians, then interest in them, however solicitous, was bound to become indirect or indistinct.

3. As the consumer/materialist ethos advanced, some Hungarians became less anxious to regain their lost brethren.

4. The corrective impact of "Europe." The prospect of joining, or rejoining, Europe has undoubtedly affected Hungary's international behavior. Both the EU and NATO were firmly against border revisions and anything held to be international incitement. Western associations and their accruing benefits have taken precedence over any slender hopes of "righting the wrongs of history."

5. Hungary was also readier than ever for regional as well as international cooperation. The Socialist government under Gyula Horn soon indicated that it would drop the issue of militance over the minorities that had characterized its predecessor. Its reward was a growing international reputation, promises of further foreign investment, and the prospect of a rising standard of living.

After the FIDESZ victory at the Hungarian parliamentary elections in May 1998, many were asking whether this moderation would continue. FIDESZ was in a governmental alliance with the Smallholders Party and the Hungarian Democratic Forum. The reappearance of István Csurka and his followers in parliament (many of whom, like their leader, were still unashamedly irredentist) and some of the nationalist promises made by Viktor Orbán himself cast some doubt on this question. Orbán is reported saying after his election that he wanted changes made in the bilateral state treaty that Hungary had signed with Romania in 1985 (see below), although he ruled out demands for any territorial changes.[4] This possibility raised fears, even among moderates in Bucharest; among the Romanian right it seemed a heaven-sent opportunity to revive the feud with Hungary—as well as their own political fortunes. It also threatened to revive agitation among the Hungarian minority itself in Romania. Orbán was intelligent enough to know what was at stake here—domestically, regionally, and internationally. In the event, he showed himself keen to be solicitous about the Hungarians abroad, but diplomatic enough not to offend their governments by actually being so. One of his imminently most serious problems is likely to be with Brussels, not with these neighboring governments. When Hungary joined the EU, it became technically obliged to obey the Schengen agreement, necessitating visas for members of the Hungarian minorities to enter Hungary. (For Poland's similar problem, see chapter 9.) It is vital that Hungary get an exception here if the concept of a Magyar nationality is not to be weakened.

The treatment of Hungarian minorities in the neighboring countries has varied in terms of both intent and circumstances. In Ukraine during the Soviet era, the situation was grim, but it was only slightly less grim for everybody else. Since Ukrainian independence, the Hungarian minority (like the Polish minority) has largely had the existence of the huge Russian minority to thank for the relative liberalism with which it has been treated. The need to appease the nearly 12 million Ukrainian Russians led the new government in Kiev to grant them concessions, which it could not then refuse to the other, smaller minorities. Many Hungarians in former Yugoslavia, in Vojvodina, and especially in East Slovenia, generously treated under Tito, had nightmarish experiences during the wars and the ethnic cleansing of the early 1990s, and it will take many years of peace and international pressure before they regain even a part of the stability and prosperity that they once enjoyed. (The Hungarian population in Vojvodina declined from about 400,000 to about 300,000 during the wars in former Yugoslavia. Apart from refugees fleeing destruction, many young men had gone to Hungary or elsewhere to avoid conscription into the Yugoslav [Serbian] army.)

But Romania and Slovakia have been the site where the future of Hungarians as minorities has been tested (see also chapter 2). In Romania after 1989, not so much a policy as a set of attitudes—negative, defensive, opportunistic, and provincial—was shown toward the Hungarian minority. True, the widespread conflict and serious violence expected by many observers did not occur, but tension and some violence persisted in mixed ethnic districts. Most dangerous of all was the undue influence that ultranationalist political groupings came to have on Romania's postcommunist governments under the aegis of President Iliescu. The support of these groupings kept the postcommunists in power. They helped destroy Iliescu's own reputation for ethnic tolerance, seriously compromised Romania's international reputation, and prevented any real improvement in the status of the Hungarian minority and in relations between Bucharest and Budapest.

The democratic election victory of 1996, however, altered the situation. The new Romanian president and the government owed nothing to the retreating ultranationalists and were ready to turn a new page in minority relations. The government in Budapest and some (though not all) of the Hungarian minority's own leaders responded favorably. Its political representatives in the Romanian parliament not only supported the new government but accepted a ministerial post in it for one of their own. Serious difficulties over higher educational facilities for Hungarians, in the Hungarian language, still remained, and the government split into "liberal" and "conservative" factions on minority issues. But an important step forward had been taken in ethnic relations in Romania. It remained to be seen whether any new government in Romania would slow or halt the progress made. The promise of Europe—close in Hungary's case, more distant in Romania's—should, however, help to make that step irreversible.[5] So should the changing attitude of the Hungarian minority as a whole. That minority officially accepted the fact that reunion with Hungary was now out of the question, and it rejected the irresponsibility of its own ultranationalists and of those in Hungary itself. If many of the minority's kinsmen in Hungary were becoming resigned to losing them, many also were becoming resigned to being lost.

But few Hungarians would ever become resigned to losing their Hungarian ethnic and cultural identity. And in this unnegotiable resolve, they realized that their own language must be preserved and fostered, not only in the home but also in public and in their own schools. The struggles of the Hungarian minority in both Romania and Slovakia for the preservation of its language, though differing in details, were essentially the same. For much of the communist period, the struggle had seemed to be lost. After 1989, with atavistic nationalism threatening to take hold everywhere, minority causes seemed at first to be in mortal danger. Then came "Europe"—which created the desire to get in and the need to avoid giving excuses for being kept out. Thus, minority rights were saved. And as the behavior of the majority nations became less antagonistic, the minorities became more realistic.

The long march to a modus vivendi had begun. But many obstacles had to be confronted along the way. On language and education, the Hungarian minorities had to stand particularly firm. Increasing minority demands were now heard for establishing a Hungarian university in Transylvania (to replace the old one in Cluj that virtually disappeared in the late 1950s). The Romanian government, ostensibly on legal grounds, opposed this move. In 1999, momentum gathered to found a multilingual institution in Transylvania—the "Petöfi-Schiller" University. This was becoming an important issue. It also could affect relations between Budapest and Bucharest. What many Romanians feared was that any such new university would become a hotbed of Hungarian nationalism, reviving the waning militancy of the Hungarian majority at large. (The University of Priština in Kosovo was a disturbing warning.) This issue was indeed one obstacle that would have to be negotiated because it could hardly be avoided. If it could be negotiated successfully, the modus vivendi would be in sight.

In Slovakia, premier Mečiár had been an experienced Magyar-baiter. He had also been beholden to the Slovak National Party for political support in the same way that Iliescu had been indebted to the Romanian ultranationalists. Ethnic relations suffered, and Slovakia's exclusion from early consideration by NATO and the EU could partly be explained by this discord. But the firm line from Brussels seemed only to steer Mečiár to more vindictiveness. Most leaders of the Hungarian minority's political groupings, partly because they had no alternative, reacted with restraint to the Slovak government's demagogy. What minority leaders hoped for was a change of government, as had occurred in Romania, and a fresh start. Like their counterparts in Romania, they too had become resigned to the reality of their citizenship and their minority status. They wanted Slovakia to get into "Europe" quickly. A Europeanized Slovakia was now their main hope for improvement and their best chance of remaining Hungarian.

After the elections of September 1998 and the ousting of Mečiár, minority leaders' wishes seemed much closer to fulfillment. And, as an earnest of its good intentions, the new Slovak government expressed its willingness to help rebuild the Marie-Valerie bridge (destroyed in 1944) across the Danube, connecting Esztergom on the Hungarian side of the border with Štúrovo on the Slovak side. For many Slovaks, this bridge had symbolized Hungarian historical domination. After 1989, Mečiár and the Slovak nationalists also objected to rebuilding it because it would link Slovakia's Hungarian minority with their brethren in Hungary itself. In 1998 the intentions of both sides seemed more reasonable, and some trust was returning. But then Mečiár bounced back and tried to strengthen his followers by raising national hackles over a relatively liberal minority language bill. If he could be kept out of power, then reasonableness could prevail on the minority issue.

The Bulgarian Turks

For well over a century, no national minorities were legally recognized in Bulgaria. Nor in Greece or Turkey, for that matter. Nonethnic Bulgarians, along with ethnic Bulgarians, were all considered as members of the Bulgarian political nation.

The Bulgarian refusal to entertain the notion of minorities began to waver during 1997 when it signed the Council of Europe's Framework Convention for the Protection of National Minorities. This wavering occurred amid some domestic intellectual pressure in Sofia for full minority recognition for Bulgaria's Turkish population. It seemed only a matter of time before recognition was officially granted.

Just how many Turkish Bulgarians there were at the end of the twentieth century was not known. Up to 1984, when the Zhivkov communist regime began its forced assimilation campaign (see chapter 2), more than 800,000 Turks were officially counted, about one-tenth of the total population. According to the Turkish government, Bulgarization set off a migration to Turkey of more than 322,000 Bulgarian Turks. After the fall of Zhivkov, nearly 100,000 returned to Bulgaria. But then, from 1989 to 1996, nearly 250,000 Bulgarian Turks applied for visas to enter Turkey; of these, more than 86,000 were allowed entry on the grounds of reuniting with their families.[6]

These figures helped to confirm two salient facts about the Turkish minority. (1) It has declined considerably over the last fifteen years, and because of emigration to Turkey, it will probably continue to do so, despite its traditionally high birth rate. (2) The Bulgarian Turks are now probably less numerous than the Bulgarian Roma. Many Bulgarian Turks still want to leave for Turkey despite the unfavorable conditions there. Their economic situation in Bulgaria has generally deteriorated since 1989. Tobacco cultivation, always a major export earner, has been seriously hit by falling prices, and some Turks (like ethnic Bulgarians) have been deprived of their land through laws restoring it to precommunist owners.

Still, writing in 1995 about Bulgarian Turkish grievances, the *Economist* concluded on an optimistic note: "But few now believe they will suffer the fate of other afflicted Balkan minorities. 'The situation will never explode here as it did in Bosnia,' claims Yunal Lutfi, the vice-president of the ethnic Turkish party in parliament, 'because Bulgarians and Turks are not extreme nationalist or fanatics. They have a tradition of peaceful coexistence.' Fingers crossed."[7]

Fingers crossed, indeed! Complacency should not creep into the West's view of ethnic relations in Bulgaria. The former president of Bulgaria, Zhelu Zhelev, saw dangers of a "Bosnia in Bulgaria" unless the communist Bulgarization campaign had not been stopped.[8] And, "the vice-president of the ethnic Turkish party in parliament," quoted by the *Economist,* might not be the most authoritative spokesman for Bulgarian Turks at the ground-floor level. Many Bulgarian Turks regard their representatives as having been caught up in the cushy life in Sofia. (Many Macedonian Albanians regard their representatives in Skopje the same way.)

A potential for danger exists here, destabilizing not only for Bulgaria, but for the entire southern Balkans, including Turkey and therefore Greece. The Bulgarian state can ill afford a prolonged period of tension with its Turkish minority, especially if that minority were supported, however indirectly, by Turkey. For many years now in Bulgaria—in both communist and postcommunist periods—fears have mounted of Turkey performing an "Anschluss" (the word is sometimes used) or a "Cyprus" on parts of Bulgaria. The fear, of course, is rekindled regularly for nefarious political motives. But it could not be rekindled if the kindling were not there.

Four things would help to permanently improve the Bulgarian minority's relations with its Turkish minority.

1. Successive Bulgarian governments must convince the Turkish minority that the government is sympathetically and boldly aware of the minority's aspirations and problems.
2. The minority itself must not question the Bulgarian state framework.
3. The United States and especially Western Europe must begin to realize that Bulgaria is as frail as it is strategically important; it must (conditionally) be given the necessary economic, political, and psychological support.
4. Turkey would not go beyond a role of non-interfering concern with regard to the Turkish minority. Internal Turkish developments and the course of bilateral relations between Ankara and Sofia will have a

profound effect, and these relations were improving.[9] They would be seriously tested, however, if Turkey became either more nationalistic or more Islamic, and Turkey was showing some signs of moving in both those directions.

What was needed was the arrival of both sides at a stable point where one serious incident would not endanger whatever progress had been made. That point of stability was still some way off.

Roma Awakening

Are the Roma basically irrelevant? Or are they just a local problem? At one time perhaps, they were both. But today they are neither. Just as the Albanians are emerging, the Roma are awakening. They are pressingly relevant and have become a regional problem throughout Eastern Europe. They have contributed to their being considered a problem, but they have not caused it. Others have placed the blame on them. The Roma have become Eastern Europe's new big hate object. They bring out the worst in nations as different as the Czech and the Romanian. Two Czech cities in 1998 wanted to ghettoize the Roma. In May 1999 the Czech cabinet was trying to prevent a wall from being built in one city to segregate Roma from Czechs. Minor pogroms, both orchestrated and impromptu, occur regularly throughout the region. The Roma's most protected period took place under communism. Freedom has not healed their wounds; it has only rubbed salt in them.

Some of the reasons for this situation are complex; others are simple. One of the simplest is the sheer proliferation of the Roma during the past forty years. Another is the increasing misery and uncertainty of some East Europeans in the past decade. For those penalized rather than benefited by market democracy, the craving for scapegoats has intensified. The Roma perfectly fill the bill. But their own situation also has markedly declined, not only in terms of their security, but of their economic hardships, too.[10]

It is impossible to even approximate the numbers of Roma today. The estimates in table 2 are probably less unreliable than most, although many analysts might contend that they are too low.

The decline of the old Gypsy traders and crafts has been mentioned. But since the fall of communism, Roma unemployment has increased alarmingly. In Bulgaria it has reached 60–70 percent. In some Bulgarian villages, and in towns where the Roma population is compact, it has reached 80–90

Table 2. Estimated Numbers of Roma in Eastern Europe

Albania	65,000
Bulgaria	800,000
Czech Republic	300,000
Slovakia	500,000
Hungary	600,000
Poland	20,000
Romania	1,800,000
Former Yugoslavia (Macedonia, Serbia, Montenegro, Croatia, Bosnia-Hercegovina, Slovenia)	1,000,000

Sources: Thomas S. Szayna, *Ethnic Conflict in Central Europe and the Balkans* (Santa Monica, Calif., RAND, 1994), 20. Szayna, as he says, extensively used the article by Andre Liebich, "Minorities in Eastern Europe: Obstacles to a Reliable Count," *RFE/RL Research Report*, May 15, 1992; *Economist*, March 20 and September 11, 1999. I also have consulted official and expert East European sources.

percent of the ablebodied population. (The average unemployment figure for Bulgaria as a whole is about 20 percent.) Unemployment relief is available, but in South Eastern Europe especially, it is not distributed fairly, regularly, or efficiently to the Roma. Much rural unemployment for Roma throughout Eastern Europe stems from dissolution of the collective farms. Some of this former collectively owned property has been restored to its former private owners or their families. No Roma are among the claimants because before the communists seized power, virtually none of them owned land. But restitution has only aggravated their condition. Many Roma had built cottages on their sections of the collectives, and some of them derived a livable income from their private plots. Now these have gone, too.

Rural destitution has led to migration into towns and cities. There, Roma ghettos have developed, often with shocking health and housing conditions. Child health and child education cause particular concern to the many responsible members of the Roma community and to non-Roma who take up their cause. One of these non-Roma is Dr. Antonina Zhelyazkova, a brave and learned woman at the University of Sofia. Her view of the situation of Roma children in Bulgaria is grim.

More and more Gypsy children no longer go to school for the simple reason that they lack clothes, they lack shoes, their parents do not have enough money to buy textbooks. The state can cover the textbook expenses for the first four or five years, but after primary school they [the children] just abandon school because their parents have no money to secure other things for them. About 60 percent of the Gypsy children have ceased attending school, and this means illiteracy, this means future criminality and future offenses. . . . Abandoned children also come from Gypsies who are unemployed. I do not wish to make my speech emotional; I am not going to dwell on the sufferings of the children themselves. But from a purely sociological point of view this is among the most complicated problems that have to be solved urgently because these . . . children are the potential source for future . . . criminal offenders.[11]

Against the background of this somber Bulgarian picture, it is encouraging to note that a National Program for the Roma People was announced in Sofia in March 1999. Aimed at improving the life and the status of the Romany people in Bulgaria, it was drafted by the country's Roma organizations. The program was scheduled to last ten years. It is a brave gesture that needs success.

Crime among the Roma already is high enough for everyone to be concerned. But unless the obvious causes of this crime are tackled, it will swirl totally out of control, as will the prejudices against Roma everywhere. As it is, these prejudices are being whipped up by sensationalist reports in the East European media and by demagogic politicians out to make easy capital of a profound ethnic and social dilemma.

Roma crime easily gets mixed up by the public at large with "foreigners' crime"; it is all part of the syndrome of the "other." No doubt the serious and petty crime committed by foreigners, transient or resident, has increased enormously throughout Eastern (and Western) Europe in the 1990s and will continue mounting in the new century. But, again, the reality is much less dramatic than impressions of it. True reality, however, will never be accepted as long as public figures and private interests can gain from spurning it. A speech in February 1998 by the then-premier of Hungary, Gyula Horn, obviously with the approaching general election in mind, illustrates this point. Horn, speaking after the murder of one of the nation's most prominent businessmen, flatly declared that 80 percent of the murders and robberies in Hungary were committed by foreigners. The most recent figures at that time actually showed that the ratio was 3–4 percent. The usual "clarifications" followed, but the damage was done.[12]

The real point was that many Hungarians wanted to believe Horn's lies. Such lies justified their concerns, identified a target, and rationalized their prejudices. True, the Roma were not exactly the target that Horn had in mind. But what did that matter? All Roma were the "other."

The social and political consequences of the situation are potentially critical. The only solution for the Roma is their slow but steady integration into the societies, politics, and economies of the lands where they live. Culturally, they can never be integrated. Why should they be? Their culture ensures their own survival and could enrich the societies in which they live. But in every other respect, the need for integration is urgent. Yet nowhere can the economic means or the political will be found.

A well-known case in Hungary in 1997–98 illustrates this point. In a house in Székesféhervár in western Hungary, thirteen Roma families lived cheek by jowl.[13] The town council was authorized to move them into more suitable quarters, but wanted to house them provisionally in newly constructed "containers." This led to demonstrations by human rights activists, many from Budapest, including well-known cultural personalities. The minister of the interior himself then stepped in and ordered the move stopped. The town council put the equivalent of about U.S. $150,000 for the Roma to buy houses. It was enough for decent rural houses in villages. But no villages would have them, or, at best, only three of the thirteen families could be housed. The others were forced by various violent means to get off the property they had legitimately bought. They then had to move into a Red Cross hostel.

A familiar type of story, although this one occurred in a relatively prosperous community in which by no means did all the non-Roma behave badly. In most other towns throughout Eastern Europe, much worse could have happened. But—all the more so because it did happen in relatively enlightened Székesfehérvár—this story throws light on four depressing facts about East European attitudes to the Roma:

1. Most East Europeans disapprove of affirmative action (or extra social welfare) to help them. Taxes, they say, should not be "squandered" on Roma! As one commentator ruefully put it, no one feels responsible for, or guilty about, the fate of the Roma.[14]

2. East Europeans oppose integration, at least on the scale necessary.

3. They turn a blind eye to discrimination against Roma and intimidation of them.

4. They regard white as the only acceptable skin color. Racism is the nub of the problem. One Slovak, echoing a common *tu quoque* defense, stated succinctly: "In the West you have your blacks, we have our Gypsies." By no means was this the first time that such things had been said.

What all of these attitudes and actions mean is that more and more Roma will attempt to migrate to Western countries, where they will face increasing problems and prejudice. Those who stay put will become, not integrated, but increasingly excluded. Their ghettos will become virtual no-go areas for the central authorities. The Roma will take what is available in terms of material handouts, but they will give nothing back—certainly not loyalty.

On a continental basis, or even a regional basis, the Roma remain almost as disunited as they ever were. But in smaller, local areas, they are showing some signs of cohesion and political awareness. Leaders are emerging, too, educated, forceful, and aware of the Roma's potential power. Most of them still want integration; they realize that in ghettos, only one-way streets can be traveled. They realize, too, that violent confrontation can be the only consequence of a proliferation of "Romistans" born of an apartheid policy. But even the best-willed among them will get impatient if no good will is shown toward them or their efforts. The Roma are no longer irrelevant. They have become realities in local and even general elections—in international relations, too. But the preoccupation of governments still centers not on what can be done *for* them, but what can be done *about* them. This approach usually means, in truth, what can be done *against* them. If that attitude does not change, the Roma will become Europe's unsolvable problem.

This discussion of the Roma ends with a comment I made at a conference in Sofia in 1997:

Most minority issues have never lacked attention. What they have lacked is solution. The Roma issue has lacked both. Hence, it was both refreshing and disturbing at this conference to hear the remarks of the Roma mayor of a predominantly Roma section of the town of Stara Zagora, in central Bulgaria. What emerged forcefully from his remarks was precisely the opposite of the Roma stereotype in the minds and prejudices of almost all East and West Europeans: that the Roma are unassimilable, anti-social, irresponsible and incorrigibly individualistic. Many Roma in Bulgaria *do* see themselves as Bulgarian: they *do* want education, jobs and decent housing. But they feel they come at the bottom of the list in everything and are ill-equipped to get any higher. Out of over 20,000 Roma in Stara Zagora there is one college graduate. Time is running out, in Bulgaria, in the Balkans, in the whole of Eastern Europe. This is not the *message* from Stara Zagora: it is the *lesson* of Stara Zagora.[15]

Key Questions

The big question about minorities concerns their collective status. In this context, it is worth recalling that the Romanian and Slovak governments added riders to their state treaties with Hungary in 1995 disabusing all and sundry of the notion that these treaties implied any suggestion of collective status for their Hungarian minorities (see chapter 5).

These two riders reflected the growing controversy about the status of minorities, not only in Eastern Europe, but throughout Europe, and even worldwide. The Council of Europe's Recommendation 1201, para. 11, part of a Framework Convention on National Minorities, adopted in November 1994, states: "In the region where they are a majority, persons belonging to national minorities have the right to dispose of local authorities and auton-omy to enjoy a special status in conformity with the specific historical and territorial situation and with the internal legislation of the state."[16] This is Council of Europe fudge, an imprecise recommendation that gives any dissenting central government the opportunity of opting out, which is what the Romanians and the Slovaks did. But, however imprecise, Recommenda-tion 1201 could become a landmark in the history of ethnic relations. It did not introduce the notion of collective rights for minorities, but it made that goal a plank in the programmatic platform of a West European institution and a policy guide for both the EU and NATO.

Most majoritarian nations take the unitary approach on minority ques-tions. They insist that individual rights, nondiscrimination, and equality before the law are the best principles for the governance of multiethnic states. The whole concept of citizenship in most Western countries is based on these principles. Majoritarian nations consider that collective rights for minorities would create not only divisive tensions, even secession, but would encourage minority disloyalty. Many members of the larger minor-ities, however, now see collective or group rights as the only means of preserving their own language and culture, and therefore their distinctive identity. It is no good arguing, they insist, that the civic, universalist principle means no discrimination if, as is inevitable, its implementation is mainly in the hands of the majoritarian nation. Majority implementation, in effect, ensures discrimination at every level. The eventual solution to ethnic relations, these minority members argue, is to recognize ethnic differences and to legislate on that basis. That means collective rights—at least for the minorities that constitute a certain proportion of the population. Equality in law need not mean equality in fact. In practice, it often can mean the opposite.

An immense volume of literature (and heat) has been generated over collective rights, and it gets to the heart of our understanding of what citizenship, law, and statehood are. One thing is certain, though: for the Hungarian minorities in Romania and Slovakia, collective rights are a legitimate aspiration, and, as closer association with Europe progresses, this aspiration will force itself onto the agenda.[17] More important, the closer the association with Europe, the less dangerous the aspiration will seem to majoritarian nations and the better its chance of being accepted.

Collective status cannot be introduced all at once. It should be realized as a culmination rather than as a full introduction. In this context, proposals made by the Democratic Federation of Hungarians in Romania as early as 1993 are worth noting. They set out three principles for achieving "inner self-determination": (1) personal autonomy, (2) local autonomy, (3) the acceptance of regional autonomy. These goals could mean a slow process, but if progress were steady, it could effectively blunt the thrust of opposition.[18]

In the meantime, Tibor Várady, a man of experience and insight, has provided some useful general lessons on how minorities can be best protected.[19] His syllabus can be summarized as follows:

1. Popular attitudes can be influenced by law. In relatively stable societies, laws can do much, if not to promote ethnic harmony, then to deter the manifestations of racial tension.
2. Popular attitudes also tend to reflect the level of political culture in the society concerned. The higher it is, the less the tension.
3. Provisions for the protection of minorities should be embedded in the state constitution and not solely be contained in its laws, which can fairly easily be reversed or modified.
4. Minority rights should be spelled out as specifically as possible, not left in general terms for the interpretation of local officials (often of the majoritarian nation).

5. With all laws relating to minorities, the guiding principle must be that they exist to *neutralize* rather than *reflect* changes in the status of any territory or nation.

Várady then imparts a general piece of wisdom:

> Racial problems need racial-conscious remedies and minority problems need minority-conscious remedies. The principle of equality of individuals is a most important precondition to viable solutions; but without recognizing race as an effectively existing added dimension, one cannot deal successfully with racial problems, and the same applies to the problem of ethnic minorities.[20]

Finally, Várady quotes the late Justice Harry A. Blackmun of the U.S. Supreme Court: "In order to get beyond racism, we must first take account of race. There is no other way. . . ."[21] The wisdom of Blackmun's words needs to be taken into account in Eastern Europe.

9

Looking Outward and Inward

FACE WEST AND KEEP GOING! After more than forty years of Russian communist domination, it was not surprising that most East Europeans saw their new international relations in simple terms. True, the Poles were a little slow in realizing how much the Germans had changed, and the Bulgarian postcommunists still felt the tug of Russia and the lost cause. But the new orientation was well-nigh universal, and many East Europeans, even some of the more sophisticated, thought it would be simple: the West would welcome them with open arms and open hearts; rejoining Europe would be as easy as rejecting Russia.

Now, in the perspective of more than a decade since 1989, those hopes seem touchingly naive. The East Europeans grossly overestimated the West's sense of purpose, its unity, and its material and spiritual generosity. They also underestimated the West's genuine difficulties in changing a habit of mind predicated on international confrontation and in redirecting it to shape a new European policy. They also overlooked issues like their own fitness or readiness to be taken back into the European fold. The recovery of their freedom, they thought, was all that they needed, the only passport necessary.

The East Europeans were in a hurry; the West was not. The East Europeans wanted accelerated admission to the Western mainstream, but they were soon disappointed. The West insisted on a waiting period, which for the East became an inexcusable delay. Then, by the end of the century, the pace quickened. Poland, the Czech Republic, and Hungary were accepted by NATO and the EU was negotiating the "early" accession of these three countries along with Slovenia and Estonia; the EU also had agreed to enter negotiations with Romania and Bulgaria. Altogether, ten East European countries applied for EU entry. After the delay, therefore, comes the "process." Even for the favored applicants, the EU process is likely to be exasperatingly long. Indeed, for a time Europe will become not more united but less so, and the division between West and East will be more evident. In the meantime, the chasm between East Central and South Eastern Europe will become wider and deeper.

NATO Enlargement

First, though, to NATO. In 1998 the issue was settled; negotiations began with Poland, the Czech Republic, and Hungary. In early 1999, they were admitted. But it is still instructive to look back on the "expansion" debate before moving forward to examine the consequences.

In both the United States and Western Europe (except, perhaps, for recently reunited Germany), the public showed little interest in the issue of NATO membership for East European nations. But among the policy elites, especially those of the U.S. Eastern seaboard, the debate was hot, loud, and sometimes bad-tempered. And it was difficult to predict from previous political or policy alignments who or what would be for or against NATO enlargement. The *Washington Post,* for example, was for it; the *New York Times* was against, as was (narrowly) the Council on Foreign Relations. Some Republican senators were for; others were against. The Democrats were similarly divided.

In Europe, it was much the same. The serious press debated the question, but the politicians stayed quiet, and, as in the United States, the governments wanted to push the matter through, looking the other way, with their voters not looking at all. There the matter was likely to rest—except, of course, if the costs of NATO enlargement to Western treasuries, estimates of which have varied hugely, creep alarmingly upward.

The *arguments* for and against enlargement could be grouped as follows.[1]

FOR ENLARGEMENT

1. Eastern Europe deserves the Western protective embrace. Rudely denied their European heritage for nearly half a century, the East European nations should now be helped to reclaim it through NATO and EU membership. That is not the only reason for enlargement, however. Europe would be incomplete without East European membership in both organizations. Apart

from East Europeans, many West Europeans and Americans made this point their main argument for enlargement.

2. International relations are still in a state of nature, the sole safeguard of which consists in keeping your guard up and your national interest uppermost. Russia, therefore, however much weakened, has to be contained. This Realpolitik was preached by masters like Henry Kissinger.[2]

3. The "no foe nightmare." The United States needs an enemy. If none exists, one needs to be invented. Russia is eminently recyclable in this regard. Why not, therefore, move NATO into the Baltics, or even Ukraine? "Rub Russia's nose in it." This psychosis was expressed by pundits like William Safire.[3]

4. Russia is still a potential threat to Europe in general and to Eastern Europe in particular. Russia will never be "European," and, with its economic and political situation increasingly precarious—the financial meltdown, the ascendancy of new Russian leadership—the time to enlarge is *now*. Russia is in no position to resist this move, or anything else the United States might want to do. Moscow certainly must not have a veto on Western policy; this view was expressed by most East Europeans and their leaders, by many U.S. politicians, and by spokesmen for East European ethnic lobbies in the United States.

5. The expansion of NATO plus "partnership with Russia" will give a new post-cold war dimension of security and solidarity to the whole of Europe. Expansion and partnership, it was argued, were by no means incompatible. Look at the 1997 NATO-Russia Council aimed at precisely allaying Russian fears about NATO expansion. Several public figures in the United States made this argument and it became the public view of the Clinton administration.[4] Several Western European commentators also took this line.

AGAINST ENLARGEMENT

Michael Mandelbaum emerged as one of the most persistent and effective American campaigners against the enlargement of NATO. (Mandelbaum, it must be emphasized, was no isolationist; nor did anyone doubt his interest in, and sympathy for, Eastern Europe.) His arguments are best summed up in the executive summary of an extensive paper published in 1997 and archly titled "NATO Expansion: A Bridge to the Nineteenth Century."[5] In it, Mandelbaum took up George Kennan's judgment that NATO expansion could be "the most fateful error of American policy in the entire post cold war era."[6] Kennan is right, Mandelbaum says, for two reasons:

First, expanding NATO would bring no benefits. None of the reasons cited in favor of it stands up to scrutiny. It will promote neither democracy nor stability; nor will it fill a security vacuum between Germany and Russia or discharge a Western moral obligation to the Central Europeans. . . . Finally, enlarging the alliance is an unnecessary and ineffective way to contain a potentially resurgent Russia.

Because there is nothing to be gained from it, NATO expansion is a bad idea. It is also a dangerous idea, because there is a great deal to be lost if it goes forward. Expansion would impose costs on Europe and the United States. Just how great they would be cannot be known in advance: the future is, after all, unpredictable. But they might be substantial. This is the second reason that expansion would be a fateful blunder.

The prospect of expansion has already damaged the West's relations with Russia. Furthermore, the reality of expansion would draw a new line of division in Europe, creating a "grey zone" of vulnerable countries between NATO's new eastern border and Russia. In this geopolitical no-man's land would be located new democracies whose survival and prosperity are important to the West but whose security the expansion of NATO would jeopardize.

Sir Michael Howard, in late 1997, offered three succinct arguments that underline and amplify Mandelbaum's:

Unless such extension is accompanied by the necessary military measures, it will be as useless and counterproductive as the guarantee that Britain gave Poland in March 1939. If it is so accompanied, it will certainly provoke countermeasures on the part of the Russians, and the whole merry-go-round will get going again.

The fact that the Russians are too weak to do much about an expansion at the moment is hardly relevant. Nations have long memories for this kind of humiliation.

In any case, placing Central Europe on the front line of a new confrontation is an odd way to ensure its security.[7]

Many advocates of an expanded NATO were aware of the need to placate Russian opinion.[8] But the most powerful single argument against NATO expansion centered on Russia, on the imperative that Russia be brought "into Europe," into the European comity of nations. Most opponents of expansion were under no illusions about how difficult that act would be, but they considered that the present was the best possible moment in history to try. (The collapse of the Russian financial system in 1998 and the ensuing threat to postcommunist progress in Russia only strengthened many of them in this conviction.) Obviously, diplomacy and patience were needed, which meant taking into account Russian concerns, sensibilities, and, to some extent, neuroses, as well as the dangers of a rejection of democracy in Russia and the surging of an aggressive nationalism. Expanding NATO eastward in the face of universal Russian condemnation was obviously not the best way of rescuing Russia from economic and political recidivism. In fact, it was likely to produce the opposite result. And, instead of protecting Eastern Europe, it could eventually endanger it, thus threatening the stability of the entire Continent.

Proponents of NATO expansion rejected—sometimes derided—these arguments centered on Russia. It was giving Russia a veto over Western policy, they said; it signified the return of the appeasement mentality; it revealed a romantic lack of realism about Russia; and it betrayed a naive misjudgment of how international relations really worked.

An expansion of NATO was indeed a historic issue, one that demanded an opinion, and one on which compromise was virtually impossible. I expressed my hesitation on NATO expansion in *Hopes and Shadows*, published in 1994,[9] arguing that EU expansion should at least receive priority. My hesitation subsequently hardened into opposition. But expansion was decided and became fact; the debate is therefore over. Trying to continue it would be testy and pointless. What we have now is East Central Europe in NATO, and NATO in South Eastern Europe, where it is likely to stay indefinitely. Discussion must proceed from there.

European Union Enlargement

In contrast to NATO expansion, little dispute has occurred over the *principle* of EU enlargement. Practically everybody now, including Russia, is for it. But the question remains whether anybody is *ready* for it—either the EU itself or the Eastern aspirants.

It is worth emphasizing yet again how much more complex the EU is than NATO. The *Economist* put it best:

It is technically far trickier to join the EU than NATO. One Central European ambassador to the EU often tells his government that NATO entry concerns only his defence and foreign ministers; EU entry affects the entire cabinet. Applicants have to sign up to all the EU's swaths of accumulated legislation, the *acquis communautaire,* with only temporary waivers. The administrative task is immense. One official in the commission says that each of the current 15 members has perhaps 1,000 senior civil servants who are fully conversant with EU practices. In some applicant countries, the number is more like 20.[10]

This complexity needs to be unraveled, and no Gordian knot solution is evident. The complexity just grows; the sheer tonnage of bureaucracy takes on a life of its own, enveloping everything. Paul Lendvai, in a brilliant article on "The Dangers and Risks of EU Enlargement," put the problem succinctly: "Verwaltung statt Gestaltung" (Administration Instead of Concept).[11] Leaders in Brussels could, of course, argue that initiatives like the European Monetary Union (EMU) and the Euro currency, the idea of eastward expansion itself, showed that concepts were alive and kicking. In fact, the very idea of the EU was one of the most audacious grand designs in world history. But the question was whether the proliferating weeds of the Brussels bureaucracy would not blight the flowers seeded by the EU founders.

Moreover, the very fact that the EU throughout the 1990s has been going through the most crucial stage of its own entire development, and that the EU Commission was beset with the worst crisis in its history in early 1999, hardly made this a suitable time to begin considering new and difficult applicants, applicants still sloughing off the political and economic effects of communist rule. West European leaders, beset by problems of deepening the EU, had become muddled about widening it. Eastern Europe was becoming almost an afterthought. Lendvai made his point by quoting the *Economist:*

> Before the Luxembourg summit (in December 1997) *The Economist* spoke cynically, but quite accurately, about the hidden feelings of some EU politicians and bureaucrats about the oncoming negotiations for entry (of the East European states and Cyprus): "Can you say no, but pretend you are saying yes?" These sceptics fear that instead of the ever cohering European Union of the present, the future will bring a much bigger and more diffuse entity of between 18 and 25, perhaps even 30, member-states.[12]

It would be unfair to accuse the EU of having moved from rashness to hypocrisy in its enlargement policy. But at the end of the century, the EU seemed unready for the task. Many East Europeans, as well as some of their supporters in Western Europe, who argued that a steadily uniting Europe should have been at the top of the agenda after 1989, bemoaned the fact that little had been done to prepare for expansion. It was not simply a question of procedural measures. Some necessary policy reforms had not been put in place. What successive EU summit meetings showed was that, though its members knew some sacrifices would have to be made to accommodate Eastern Europe, each of them was determined to make its sacrifice as small as possible. The less their sacrifice, the greater their numbers of votes back home. A key question centered on agricultural subsidies. By how much would they be changed? This problem most affected Poland with its legions of small private farmers and its own unwillingness to make concessions that would go down badly at home. Poland at the end of 1998 had slightly more than 2 million farms, only 300,000 of which were of more than ten hectares, or yielded enough money for future development.[13] The whole EU Common Agricultural Policy (CAP) had to be changed, but it was only being timidly diluted.

Poland as well as Hungary (see chapter 8) presented problems of another sort. Its relations with its Eastern neighbors, successor states of the old Soviet Union, could fall afoul of the EU's overall border control policy. Though the Poles had been cautious about collaboration with the Visegrad countries, they had developed promising relations in the mid-1990s with Lithuania and Ukraine and would have done the same with Belarus but for the eccentricities of its president, Aleksander Lukashenka. Several reasons accounted for Poland's Ostpolitik: (1) Mutual economic gain. Tens of thousands of Belarusans, Ukrainians, and Lithuanians peacefully invaded Poland practically every day, selling, buying, and bartering. (2) Safeguarding Polish minorities. About 260,000 Poles lived in Lithuania, 420,000 in Belarus, and 220,000 in Ukraine. (3) Poland's self-image as a "power." (4) A genuine Polish desire not only to ease historic tensions, but to be the "conduit to Europe" for its Eastern neighbors. (5) To thumb its nose at Russia generally. (6) To try to neutralize the intimidating aspects of Russia's enclave at Kaliningrad. Poland's Ostpolitik was going well, but what about the EU's tight border control policy as contained in the Schengen agreement? Its restrictive policy was based on the all-too-genuine fear of uncontrolled mass immigration. It wanted visa travel only. Poland wished to continue its visa-free openness, insisting that, whatever problem might exist, it could handle the matter. The EU was reluctant to take that risk. In any case, Brussels did not like exceptions, especially for new, needy entrants.[14]

And overshadowing much of the enlargement debate (as in the case of NATO) was the imperative to be sparing with money. The EU countries, including Germany, the great benefactor, were strapped for cash. Their economies were facing problems, their welfare states were too expensive, and massive cost-cutting had been needed to qualify for the Euro-club. Western Europe's days as the Cheerible Brothers were over; those of Scrooge and Jacob Marley had set in.

In their own way, the East European countries were just as unprepared as the West Europeans for EU enlargement. Even among the best of them like Slovenia and, say, the Czech Republic, their economic situation was inferior, not just below the EU average, but lower than the EU worst (see chapter 3). Even if the East European economies grew at a rate 2 percent faster than the EU average, it would take until 2005 for the Czech Republic and Slovenia to be able to equal the per capita performance level of the Portuguese and Greek economies.[15] Economically, the East Europeans were not applicants but supplicants.

But the most basic danger to the prospects of real European unity had been the failure of the EU to develop its own foreign and security policy. Politically and militarily, despite all the hand-wringing and New Year's resolutions, it had remained largely impotent. But by the year 2000, the EU seemed to be making a serious move toward a combined military capability. The problem was that Washington, always critical of Europe's impotent dependency, now seemed to be of two minds once Europe began to take action. Some applauded Europe's efforts, but others feared that any new European military force would inevitably become an independent, or semi-independent, force (certainly if France had anything to do with it!). Thus NATO would be weakened and America's authority diluted. From several points of view this question needed resolution. For Eastern Europe it needed resolution quickly and clearly.

The Impact of Russia

Russia, even in its present weakness, still influences much of the thinking of East Europeans about their own place in the world. Russia is what they want to get away from, but they know they cannot—not completely—because Russia is and always will be European. Johann Gottfried Herder put it as well as anybody in 1802: "Wohin gehört Russland? Zu Europa oder zu Asien? Zu beiden. Dem grosseren Erdstrich nach zwar zu Asien, sein Herz aber liegt in Europa!"[16] (Where does Russia belong? In Europe or Asia? In both. Its bulk rests in Asia, but its heart lies in Europe.)

But Russia is different from Europe—very different. Immediately after the collapse of the Soviet Union and the communist system, some Westerners, especially the ideological triumphalists in the United States, were totally deceived by what seemed to be the "new Russia." The pace apparently was being set by a largely Moscow-based group of personable, democratic, internationalist, market-oriented, pro-Western, learn-from-America, thoroughly amenable intellectuals. Russia at last seemed on the right track. All it needed was freedom! But this euphoria did not last. Soon the real Russia stood up—a murky muddle of types and trends, with the only common denominator a proud, bewildered, and aggrieved nationalism. This nationalism had various shades and different intensities. But such confusion took over to become the Russian "mainstream," engulfing its public life.

This is the real new Russia that the United States, Western Europe, and Eastern Europe now have to cope with. The elections of 1996 removed the threat of old communism's return to power, but the 1998 financial disaster showed that much of the optimism had been premature. After that, Russia's leadership became still more erratic, and the threat to the very unity of the country seemed to increase. Only with the election of Alexander Putin as president in early 2000 was some strength and coherence restored to Russian leadership—for the first time since Stalin.

Historically, the attitudes of East Europeans toward Russia have varied. At times, those attitudes have not been nearly so hostile, fearful, or contemptuous as some of them now are. Generalizations are patchy and can be misleading, but, briefly, the South Slav nations—especially Serbs, Bulgarians, and Montenegrins—saw Russia as liberator and protector. Until 1917, Christian Orthodoxy was a powerful religious and cultural bond linking Russia with these nations. At times, intellectual pan-Slavisim also was strong. Greece, too, shared the bond of Orthodoxy with Russia, although its religious allegiance was more to Phanariot Constantinople than Slavic Moscow. Russia also had played an important role in the liberation of Greece from Ottoman rule, and, after liberation, Russia was viewed with sympathy by many Greeks worried over the dominance of Western influence in their affairs.

But for the Romanians, non-Slavic and next-door, the Russians were alien invaders, periodically trampling them underfoot in their drive westward and southward. For the Balkan Muslims, too, whatever their ethnic provenance, Russia was the enemy of the Ottoman empire and the self-proclaimed champion of their downtrodden Christian neighbors.

Moving northward, Russians were shown mostly dislike and fear. This response was especially true of Hungary. Hungary's 1848 revolution was crushed by Russian troops acting on behalf of Austria. Hungary fought against Russia in both world wars, had its revolution crushed again by Russians in 1956, was garrisoned by Soviet troops for nearly a half-century, and forcibly kept inside Moscow's imperial system. In contrast, Croatia and Slovenia, adjuncts to Central Europe and now aspirants to it, brushed against Soviet Russia while they were part of communist Yugoslavia, but they seldom were involved with it.

Still farther north, in East Central Europe, considerable popular and intellectual admiration for Russia was always present among the Czechs. Russians were seen as offsetting Germans. This sympathy was finally drained only in August 1968, when the Russians' ideas of deliverance were brutally at variance with the Czechs'.

Lastly, the Poles have generally hated, despised, and feared the Russians for three centuries. Russia (with Austria and Prussia) partitioned the Polish state out of existence at the end of the eighteenth century, tried to strangle the reborn state after World War I, partitioned it in collusion with Nazi Germany in 1939, and then incorporated it in the Soviet empire after 1945. But with Poland doomed to lie in perpetuity between Germany and Russia, a strong body of nationalist-realist opinion emerged there during the brief interlude of independence between the two world wars. This viewpoint saw Russia as the lesser evil and advocated that Polish foreign policy reflect that assessment. This view experienced a flickering revival after 1989 when some influential Poles saw the newly reunited Germany as possibly the main danger.

How does Russia view the East European states, the new empire it gained in 1945 and then lost almost a half-century later? Virtually no serious hankering to regain them is apparent, but most Russians—including some of the best and the brightest in Western eyes—still would put Eastern Europe in a special category as far as Russia's national security, interests, and sense of self-esteem are concerned. Russia no longer may be a superpower, but it still regards itself as an unbowed, great European power with legitimate interests that should be respected. In the early days of cold war defeat, collapse, and confusion, interest in Eastern Europe, the former satellite area, shrank to virtually nothing. Oleg T. Bogomolov, a genuine and influential liberal and friend at court for the East Europeans from the end of the 1960s, lamented this development: "Like others, I'm concerned about our loss of interest in the group of [Eastern European] countries seen until recently as a Soviet foreign policy priority. We used to assign them a special place in our policy, but everything changed almost overnight. We are beginning to forget that we will have to live with them in the years ahead."[17]

That statement was made nearly ten years ago. In the meantime, many other Russians have recovered their awareness of Eastern Europe. Eastern Europe matters again; it is special. Not as the "near abroad," certainly, but perhaps as the "intermediate abroad," ideally seen as independent but not unrestrainedly so, sovereign but not uninhibitedly so, free but not irresponsibly so. The Russians would have liked to regard Eastern Europe much as the Americans regard Central and South America—in short, as covered by a Russian Monroe Doctrine. The realists see this state of affairs as impossible, but perhaps not totally beyond reach; the romantics see it as denied them, but only temporarily. Where most East Europeans want to turn their back on Russia, however, few Russians want to do the same to them.

Kaliningrad, broken down, shoddy, and economically bankrupt, truly symbolizes present-day Russia, but it also symbolizes Russia's determination to stay in Eastern Europe, even if only by a toehold. Russia's military force there has severely run down, but Kaliningrad's very existence still reminds Poles, Belorussians, and Lithuanians of Russia's presence. Similarly, in South Eastern Europe, Russia seems to be looking to a portion or all of the Dneister Republic in Moldova as a counterpart to Kaliningrad. Moscow certainly would see itself as having the right to veto any merger of Moldova with Romania, if that were ever to become a possibility.[18] The firmly held conviction in Moscow, among both the political class and the military, is that history ordained the Balkans as an area of Russian influence and concern. Not surprisingly, therefore, that bitterness and humiliation are felt over what Russians regard as American exploitation of their current weakness by moving into parts of Yugoslavia, "adjudicating" on Kosovo, and attacking Serbia. In short, the Americans have overrun their turf.[19]

Responding to Russia

These Russian reactions to the momentous changes in the "correlation of forces" have yet to cohere in a consistent policy. That outcome could take a very long time. But the West, as well as the East European countries, would do well to take the Russians seriously. The West—in particular, the United States—will play an important role in how Russia's East European policy unfolds and in how flexible, rigid, or predictable it becomes. Despite its military strength, what the world's sole superpower now needs more than ever is a twenty-first-century diplomacy. American global diplomacy was born and raised in the confrontations of the cold war. The zero-sum habit of mind engendered by that decades-long opposition, and then reinforced by victory in it, has not yet been flushed away. It is essential, too, for East European leaders, no matter how Western-oriented they might be, to act as if they understood the long-term implications, opportunities, and restrictions of their geopolitical situation and to see their national interests not as provincial, short-term imperatives, but as part of a continent-wide interplay of interests. In other words, they must get themselves in perspective.

All East European countries genuinely fear a revival of what in terms of power would be the former Soviet Union. Just as Russia dominated and drove the Soviet Union, so, East Europeans often contend, it now seeks, especially under Putin, to make a reality of and then to dominate the lands of the former Soviet Union. What is now the "near abroad" therefore would meld into the new imperial power, and Eastern Europe, once the "intermediate abroad," would become the new near abroad. This fear is understandable, as is its corollary: gain entry into NATO as quickly as possible and lower the portcullis behind you.

It sounds simple and final, but it is neither. First, the United States and Western Europe, despite or because of NATO expansion, have constantly tried to assure Russia that it has an important place as a partner in any new European or international arrangements. That eventually means a substantial degree of Russian-East European interaction.

Second, Russian exclusion would only strengthen Moscow's efforts to increase its influence in Belarus, Ukraine, and Moldova, and to exert its pressure on the Baltic republics. If that were to happen, some East European states might feel formally secure behind NATO's perimeter fence, but tensions throughout the region could become more palpable than ever. Life would become more complicated, not less.

Third, normal relations with Russia, especially economic relations, eventually could be beneficial for all East European countries, even for those like the Czech Republic, Poland, and Hungary that were first in line to join the European Union. These three countries have achieved remarkable success during the 1990s in redirecting their trade westward. Poland, for example, now carries on less than 10 percent of its trade with Russia. But eventually, room for some expansion on a commercial basis, particularly in fuels and raw materials, might seem not only possible but advantageous.

For some countries farther back in the queue for EU entry, trade with Russia remains important and could become even more so. In March 1996, considerable commotion developed in Sofia and some Western capitals when Russian President Boris Yeltsin mentioned Bulgaria as a possible candidate for inclusion in an economic association comprising several CIS states.[20] Whether Yeltsin had something specific in mind or was simply ruminating was never clear. But for Bulgaria and other Balkan states, a closer economic association with Russia might prove to be more advantageous than dangling interminably on the West European hook. In March 1998, Bulgaria finally concluded an important agreement with Russia on the supply and transit of natural gas. It was a sensible, self-confident step by the (strongly pro-Western) government in Sofia.[21]

Finally, a prediction about President Vladimir Putin. In Chechnija, he has seen that nationalism pays electoral dividends. He believes in Russia's power as well as its territorial integrity. He presumably also believes in Russia's place and influence in the world. Short of war, he may use any means, not just to preserve that position and leverage, but to recover what can be recovered.

Pivotal and Precarious Ukraine

Ukraine needs special mention. It is, after all, Ukraine and not Russia that borders four East European countries. It is also a major state in its own right. Ukraine's future still mainly depends on how well it gets along with Russia, with which it has a complex set of relationships. Sometimes this connection has seemed perilously close to breaking down; it has survived because of the good sense of both sides. Ukraine's economic requirements force it to gravitate toward Russia, at least for the foreseeable future. So does its large ethnic Russian minority. Its independence in the longer term, however, depends on a partial gravitation westward. Polish-Ukrainian relations, once full of enmity but now much improved, can play an important role in this shift. Ukraine also is intimately connected with Romania (see chapter 5).

Toward the end of the century, it was not Ukraine's foreign policy but its very survival that had become its uppermost concern. The West, in general, especially the United States, which had placed Ukraine fourth on its list of foreign aid recipients, were increasingly worried about political and economic developments there.[22] Many Ukrainians also were becoming fearful about their country's future. Their misgivings only increased after the inconclusive parliamentary election results at the end of March 1998. The differences between Uniate, "European," Western Ukraine as opposed to Orthodox, "Russian," Eastern Ukraine seemed to be growing. About one-half of the total population was then estimated to support reunion with Russia.[23] Massive corruption and economic gangsterism reached to the very top levels of government. That, together with common criminality and general economic failure, were the main reasons for disaffection. Indeed, the Ukrainian situation began to look as alarming to the political future of Europe as the crisis set off in Russia in 1998. Ukraine's instability, the inevitable Russian concern, and then Russian interference could undermine the post-1989 pattern that had been emerging throughout the entire formerly communist domain. And Ukrainian discomfiture was not at all unwelcome to most Russians, who still were not psychologically resigned to "losing" Ukraine. But the culminating crisis that many had feared was averted, or at least postponed, toward the end of 1999. Leonid Kutschma was reelected president with an unexpectedly clear majority, defeating his communist challenger and polling very well in even some of the "Russian" industrial regions. Kutschma had not been successful in his first term, but the political fates had conspired to give him and Ukraine a second chance.

Belarus was always a doubtful proposition for independence, and it now appears to be politically, economically, and psychologically unviable.[24] President Lukashenka is probably more the symptom than the cause of this condition, although his eccentricities have been immeasurably damaging. Still closer association between Belarus and Russia looks inevitable, incorporation into Russia quite possible. If (when) this happens, support in Ukraine for closer association with Russia probably would increase. These developments undoubtedly will be unsettling for all East Central European states. But the security of those states need not be threatened. Russia's closer interaction should not create panic; rather, it simply should call for greater nerve.

Pax Americana

Yesterday, Pax Sovietica. Today (and tomorrow), Pax Americana. The one based on force, the other on strength.

American influence in Eastern Europe is one of this book's main themes. "Long may it continue," say most East Europeans. That influence is likely to be needed, too. Suggestions being made during the U.S. elections in 2000 in favor of considerable reductions of U.S. forces in Europe, including the Balkans, would, if implemented, constitute the most serious error in U.S. European policy since the withdrawal from Europe after 1920.

Something else is probable, and important, too: namely, the popular cult of the United States in Eastern Europe is likely to persist and grow. Over the past twenty years, the extent to which U.S. pop culture has swept across Eastern Europe and some parts of the former Soviet Union, especially throughout the youth scene, has been astonishing. In a sense, it has served to unify. Young Germans and young Poles in Silesia, once separated by centuries of different cultures, now drink Coke, smoke pot, bawl the same ballads, and boggle at the same videos—the common denominator of all their frenzy being the United States. It is the same with Hungarian and Romanian youth in Transylvania, with Croat and Serb youth in former Yugoslavia. Whether these shared enthusiasms make them more friendly to each other, more understanding and tolerant, remains to be seen. But what is telling is that through the magnetic mass appeal of American popular culture this has happened at all.

Nor is it just U.S. *popular* culture that is supreme. The United States is now preeminent in many of the creative and performing arts, in the sciences, in scholarship, and in advanced education. The younger intellectual elites in Eastern Europe's capitals today look not to Paris, Rome, Berlin, or London, as their predecessors did, but to New York, Los Angeles, Boston, Chicago, and San Francisco. Culturally, intellectually, and academically, the United States sets the pace. Some West Europeans accept this state of affairs; others refuse to. Yet their acceptance or lack of it is largely irrelevant. What does matter is that the U.S. government, with American cultural foundations and academic institutions, has a marvelous opportunity to consolidate the prestige and goodwill that the United States enjoys. This prestige can further enlarge the opportunities for young East Europeans (Russians, too) to visit North America. The resulting reservoir of goodwill for the United States would make it worthwhile. A pro-American elite, not necessarily liking everything the United States does, but liking the United States, could be in the making.

But the United States cannot be complacent, as it shows some signs of being. Globalization (see chapter 3) has only added to its supremacy, its unrivaled superpower status. But enhanced power does not necessarily mean enhanced popularity. It can mean just the opposite, in Eastern Europe as elsewhere. Signs of unpopularity have already appeared. The widespread popular opposition to NATO's action against Serbia in 1999, not only in the Balkans but in other parts of Eastern Europe, was one symptom. The United States needs a *sensitive* public relations campaign to offset such unfavorable views. Policies are not the problem as much as the very fact of power. And no matter how affected by American culture East Europeans might be, they could still become anti-American if the United States is content simply to rest on its leadership laurels and assume that it will be liked. Popularity, with power and influence, was possible in the euphoria after 1989. Now it must be earned.

Germany: Doubts among the Hopes

"Die Deutschen sind wieder da." East Europeans were repeating this sentence well before the walls came tumbling down in 1989. From the early 1970s, in the framework of Ostpolitik, West German businessmen, the modern Hansa, began reappearing, first in a trickle, then in a flood. After 1989, whole armies of ordinary Germans flocked into Eastern Europe, this time as spenders, not soldiers.

Many East Europeans were not unduly worried about the new Germans filling some of the vacuum created by the end of the cold war and the defeat of Soviet Russia. They realized that the new, powerful Germany was very different from the "old" Germany and that part of the difference was due to its membership in NATO and the EU, international organizations that molded and contained Germany's role in the international order. Nor was condemnation of the "old Germany" as universal as some Westerners think or as many East Europeans now try to make out. Among Poles, condemnation certainly was constant; among Czechs, too, the same could be said, despite their extensive collaboration with Nazi Germany during World War II. Among Serbs, condemnation also was steady. But many Slovaks, Slovenes, Croats, Albanians, Hungarians, Romanians, and Bulgarians regretted little about World War II, except losing it. Still, whatever East Europeans once may have thought, Germany again had become the most powerful country in Europe, and that power was making a strong showing in Eastern Europe.

Now, with its capital moved from Bonn back to Berlin, Germany is moving eastward. The change cannot remain solely symbolic; it will have a political, economic, cultural, and psychological impact. It is bound to raise questions, including these:

1. Will the internationalism in which Germany is embedded be strong enough and flexible enough to facilitate legitimate German interests and yet blunt the possible dangers of German reassertiveness?

2. Will NATO and the EU be able to reconcile Germany's nationalism and internationalism? More specifically, will the present plans for the eastward enlargement of these two bodies maximize the constructive effectiveness of Germany in Eastern Europe?

3. Will Germany and Poland eventually be able to create an effective partnership similar to the one between Germany and France? The good bilateral relations that had developed since 1989 showed signs of deteriorating in 1999. But the real question was: Could Germany combine good relations with both Poland and Russia? Russia would have to take priority, and this choice could hurt the Poles and certainly make them nervous.

4. Will the German domestic situation—especially regarding the reintegration of the former GDR and the absorption of immigrants—proceed in a way that will enable Germany to continue playing a constructive role in Eastern Europe?

5. Will the German economy revive to the point where it can continue being a motor of East European economic development?

At the end of the twentieth century—in fact well into its last year—the answer to all five of these questions would have been a fairly confident "yes." Just one year later it was more likely to be a nervous "hopefully." The German economy would, indeed, probably revive, but its revival would require a drastic revision of the whole economic and social culture on which the Federal Republic of Germany had always been based. The other questions, though, must now be considered in a new, disturbing, light. Germany was being weakened, not strengthened, by reunification.

The question now was how long it would take to reverse that weakening. Moreover, the internationalism that had once been a characteristic of West German public life was now shifting toward a defensive, sometimes xenophobic, nationalism. The EU expansion eastward was becoming a controversial issue. For many Germans, only Hungary was now seen as a suitable member, Poland much less so. Officially, relations with Poland were deteriorating. Even when Poland eventually joined the EU, those relations would never return to the near intimacy of the early 1990s, if only because of Germany's growing preoccupation with Russian relations. At the popular level, attitudes toward Poles were noticeably hardening. Too many Poles were knocking about in Germany! Germans, who historically had made a habit of invading Poland, were now miffed at seeing so many Poles in their own country.

In short, the "ethnic" factor was again making inroads into German public life at the expense of the "civic." (It was doing this in the rest of Western Europe, too, but German "civicness" was newer and more fragile than, say, French, British, Benelux, or Scandinavian "civicness.") True, West Germany had opened its doors to hundreds of thousands of *Gastarbeiter* from Southern and Eastern Europe from the 1960s onward. It did not exactly welcome this massive influx but regulated it in an orderly and decent fashion. And the *Gastarbeiter* helped to build the economy and were willing to do the kinds of jobs that many Germans were not. But when the walls came tumbling down at the end of the cold war, "new kinds" of foreigners were pouring in, not only from Eastern Europe but from the former Soviet Union and the developing world. These foreigners were not only unwanted; they became easy scapegoats for rising dissatisfaction and insecurity.

Germany was becoming rather like Austria in its attitude toward the new immigrants. These countries were the two "frontline" states, in the opinion of many citizens of both. (The concept of the "ethnic frontline," so much touted in South Eastern Europe, was also moving to Central Europe!) A new defensive Anschluss mentality could indeed be forming, unacknowledged and even surreptitious. Such speculation is, of course, irrelevant in the context of this book. But a relevant point is that the regenerating confidence that Germany first had in its relations with the new Eastern Europe, and the hope that Eastern Europe had in this confident Germany, could be seriously eroding. Even more serious: a dreadful irony would result if the "civic" at last prevailed over the "ethnic" in East Central Europe, but at the same time lost ground in Germany.

France: Assertive Diplomacy

In the twenty-first century, French diplomacy will presumably continue to be as active, skilled, and self-centered as it was for most of the twentieth. This expectation applies to Eastern Europe as well as to anywhere else that France sees itself as having interests. In Eastern Europe after World War I, France formed a series of alliances often known as the French system. President Charles de Gaulle's Fifth Republic after 1958 resumed active French interest in Eastern Europe, and, though this interest became less spectacular after de Gaulle's retirement in 1969, it has continued to be forcefully pursued. Now, since 1989, the French calling card remains prominently displayed throughout the region.

Pierre Hassner has discussed the issues that have historically influenced French policy in Eastern Europe. He begins with the remarkable exhortation of Charles Maurras, written as early as 1910 but having considerable resonance throughout the twentieth century.[25] "Circumstances are propitious," Maurras wrote, "for the interposition of a state of medium magnitude with a robust and firm makeup like our own." He went on: "we would need neither to seek friends nor to invite them. The secondary states would be driven in our direction by the force of circumstances. It is up to us, then, to be wise enough and show ourselves vigorous enough to inspire confidence." Hassner then continues this train of thought himself: "From Napoleon III to Mitterrand via de Gaulle, French policy can be interpreted as an attempt to resurrect past grandeur in the absence of the means that had once made it possible. Yet it is true that the most fundamental French self-perception is not of strength but of physical limitations in men, territory, or wealth, limitations that have to be made up by superior diplomatic skill, historical lucidity, institutional privileges, or moral authority."[26]

The "most basic device," according to Hassner, in pursuing this policy is the so-called *alliance de revers*, the alliance with the neighbors and potential rivals of one's potential enemy. He gives examples of this alliance: the anti-German strategies adopted by France between the two world wars and then by de Gaulle immediately after 1945. But concomitant with all of these self-interested strategies, tactics, and maneuverings has been the support of self-determination, national independence, and individual freedoms that were inspired by the French Revolution.[27] Reconciling the two has sometimes not been easy; its difficulties have sometimes exposed France to charges of hypocrisy and imposture. But, generally, the French have little to reproach themselves for. Their foreign policy has been both principled and consistent.

How will these French principles specifically apply today and tomorrow? If France sees American power as a potential menace to "European" interests (i.e., its own interests), then France will use *Russia* as an ally against the United States. And, at a more local level, if France still sees German power as its main challenge among the European powers, then it will use new Eastern European allies, along with old West European associates, to curb Germany.

The following will likely take place:

1. France will continue to make life awkward for the United States in Europe.
2. Russia will be brought toward the center of European affairs as an instrument of French diplomacy—perhaps, when necessary, to the detriment of East European nations' perceptions of their own interests.
3. Especially if Germany falters, France will vigorously pursue its own interests in Eastern Europe early in the twenty-first century along the lines that Charles Maurras envisaged at the beginning of the twentieth. What this means is simply that France will bring diplomacy back to normal. That is where French principle and consistency come in.

Yesteryear Nations

At different times, Britain, Austria, and Italy have all directly and indirectly, exerted strong influence on Eastern Europe. None has done so more, of course, than Austria during Habsburg times. Along with Britain, Austria was one of the powers that settled the region's fate at key moments in both the nineteenth and early twentieth centuries. Now, however, the influence of Austria and Britain is strictly limited, and it is likely to remain so. But Italy's influence could grow, provided the Italians begin believing in themselves as a nation and in the responsibilities that go with their geopolitical importance.

GREAT BRITAIN

Britain has generally had a dismal record in Eastern Europe. In the nineteenth century it backed a status quo in the Balkans that could not last, and a horse, Turkey, that could not win. In the twentieth century it left diplomatic management of Eastern Europe to France after 1918, appeased Nazi

Germany, and then deserted Czechoslovakia in 1938. It did honor its pledge to Poland in 1939, which Hitler ignored when he went to war. So Britain could not help Poland.

The British people's steadfastness in World War II recovered the nation's honor. But Britain did not draw the right lessons for the future from their determined victory. Europe remained foreign and mistrusted. Only the Poles among "Europeans" had Britain's grudging respect (except for the distant Russians). The British view of the lands beyond Calais was condescending, to say the least, and the perceptions of those lands toward Britain became dim and bewildered. To Eastern Europe under communism, Britain became virtually irrelevant. A writer like Timothy Garton Ash, continuing a fine crusading tradition, did more for his country's prestige than did successive British governments. Margaret Thatcher in the 1980s was greatly admired by many East European dissidents, but they knew enough about the world to understand that her bark was much stronger than her country's bite.

Then the Kosovo crisis brought to the fore a moralistic strain in British foreign policy that had not been seen for well over a century. And once again it was a devoutly Christian prime minister who was the mover. William Ewart Gladstone in the 1870s conducted an indignant crusade against the "Bulgarian atrocities" committed by the Turks, and he spoke out for the independence of the Balkan nations. In 1999, Tony Blair saw Kosovo as a moral test for Western civilization: "We have seen scenes of terror and murder. . . . This is not a battle by NATO for territory; it is a battle for the values of civilisation and democracy everywhere. . . . We bring justice and hope to the people here. . . . They are our cause, and we must not, and we will not, let them down. . . . Our promise to all of you is that you shall return in peace to the land that is yours."[28] This call was responded to by many Americans and Europeans. Combined with the vigor with which the British government conducted its war and diplomacy against the Milošević regime, it gave Britain a new prominence and a reputation in the Balkans.

AUSTRIA

In *Hopes and Shadows*, under the rather mawkish subtitle "Not As a Stranger," I speculated on the possibilities of Austria assuming a more active role in the newly liberated Eastern Europe.[29] Economically, it did take such a role. Austria's trade with several East European countries increased at a much higher rate than it did with Western Europe. From 1989 until 1996,

Western trade with Eastern Europe more than doubled, with exports considerably exceeding imports. Austrian investments in Eastern Europe also grew substantially, reaching a peak in 1995, when nearly 60 percent of all Austrian money went to former East bloc countries.[30] Politically, though, few signs were evident of the Austrians making any effort to move back into their old hinterland.

During the Yugoslav wars, Austria was vociferous from the sidelines. Avoiding intervention, ostensibly on the grounds of its neutrality, it invoked its historical experience in the region to justify showering advice and homilies like confetti. For old-time's sake, it strongly supported Slovenia's and Croatia's fight for independence. Its provincial posturing did little harm, although it annoyed those Western countries that became embroiled in the struggle. Many of those nations felt that Austria would have served its reputation better had it remembered one of the basic rules of good form among nations: no pontification without participation.

The imminence of European Union's eastward enlargement caused a heated debate among Austrians in regard to its advantages for them. Opinion was roughly divided between the romantic enthusiasts, the cautious bottom-liners, and the strict rejectionists.[31] The romantics reveled in the prospect of three former Habsburg lands—the Czech Republic, Hungary, and Slovenia (plus a part of Poland)—"reclaiming their heritage." The region would rediscover its bloom and Vienna its past glories! Big business, backed by the government, was generally in favor of expansion on economic grounds. But it wanted protection, at least for a period, against the inroads of cheaper Eastern goods and agricultural products. By contrast, the trade union organizations, the farmers, and many workers saw expansion as causing a massive rise in unemployment and much impoverishment. Their spokesmen argued that the average wage in Hungary was only 10 percent of that in Austria. Until it reached 70 percent, no question should be entertained of Hungary being admitted to the EU. Overshadowing such arguments was the Austrian fear of further immigration from the East. To counter apprehensiveness and the political capital being made out of it, the term "eastward extension" began to be dropped in favor of the simple "extension." The pope on a visit to Austria in the summer of 1998 urged Austrians to think of their country as not being on the "border" of Europe, but at its "heart."[32] It was a semantic stratagem that did not cut much ice, and many Austrians still would tend to agree with Metternich that "Asia begins at the Rennweg."

The crucial question, though, was not where Asia might begin, but where Austria was, and where it was heading. The historic question of a distinct Austrian identity seemed to have been settled by the disaster of collaboration with the Hitlerite Germans in and after 1938, by wartime defeat, by the benefits of being deemed the "first occupied nation," and then by the rewards of neutrality during the cold war. The question of Austria's future role would be more difficult to settle. It is now a member of Western Europe's international community, the EU, which is in the process of expanding eastward. What part can Austria play in this historically new configuration and situation? What part would it want to play? These questions form the core of the debate in Austria itself. Its outcome could have important consequences well beyond the confines of Austria.

The debate was already getting lively but then, early in 2000, the Haider furore, after seething for several years, burst onto the Austrian and European scene. His "Freedom Party" became part of the new Austrian government.

Jörg Haider is the latest figure in the long line of Austro-fascism that began in the second half of the nineteenth century as the Habsburg empire sped into terminal decline. As Shlomo Avineri points out, Haider's real predecessor was Karl Lueger, "der schöne Karl," mayor of Vienna at the end of the nineteenth century.[33] Later, Austro-fascism was swallowed up by German Nazism, led by another Austrian, Adolf Hitler, although comparisons between these two figures should not be pressed too far.

Haider's relevance for Austria lay in his central role in the great debate in which his countrymen were engaged. After almost a half-century of being cosseted by the cold war, Austria after 1989 had to make its own decisions and to assume responsibility for them. Its biggest decision was to join the European Union. Most Austrians supported this decision. But immigration from Eastern Europe was the dominant issue in Austria's domestic politics, an issue obviously connected with the question of the eastward expansion of the EU. As the immigration issue took on strong racial overtones everywhere in Europe, Haider exploited it throughout the 1990s. His stance was popular with the electorate and brought his Freedom Party into government.

Eastern Europe's reaction to Haider was ambivalent. On the one hand, its governments, anxious to join the EU on the best terms possible, resented his trenchant reservations about the dangers that admission of their countries would pose to Austria. On the other hand, they and the people they governed were basically in sympathy with Haider's racist approach. They generally opposed the partial ostracism of Austria by other member countries of the EU on account of the Freedom Party's inclusion in the Austrian government. (Poland, with virtually no ethnic problems, stayed aloof.) This opposition was ostensibly based on their rejection of interference in any country's internal affairs, but it was certainly not just that.

ITALY

Inhibited by fascist imperialism in South East Europe before and during World War II, Italy was loath to assert itself there after the peace. But following the collapse of communism, it showed signs of renewed activity, this time wholly benevolent. Italian companies, state-assisted, have invested heavily in the Balkans. Italy also has helped in Yugoslav peacekeeping and reconstruction. In April 1997, in the midst of Albania's bloody chaos, Italy led a force of 6,000 European soldiers in "Mission Alba," under the auspices of the EU. Italian troops went to Albania not so much to fight as to stabilize the situation, help the population, and, above all, discourage Albanian "boat people" from crossing illegally to Italy. Mission Alba was on the whole successful, and Italy, almost in spite of itself, was accorded considerable international credit.[34] Italy also has gained regard for the relatively humane way it handled the dreadful problem of tens of thousands of Albanian boat people who did make it to Italy. But it began to waver over the Kosovo conflict. Unless it stiffened its resolve, Italy might throw away the reputation of greater seriousness that it was building.[35]

East European Cooperation: Needed But Not There

East Europeans need the West, and need it sorely, but they would be more internationally credible and stronger, severally and collectively, if they could forge meaningful regional or subregional cooperation among themselves. They have scarcely tried to do so. In East Central Europe, there was (and still is) the Visegrad grouping of the Czech Republic, Slovakia, Poland, and Hungary. But, despite protestations, press releases, and attempts to reinvigorate, Visegrad has remained more dilettantism than serious business. More genuine, purposeful cooperation before 1989 was forged among Czechoslovak, Hungarian, and Polish dissident intellectuals than now can be found among their free, democratically elected governments. Perhaps Hungary has been the keenest on regional cooperation. Poland is less dismissive of it now than under Wałęsa, but Poland still sees itself as a major league team among minor leaguers. Mečiar's Slovakia was impossible to cooperate with. The Czech government under Václav Klaus was contemptuous of the whole notion. (Klaus is reported as saying that the only Visegrad he took seriously was the cemetery of that name on the outskirts of Prague.) And without the Czech Republic, which wants to strap itself exclusively to the West, no East Central European cooperation can be effective. Neither Hungary nor Slovakia, already divided by the minority controversy, would want to be part of a Polish-dominated grouping. Historic memories, especially the forty years of socialist "togetherness," would always make regional cooperation difficult.

Although now the lure of "Europe" and of the "West" is not exactly beckoning, it is magnetically attracting. And for almost all East Europeans, this "Europe" makes their resources of every kind appear to be inferior, provincial, or demeaning. Could Visegrad ever compete with Brussels? Perhaps not, but it could compete against others *in* Brussels. Once its members get settled in the EU, it could form a negotiating group of which the others would have to take some notice. It might occasionally even get its way. But the depressing truth seemed to be that the intellectual enthusiasm for Central Europe that existed during the years of oppression before 1989 had come to little or nothing practical in the years of freedom that followed.

In South Eastern Europe the war in former Yugoslavia and the crises, actual or potential, elsewhere have made the need for cooperation all the greater, but the will for it all the less. Slovenia slid off the top-left corner of the Balkans into Central Europe with little fuss. Croatia now disclaims any Balkan connection and asserts Central Europe as its birthright. Bosnia-Hercegovina may not survive. Serbia has only just revived. It is too much to expect the former warring nations in Yugoslavia to cooperate fully. Elsewhere, neighbors, if not considered potential enemies, are seen as a potential problem that is better left alone. A strong ashamed-of-the-neighborhood complex also exists in the Balkans. We are all right, but the rest are Europe's dregs. Besides, our problems are too big for us.

It is true that since the end of the Kosovo conflict, some apparently serious efforts have been made toward better state relations, with Bulgaria and Greece playing notable parts. Indeed Greece, under the Simitis government, is now seen as a potential Balkan leader, because of its partial rapprochement with Turkey and its eagerness to mend fences with Macedonia, Albania, and Bulgaria. In this connection it is worth recalling remarks made in November 1995 by Branko Crvenkovski, then prime minister of Macedonia, to a group of visitors, of which I was one. When asked to sum up Macedonia's policy toward its neighbors, Crvenkovski routinely responded, "Equidistance with all." Asked whether any neighbor was more equidistant than others, he replied, "Greece." At this time Greece was still making his country pay for taking the name Macedonia and for adopting national symbols that offended the Greeks. Greece, Crvenkovski said, as a member of both NATO and the EU, and as a nation of seafarers with far-flung contacts, could be his land-locked country's conduit to the outside world. Greece is, indeed, well placed for a regional leadership role.

The Balkan countries are also being urged under the aegis of the Stability Pact to cultivate closer cooperation. Such cooperation could become a condition of assistance. But in the Balkans one finds too much history, too much suspicion, passivity, and parochialism—all militating against real cooperation, all engendering a whinging fatalism and an inordinate self-centeredness, often shot through with the inverted naïveté mentioned earlier (see chapter 6). These characteristics will recede only when the Balkan nations stop concentrating on each other, start becoming involved "continentally," and start thinking internationally. They must think of Europe and the Atlantic community, and of their place in them. The means, the instruments, are now available for the Balkan nations to cooperate with these communities: NATO and the European Union. For the first time in their modern history, most of these nations are *willing* to be associated with an international community of nations. For the first time they have the chance to see life in a broader perspective—broader than themselves, their neighborhood, and the turmoil that has divided it. But in these new surroundings the Balkan countries will count for nothing if each remains alone, bent only on getting the best for itself. In international company they will soon realize that they have goals in common that can only be reached by acting in common. Only then will they get international recognition and respect—and a decent share of prosperity and success.

10

The Last Word: Urgency

WHATEVER HOPES EXISTED in Eastern Europe after 1945 soon turned to disillusion. Certainly more hopes arose after 1989 than after 1945. Have they turned to disillusion, too? Some opinion polls at the turn of the millennium suggested that optimism was fading. Only a clear majority of Poles supported the transition. Just over half the Czechs did but just over half the Hungarians did not. In Romania just over half those polled thought that life under Ceauşescu had been better. Most Bulgarians looked back nostalgically to the days of "Bai Tosho" (Todor Zhivkov). Most Slovaks apparently preferred life in communist Czechoslovakia. Everywhere, Poland included, large majorities thought the previous ten years had not "met their expectations." The lines waiting for visas outside American consulates were not getting much shorter.

It is easy to be cynical about the accuracy of polls. But cynicism cannot explain away all of these results. Nor can wit like that of Oscar Wilde, "The past appeals to people because it will never come back," or insights like that of Mark Mazower, "Sometimes it is easier to dream the old dreams—even when they are nightmares—than to wake up to unfamiliar realities." In fact, more immediate, tangible reasons can be found for the profound disappointment reflected in the polls.

"Protest votes" touched only the surface of the disappointment. For many older East Europeans, the post-Stalin communist past, however gray and grim, did have a certain predictability, stability, even safety. Today was like yesterday, tomorrow like today. A predictable minimum of material goods could also be expected. Socially, too, people possessed a modicum of equality. And, for those who kept their noses politically clean, professional mobility was possible, in addition to perks like free vacations in places that seemed almost exotic—the Black Sea or the Tatras, for example. In retrospect, therefore, life seemed not so bad, however much people may have groused at the time. Now—strengthening the point made in chapter 4—the guaranteed minimum had been replaced by deprivation, the assurance by disorientation. Life was no longer a continuum but a matter of two escalators, with no doubt as to which one so many East Europeans were on.

And that minimum livelihood, which had afforded them a certain dignity, had been guaranteed by the state, by the communist system. People may have disparaged the system then, but they missed it now. For many the ultimate indignity was losing the jobs that the state had provided. (Being *fearful* of losing jobs was almost as bad.) The state as a provider was now gone, but its comfort lingered in memory.

For many East Europeans, old and young, capitalism has not been just a disappointment but an outright deception. They witnessed the dawn of a consumerist abundance, which was the reason so many embraced capitalism in 1989. They were roused not by Thomas Jefferson, John Stuart Mill, or Jean-Jacques Rousseau, not by freedom, dignity, and independence—those were for the intellectuals. Materialist bonanza, instant or soon, stirred their hearts. Thus, hopes have not been disappointed as much as fantasies have been punctured. The most egregious example of a shattered fantasy occurred in Albania with the Pyramid fiasco. For a short time the get-rich-quick schemes seemed to be working and everyone was in capitalist clover. Although Albanians are the most primitive of East European nations, the magic wand of illusion was not confined to them. And when the illusion vanished, it was replaced by anger and cynicism.

The cynicism grew when it became evident that many of those benefiting from the new system were the old communist bosses now transmogrified into "new bosses"—and new millionaires. The reputation of democracy thus suffered too. The whole new order seemed something of a sham. Therefore, 1989 was not the "surge to freedom" but just another confidence trick by "them."

The popular disillusion was certainly an antidote to the ideological triumphalism about Eastern Europe that had raged in the West in 1989. But as the millennium polls indicated, this disillusion, though widespread, was not universal. In every country, most members of the younger generations, even those almost fifty years old, did support the new order. At least they preferred it to the old one. They were also more impressed than their elders with the blessings of democracy and regarded capitalism as the only way to the future, despite its ugliness.

But many of these younger generations, despite their overall approval, were still dismayed at the way their governments were run. Too many communist survivors remained, and, above all, too much "cliqueism." Promise and energy were positively discouraged. Total despair often afflicted the professions. Salaries in the medical and teaching professions and in the civil service were degrading; many professionals not only had to take extra jobs but bribes as well, from patients, students, or those seeking help or service. It is thus hardly surprising that many young people approved of 1989 just because it enabled them to emigrate.

Still, many young people hoped that things would get better. Some would even grudgingly admit that things *were* getting better. That slim hope kept some at home or induced some who left to return. But those who hoped were also impatient. They would not wait long for some signs of prosperity and some evidence of real change and better government. The need was urgent; it could not wait.

Notes

1. Coming into Being

1. J. F. Brown, *Eastern Europe and Communist Rule* (Durham, N.C.: Duke University Press, 1988), 415.

2. See Charles and Barbara Jelavich, *The Establishment of the Balkan National States, 1804–1920* (Seattle: University of Washington Press, 1977), and Barbara Jelavich, *History of the Balkans,* vol. 1 (Cambridge: Cambridge University Press, 1983).

3. Golo Mann, in his finger-wagging way, has an excellent chapter on Bismarck's character, personality, aims and strategy in his *History of Germany Since 1789,* translated by Marian Jackson (London: Pimlico, 1996), 156–98. Mann brings out Bismarck's prodigious common sense.

4. These approximate figures are based on the table in Joseph Rothschild, *East Central Europe Between the Two World Wars* (Seattle: University of Washington Press, 1974), 89. Rothschild's book, which I have used extensively in writing this chapter, is invaluable. So is the late Hugh Seton-Watson's *Eastern Europe Between the Wars, 1918–1941* (Hamden, Conn.: Archon Books, 1962). Seton-Watson's book, which has been through many editions, is contemporary history, containing misjudgments that were typical of the time. But those do not detract from its overall value.

5. This was a plan for Serb national expansion drawn up by Iliya Garašanin, one of the Serbian prince's senior ministers, in 1844. It envisaged the reestablishment of Tsar Dušan's medieval empire around the nucleus of autonomous Serbia. It remained the ideal, or, in some cases, the practical ambition of Serbia's leaders right until the end of the twentieth century. See Charles and Barbara Jelavich, 63.

6. See Brown, *Eastern Europe and Communist Rule,* 419–22. See also Robert R. King, *Minorities Under Communism: Nationalities as a Source of Tension Among Balkan Communist States* (Cambridge, Mass.: Harvard University Press, 1973). A more recent helpful study is Thomas S. Szayna's *Ethnic Conflict in Central Europe and the Balkans* (Santa Monica, Calif.: RAND, 1994).

7. For the Germans in Romania, see Michael A. Nagelbach, *Heil! and Farewell: A Life in Romania 1913–1946* (Chicago: Adams Press, 1986), passim.

8. Ivo Andrić, *The Bridge Over the Drina* (London: Harvill Press, 1994), 230.

9. On Hungary, see William O. McCagg Jr., *Jewish Nobles and Geniuses in Modern Hungary*

(New York: Columbia University Press, 1986). For Germany and Austria, see Peter Pulzer, *The Rise of Political Anti-Semitism in Germany and Austria,* rev. ed. (Cambridge, Mass.: Harvard University Press, 1988).

10 In J. F. Brown, *Hopes and Shadows: Eastern Europe After Communism* (Durham, N.C.: Duke University Press, 1994), 227, I quote the late Cyrus Sulzberger recalling a Macedonian Gypsy telling him before World War II: "There are 77½ religions in the world. Ours is the half." It was an apt summing up of the Gypsy condition and how most Gypsies took it.

11 King, 101.

12 Brown, *Eastern Europe and Communist Rule,* 443–44.

13 Nationalism again became a much-discussed subject after 1989. The best coverage and analysis that I have read is in Charles A. Kupchan, ed., *Nationalism and Nationalities in the New Europe* (Ithaca, N.Y.: Cornell University Press, for the Council on Foreign Relations 1995). The introduction, by Kupchan, is illuminating.

14 R. J. W. Evans, "The Magic of Bohemia," *New York Review of Books,* October 21, 1999.

15 Eric Hobsbawm, *On History* (New York: New Press, 1997), 223.

16 See Piotr Wandycz, *France and Her Eastern Allies, 1919–1925* (Minneapolis: University of Minnesota Press, 1962).

17 Rothschild, 5.

18 Orlando Figes, *A People's Tragedy: The Russian Revolution, 1891–1924* (London: Pimlico, 1997), 548.

19 Romania's remarkable success in Paris is analyzed by Sherman David Spector, *Romania at the Paris Peace Conference: A Study of the Diplomacy of Ioan C. Brătiănu* (New York: Bookman, 1962).

20 Rothschild, 138.

21 Ibid., 325.

22 Miroslav Krleza, quoted by Chris Hedges, "*A Yugoslav War Novel* for the 'Doomed Generation,' " *International Herald Tribune* (New York Times Service), December 31, 1997.

23 Rothschild, 10.

24 "Salami tactics" were later made famous, especially by Mátyás Rákosi, the Hungarian communist leader, after 1945. They were designed to pick off his democratic, or anticommunist, opponents one by one.

25 See Aurel Braun, *Small State Security in the Balkans* (London: Macmillan, 1983).

26 See Antonin Basch, *The Danube Basin and the German Economic Sphere* (New York: Columbia University Press, 1943).

27 Rothschild, 15.

28 Ibid.

29 Rebecca West's book, *Black Lamb and Grey Falcon,* eloquently written by a brilliant, prejudiced author, has exercised a pernicious influence, particularly on readers in her native Britain. Some Britons and Americans who should have known better have regarded her book as the main authority on prewar Yugoslavia. Her hold, though, is apparently not as great as it used to be. David Owen, for example, before starting with

the Vance-Owen peace mission, says he had "dipped into, rather than re-read, *Black Lamb and Grey Falcon.*" Later, he "glanced at her book again" (*Balkan Odyssey* [London: Indigo, 1996], 6). What he really means is not clear; but what he seems to mean is that he knows that West is not as fashionably accepted as she once was. For more on Rebecca West, see Brian Hall, "Rebecca West's War," *New Yorker,* April 15, 1996.

2. Communist Rule

1   See Hugh Seton-Watson, *The East-European Revolution* (New York, Praeger, 1951).

2   See Walter R. Roberts, *Tito, Mihailovic, and the Allies, 1941–1945* (New Brunswick, N.J.: Rutgers University Press, 1973).

3   The best book on Stalinism in Eastern Europe remains Zbigniew K. Brzezinski, *The Soviet Bloc: Unity and Discord,* rev. and enlarged ed. (Cambridge, Mass.: Harvard University Press, 1967). George Schöpflin's *Politics in Eastern Europe* (Oxford: Blackwell, 1993) is masterly. On the establishment of the Cominform and its impact, see Adam Ulam, *Titoism and the Cominform* (Cambridge, Mass.: Harvard University Press, 1952). See also Joseph Rothschild, *Return to Diversity: A Political History of East Central Europe Since World War II* (New York: Oxford University Press, 1989).

4   See Brzezinski, chaps. 7 and 8.

5   See H. Gordon Skilling, *Czechoslovakia's Interrupted Revolution* (Princeton, N.J.: Princeton University Press, 1976); see also Mark Kramer, *Crisis in Czechoslovakia, 1968: The Prague Spring and the Soviet Invasion* (forthcoming).

6   On "consumerism," see J. F. Brown, *Eastern Europe and Communist Rule* (Durham, N.C.: Duke University Press, 1988), passim.

7   On the new pope's first visit to Poland, see *The Pope in Poland* (Munich: Radio Free Europe Research, June 1979).

8   On the founding of Solidarity, see *The Strikes in Poland* (Munich: Radio Free Europe Research, October 1980). The best book on the subject is still Timothy Garton Ash, *The Polish Revolution: Solidarity* (New York: Scribners, 1984).

9   My *Eastern Europe and Communist Rule* generally reflected the pessimism (in terms of what later transpired) in Eastern Europe in the early 1980s.

10   Schöpflin, 179–81, makes some perceptive distinctions between "opposition" and "dissent."

11   This was Kádár's famous rallying cry to the Hungarian people at the beginning of his reform policy. It was reported in the main Hungarian communist party daily, *Népszabadság,* December 10, 1961.

12   Mircea Dinescu, a prominent writer, estimated that there might have been one dissident for every 2 million people. Quoted by Florin-Gabriel Marculescu, "Self Dissolution," *Romania liberă,* January 10, 1990.

13   See Richard Crampton, "The Intelligentsia, the Ecology, and the Opposition in Bulgaria," *World Today* (London), February 1990.

14   Stalin stressed this point to Milovan Djilas; see Djilas's, *Conversations with Stalin* (New York: Harcourt, Brace and World, 1962), 114. In J. F. Brown, *Surge to Freedom: The End of*

Communist Rule in Eastern Europe (Durham, N.C.: Duke University Press, 1991), I described Stalin's new type of rule as *cuius regio, eius religio,* the settlement reached at the Diet of Augsburg in 1558 whereby the religion—Catholic or Protestant—of a territory was decided according to the religion of its ruler.

15 J. F. Brown, *Relations Between the Soviet Union and Its East European Allies* (Santa Monica, Calif.: RAND, 1975). See also Robert L. Hutchings, *Soviet-East European Relations: Consolidation and Conflict, 1968–1980* (Madison: University of Wisconsin Press, 1980).

16 For a stimulating view of Comecon, see Vladimir Sobell, *The Red Market: Industrial Cooperation and Specialisation in Comecon* (Aldershot, Eng.: Gower, 1984).

17 See Brown, *Eastern Europe and Communist Rule,* chap. 2.

18 John Lewis Gaddis, *We Know Now: Rethinking Cold War History,* Council on Foreign Relations book (Oxford: Clarendon Press, 1998); Robert L. Hutchings, *American Diplomacy and the End of the Cold War: An Insider's Account of U.S. Policy in Europe, 1989–1992* (Baltimore: Johns Hopkins University Press, 1997); Lincoln Gordon et al., *Eroding Empire: Western Relations with Eastern Europe* (Washington, D.C.: Brookings Institution, 1987).

19 Josef Joffe, "The View from Bonn: The Tacit Alliance," in Gordon, *Eroding Empire,* chap. 5.

20 The soundest judgment of it is by Timothy Garton Ash, *In Europe's Name: Germany and the Divided Continent* (London: Jonathan Cape, 1993).

21 Maria Todorova, feistily, perceptively, and wisely, confounds Western myths and punctures Western arrogance about the Balkans in *Imagining the Balkans* (Oxford: Oxford University Press, 1997).

22 See "A Transylvanian Tragedy," *Economist,* January 2, 1999. A most poignant and honest account of German life in Romania is found in Michael A. Nagelbach, *Heil! And Farewell: A Life in Romania, 1913–1946* (Chicago: Adams Press, 1986).

23 See J. F. Brown, *Hopes and Shadows: Eastern Europe After Communism* (Durham, N.C.: Duke University Press, 1994), 200.

24 Quoted in Charles and Barbara Jelavich, *The Establishment of the Balkan National States, 1804–1920* (Seattle: University of Washington Press, 1977), 243–44.

25 Actually, this "re-Bulgarization" campaign was the most recent—and one of the most brutal—aspects of a long-standing historical dispute. Was there mass migration from Anatolia into the Ottoman Balkans, and does this mainly explain the presence of so many "Turks"? Or was it a question of mass conversions to Islam among the native populations with many, but by no means all, of those conversed adopting the Turkish language and becoming the "turkicized"? Many Bulgarian scholars support the conversion theory, a view that was used in attempts to give Zhivkov's campaign a certain respectable, theoretical backing. Todorova, 174–75, says that the "Islamization thesis can be scholarly [*sic*] supported far better than the colonisation one. . . ." She does not give examples of this scholarly support, although she does say that it was no excuse for "any of the anti-Muslim or anti-Turkish manifestations which, at one time or another, have been pursued in different parts of the Balkans." She does not specifically mention this most recent "manifestation" in Bulgaria in the 1980s.

3. Economics 1945–2000

1 See J. F. Brown, *Eastern Europe and Communist Rule* (Durham, N.C.: Duke University Press, 1988), 114–16. Alan Smith's comments in this passage are from his essay, "The Eastern Bloc Economic Model," in the Economic Intelligence Unit (EIU) regional review, *Eastern Europe and the USSR, 1985* (London: Economist Publications, 1985), 6. See also Smith's *The Planned Economies of Eastern Europe* (London: Croom Helm, 1985).

2 Private letter from Vlad Sobell, November 21, 1997. See also Jan Winiecki, *The Distorted World of Soviet-Type Economics* (Pittsburgh: University of Pittsburgh Press, 1988).

3 See Brown, *Eastern Europe and Communist Rule,* 117–23.

4 For "consumerism," see ibid., passim.

5 Winiecki, 173–203.

6 Private letter from Vlad Sobell, November 21, 1997.

7 See J. F. Brown, *Surge to Freedom: The End of Communist Rule in Eastern Europe* (Durham, N.C.: Duke University Press, 1991), 122.

8 Much of the following commentary is based on the European Bank for Reconstruction and Development (EBRD), *Transition Report 1998* and *Transition Report 1999* (London).

9 J. F. Brown, *Hopes and Shadows: Eastern Europe After Communism* (Durham, N.C.: Duke University Press, 1994), 123.

10 See Paul Marer, "Central and Eastern Europe: An Economic Perspective," in Dick Clark, ed., *United States Relations with Central and Eastern Europe,* proceedings of the Eleventh Aspen Institute Conference, Vienna, August 23–27, 1992. See also János Kornai, *The Road to a Free Economy* (New York: W. W. Norton, 1990), and Keith Bush, ed., *From the Command Economy to the Market* (Aldershot, Eng.: Dartmouth for the RFE/RL Research Institute, 1991).

11 Nicholas Barr, *Labor Markets and Social Policy in Central and Eastern Europe: The Transition and Beyond* (New York: Oxford University Press, published for the World Bank and the London School of Economics and Political Science, 1994), 120. See my review of Barr's book in *Transition,* October 20, 1995, under the title "Revamping the Social Welfare System in Eastern Europe."

12 *Neue Zürcher Zeitung* (Internationale Ausgabe) August 27, 1997 (no. 197). For a dire warning about the state of the Romanian economy that also has relevance for South Eastern Europe generally, see Daniel Daianu, "Rumänien kann den Reformen nicht entgehen," *Neue Zürcher Zeitung* (Internationale Ausgabe), January 6, 1999 (no. 3). Daianu was Romanian minister of finance from 1997 to 1998.

13 The *Neue Zürcher Zeitung* had by far the best coverage of any Western newspaper on the Bulgarian crisis. See especially "Bulgariens letzte Chance," in the international edition of April 18, 1997 (no. 89), and "Keine rasche Heilung für Bulgarien," in the international edition of April 3, 1997 (no. 76). See also the editorial, "Bulgarien auf dem Weg der Reform" (international ed.), April 21, 1997 (no. 91), in which the need for political as well as economic reform is emphasized.

14 See Lee Hockstader, "Hopes for a Czech 'Miracle' Evaporate," *International Herald Tribune* (Washington Post Service), December 12, 1997; also "Restoration Work," *Economist,* November 15, 1997; Hr, "Es gibt ein wirtschaftliches Leben nach Klaus," *Neue Zürcher*

Zeitung (Internationale Ausgabe), December 2, 1997 (Nr 280), and Ht, "Schmerzhafte tschechische Trendwende," *Neue Zürcher Zeitung* (Internationale Ausgabe), March 24, 1998 (no. 69).

15   On Balcerowicz's intentions, see Ht, "Polens neue Regierung setzt auf Wachstum," *Neue Zürcher Zeitung* (Internationale Ausgabe), November 11, 1997 (no. 262).

16   See Jane Perlez, "Poland's Proud Coal Miners Resist Change," *International Herald Tribune* (New York Times Service), November 4, 1997; also ruh., "Oberschlesien vor einem sozialen Kraftakt," *Neue Zürcher Zeitung* (Internationale Ausgabe), August 31, 1998 (no. 200); and T.K., "Ein weiterer Anlauf zur Sanierung des polnischen Kohlebergbaus," *Neue Zürcher Zeitung,* June 26, 2000 (no. 146).

17   Mark Kramer, "Social Protection Policies and Safety Nets in East-Central Europe: Dilemmas of the Postcommunist Transformation," in Elhan B. Kapstein and Michael Mandelbaum, eds., *Sustaining the Transition: The Social Safety Net in Postcommunist Europe* (New York: Council on Foreign Relations, 1997), 46–123.

18   Kramer, 106. Bokros resigned in 1997.

19   A.O., "Rumänien im Zeichen sozialer spannungen," *Neue Zürcher Zeitung* (Internationale Ausgabe), December 2, 1999 (no. 281).

20   Goran Lindhal, "A New Role for Global Business," *Time* January 31, 2000.

21   "Storm over Globalization," *Economist,* January 29, 2000.

22   I am indebted to Tzvetelina Tzvetkova, one of my students at the American University in Bulgaria, for information about American Standard Inc., a U.S.-based manufacturer operating in the town of Sevlievo, Bulgaria, for its own and Sevlievo's good.

23   The fluidity of the situation makes accurate figures impossible. This figure has been hazarded from conversations with several experts and does not include war refugees.

4. Democracy

1   Christoph Bertram, "Was It Unavoidable?," a review of Charles Maier's *The Crisis of Communism and the End of East Germany* (Princeton, N.J.: Princeton University Press, 1997), in *London Review of Books,* September 18, 1997.

2   For a quotation of Khrushchev's 1959 views on the future of the socialist camp, see J. F. Brown, *Surge to Freedom: The End of Communist Rule in Eastern Europe* (Durham, N.C.: Duke University Press, 1991), 19.

3   Ibid., 55.

4   Gerasimov was the Soviet foreign ministry spokesman; see Brown, *Surge to Freedom,* 62.

5   See Jacques Lévesque's *The Enigma of 1989: The USSR and the Liberation of Eastern Europe* (Berkeley: University of California Press, 1997), 254.

6   Lévesque's book is extraordinary, and indispensable in this regard, although he sometimes gives the impression that he is reporting, rather than appraising, what people told him.

7   For an excellent discussion of the various interpretations of December 1989, in Romania, see Andreas Oplatka, "Rumäniens umstritten gebliebene Revolution," *Neue Zürcher Zeitung* (Internationale Ausgabe), December 22, 1999 (no. 298).

8   Nestor Rateş, *Romania: The Entangled Revolution* (New York: Praeger and the Center for Strategic and International Studies, 1994).

9   Lévesque argues that Jaruzelski was Gorbachev's favorite among the East European leaders and that he supported him throughout. *The Enigma of 1989*, 89.

10 See Brown, *Surge to Freedom,* chaps. 5 and 6.

11 See Juan J. Linz and Alfred Stepan, *Problems of Democratic Transition and Consolidation* (Baltimore: Johns Hopkins University Press, 1996), part 4, "Post-Communist Europe: The Most Complex Paths and Tasks." This is the best analysis of democratic consolidation so far published.

12 *Economist,* Pocket World in Figures (1998), 24.

13 On political apathy, see *Hopes and Shadows* (Durham, N.C.: Duke University Press, 1994), 30–32.

14 "Upheaval," *Economist,* October 23, 1999.

15 See the chart in EBRD transition report 1999, 113.

16 See Jiri Pehe, "Civil Society an Issue in the Czech Republic," *RFE/RL Research Report,* August 19, 1994.

17 See 26–27.

18 See Andreas Oplatka, "Bildungs- Besitz- und Staatsburger in Ungarn," *Neue Zürcher Zeitung* (Internationale Ausgabe), March 23, 2000 (no. 70).

19 Robert D. Putnam, *Making Democracy Work: Civic Traditions in Modern Italy* (Princeton, N.J.: Princeton University Press, 1993), 183.

20 See my introduction to *Building Democracy,* the OMRI annual survey of Eastern Europe and the former Soviet Union, 1995 (Armonk, N.Y.: For the Open Media Research Institute, 1996), 14.

21 Julian Barnes, *The Porcupine* (London: Picador, 1992).

22 *Hopes and Shadows,* 3.

23 Ibid.

24 Stephen Holmes, "The End of Decommunisation," *East European Constitutional Review,* Summer/Fall 1994.

25 Tina Rosenberg, *The Haunted Land: Facing Europe's Ghosts After Communism* (London: Vintage, 1995).

26 See Jirina Siklova, "Lustration or the Czech Way of Screening," *East European Constitutional Review,* Winter 1996.

27 See Brown, *Hopes and Shadows,* 45–47 and 70–77. See also Wiktor Osiatynski, "Decommunisation and Recommunisation in Poland," *East European Constitutional Review,* Summer/Fall 1994.

28 See Timothy Garton Ash, "The Truth About Dictatorship," *New York Review of Books,* February 19, 1998.

29 Herman Schwartz, "Lustration in Eastern Europe," *Journal of East European Law,* vol. 1, 1994.

30 In the context of decommunization in general and of lustration in particular, it is neither fanciful nor irrelevant to quote Edward Gibbon on the instructions given by the emperor Trajan toward the end of the first century A.D. on the treatment of Christians and especially on how to respond to those who denounced them:

> Instead of displaying the implacable zeal of an inquisitor, anxious to discover the most minute particles of heresy, and exulting in the number of his victims, the emperor

expresses much more solicitude to protect the security of the innocent, than to prevent the escape of the guilty. He acknowledges the difficulty of fixing any general plan; but he lays down two salutary rules, which often afforded relief and support to the distressed Christians. Though he directs the magistrates to punish such persons as are legally convicted, he prohibits them, with a very humane inconsistency, from making any inquiries concerning the supposed criminals. Nor was the magistrate allowed to proceed on every kind of information. Anonymous charges the emperor rejects, as too repugnant to the equity of his government; and he strictly requires, for the conviction of those to whom the guilt of Christianity is imputed, the positive evidence of a fair and open accuser. It is likewise probable, that the persons who assumed so invidious an office, were obliged to declare the grounds of their suspicions, to specify (both in respect to time and place) the secret assemblies, which their Christian adversary had frequented, and to disclose a great number of circumstances, which were concealed with the most vigilant jealousy from the eye of the profane. If they succeeded in their prosecution, they were exposed to the resentment of a considerable and active party, to the censure of the more liberal portion of mankind, and to the ignominy which, in every age and country, has attended the character of an informer. (Edward Gibbon, *The History of the Decline and Fall of the Roman Empire,* ed. David Womersley [London: Penguin 1994], vol. 1, 535–36)

No one, of course, would dispute the differences between late communists and the early Christians. The point is to show the similarities between some of their persecutors and the exemplary tolerance of one of the great Roman emperors.

31 "Crime in the East," April 10, 1997. On police attitudes in the Balkans, see Stefan Krause et al., "Balkan Police Forces More Loyal to Their Leaders than to the Laws," *Transition,* March 8, 1996. The *East European Constitutional Review,* Fall 1997, has an excellent roundup on "Crime and Corruption After Communism."

32 "Crime in the East."

33 Ibid.

34 Interviews conducted on Sofia television, November 10, 1997.

35 Julian Borger, "From Communist Gold to Illustrious Corpse," *Guardian Weekly,* November 3, 1996. See also Ht., "Zwischen Staatswirtschaft und Mafia," *Neue Zürcher Zeitung* (Fernausgabe no. 303), December 29, 1994.

36 January 7, 1995.

37 On the state and "stateness" (their term), see Linz and Stepan, part 4 passim.

38 *Transition,* January 30, 1995.

39 Peter Hoeg, *Smilla's Sense of Snow* (New York: Dell, 1995), 225.

40 I quote this passage in *Transition,* January 30, 1995.

5. Country Profiles

1 See Jane Perlez, "Polish Yuppies Hit Jackpot," *International Herald Tribune* (New York Times Service), September 5, 1996; Christopher Bobinski, "Poland Finds Feelgood Factor," *Financial Times,* February 5, 1996.

2   See "Solidarity v Solidarity," *Economist* April 25, 1998; Ht, "Polen vor der Herausforderung der zweiten Transformation," *Neue Zürcher Zeitung* (Fernausgabe), March 5, 1995 (no. 53).

3   See Rudolf Hermann, "Schleppende Einigung der polnische Rechten," *Neue Zürcher Zeitung* (Internationale Ausgabe), June 11, 1996 (no. 133).

4   See ruh, "Krzaklewski-Polens neue starker Mann," *Neue Zürcher Zeitung* (Internationale Ausgabe), April 10, 1997 (no. 231).

5   *Hopes and Shadows* (Durham, N.C.: Duke University Press, 1994), 65.

6   I put these ideas about the Czech Republic in a fuller, European context in "Everybody Needs Russia—Including Eastern Europe," *Transition*, November 15, 1996.

7   See the excellent roundup, "The New Bohemians," *Economist*, October 22, 1994. Also René Höltschi, "Ein Königsweg mit Schlaglöchern," *Neue Zürcher Zeitung* (Internationale Ausgabe), July 1–2, 1996 (no. 125).

8   Czech corruption attracted much attention in the Western press. For a Westerner's intimate view of it, see Jane Perlez, "Market Place: A U.S. Fund Manager in Prague Has Found Privatization Corrupt," *International Herald Tribune* (New York Times Service), March 12, 1997. Klaus's attitude to corruption is summed up by his remark: "Jay Gould and Vanderbilt were robber barons, but one generation later they were respected people."

9   Havel's speech was more than a criticism of Klaus. It was a personal statement of his belief in democracy, civil society, and Western liberal political values. For a full translation of this speech by Paul Wilson, see *New York Review of Books,* March 5, 1998.

10 During and particularly after the election, Havel's international fame and moral standing led to a number of intrigues against him by personal and political enemies. See "Unsteady Havel," *Economist*, November 21, 1998. On the election and its aftermath, see C.Sr., "Die tschechische Angst vor dem Machtwechsel," *Neue Zürcher Zeitung* (Internationale Ausgabe), June 22, 1998 (no. 141); also ruh, "Zusammenschluss der Mächtigen in Prag," *Neue Zürcher Zeitung,* July 10, 1998 (no. 157). For an example of his wisdom, see "Paying Back the West," *New York Review of Books,* September 23, 1999.

11 Claudio Magris, *Danube* (London: Harvill, 1990), 225.

12 See A.O., "Proteste von Intellektuellen in der Slowakei," *Neue Zürcher Zeitung* (Internationale Ausgabe), April 3, 1997 (no. 76).

13 Quoted by A.O., "Slowakische Zusicherungen an die EU," *Neue Zürcher Zeitung* (Internationale Ausgabe), October 28, 1997 (no. 250).

14 See John Gould and Sona Szomolanyz, "Bridging the Chasm in Slovakia," *Transitions*, November 1997; also "Steel Stolen," *Economist*, January 2, 1999.

15 See bt, "Die Slowakei bald ein nuklearer Musterknabe," *Neue Zürcher Zeitung* (Internationale Ausgabe), February 3, 1999 (no. 27).

16 "Horn's Dilemma," *Economist*, January 28, 1995.

17 "Radical at Last," *Economist*, April 1, 1995.

18 Ht, "Folgen bittere pillen in Ungarn," *Neue Zürcher Zeitung* (Internationale Ausgabe), February 18, 1997 (no. 40).

19 Peter S. Green, "A Hungarian Model for Eastern Europe?" *International Herald Tribune,*

December 27–28 1997. See also Ht, "Gute Noten der OECD für Ungarn," *Neue Zürcher Zeitung* (Internationale Ausgabe), July 1, 1997.

20 The best analysis of the Hungarian election was in the *Frankfurter Allgemeine Zeitung,* May 26, 1998.

21 P. 86.

22 *Magyar Hirlap* (Budapest), October 21, 1996. See also Timothy Garton Ash's review article, "Hungary's Revolution: Forty Years On," *New York Review of Books,* November 14, 1996.

23 Tibor Fischer, *Under the Frog* (London: Penguin, 1993), 29.

24 For a review of Iliescu's role in Romanian politics, see A.O., "Rumänen an der Schwelle eines Wahljahres," *Neue Zürcher Zeitung* (Internationale Ausgabe), December 9–10, 1995 (no. 287).

25 For an excellent survey of Romania, see Aurelian Craiutu, "Light at the End of the Tunnel: Romania 1989–1996," draft paper for the conference "Democratisation in the Balkans," Centre for Mediterranean Studies, University of Bristol, May 16–18, 1997.

26 The *Economist* summed up Western reaction and hopes in its article, "Romania Starts to Rebuild," May 3, 1997. Its subtitle: "After four decades of repressive communism and seven years of corruption and misrule that followed, Romania has a chance to reinvent itself."

27 "New Romanian Man, Old Mess," *Economist,* April 4, 1998.

28 See A.O., "Rumäniens heikle Position gegenüber der Ukraine," *Neue Zürcher Zeitung* (Internationale Ausgabe), March 7, 1997 (no. 55), and in "Kiew und Bukarest paraphieren Grundvertrag," *Neue Zürcher Zeitung,* May 5, 1997 (no. 102).

29 "Seven Years of Democratic Communism in Bulgaria," draft paper prepared for conference, Democratisation in the Balkans, Centre for Mediterranean Studies, University of Bristol, May 17, 1997. See also the excellent "Bulgaria in the Regional Context," UN Development Programme and Centre for Liberal Strategies: "An Early Warning Paper" (Sofia: September 1997).

30 Ibid.

31 Reuters (Sofia), July 10, 1997, reporting statement by Kiril Gatev, deputy director of the National Statistical Institute, Sofia.

32 The best description and analysis of the entire episode is by Misha Glenny, "Heart of Darkness," *New York Review of Books,* August 14, 1997. On the Pyramids debacle, see Remzi Lani, "The Ashes of the Pyramids," *War Report,* March 1997; also Christine Spolar, "A Bitter Taste of Capitalism," *International Herald Tribune* (Washington Post Service), March 12, 1997.

33 For a balanced if generally optimistic view of the Albanian situation, see José-Alain Fralon, "La renaissance de l'Albanie, le pays des Aigles," *Le Monde,* May 26–27, 1996.

34 See Ht, "Die Slowenen müssen in die Hände spucken," *Neue Zürcher Zeitung* (Internationale Ausgabe), January 9, 1998 (no. 6).

35 Ibid.

36 See "Bridging Europe," *Economist,* January 11, 1997.

37 "Tudjman's Last Rally?" *Economist,* December 21, 1996.

38 "Liebst du Kroatien?" The *Neue Zürcher Zeitung* chose this appropriate headline for an analysis of Tudjman's political thinking and style; see issue of June 14–15, 1997 (no. 135).

See also Chris Hedges, "Tudjman Gives the Opposition a Taste of His Democracy," *International Herald Tribune* (New York Times Service), April 5, 1996.

39 See Marcus Tanner, "So Much More Than Just a Game," *Independent* (London), July 8, 1998. On the role of soccer supporters in rallying nationalism in Croatia in the early 1990s, see Andrej Kricković, "Football Is War," *Transitions*, March 1999.

40 See "The Croatians Are Coming," *Economist*, January 10, 1998; awy., "Kroatiens Serben vor der Integration." *Neue Zürcher Zeitung* (Internationale Ausgabe), April 4, 1997 (no. 77).

41 Quoted by Magris, *Danube*, 348.

42 Elisabeth Barker, *Macedonia: Its Place in Balkan Politics* (London: Royal Institute of International Affairs, 1950), 97.

6. The First Yugoslav War

1 The best book I have read on the collapse of Yugoslavia is Viktor Meier's *Wie Jugoslawien verspielt wurde?* (Munich: C. H. Beck, 1995). Meier's articles over many years in the *Frankfurter Allgemeine Zeitung* were sometimes controversial, but in the end he was thoroughly vindicated.

2 Tibor Fischer in *Under the Frog* has a former inmate describing the guards at a labor camp in Rakosi's Hungary: "They'd been told we were the scum of the earth, the most evil, degenerate, child-murdering, odious, verminous parasites . . . in creation" (221). Serb radio and TV were telling Serbs much the same about Muslims. For extremely thorough documentation and a brilliant analysis of the media war, see Mark Thompson, *Forging War: The Media in Serbia, Croatia, Bosnia, and Hercegovina* (Luton: University of Luton Press, 1999).

3 *The Other Balkan Wars,* a 1913 Carnegie Endowment Inquiry in Retrospect, with a New Introduction and Reflection on the Present Conflict by George F. Kennan (Washington, D.C.: Carnegie Endowment for International Peace, 1993), 96 and 98. Misha Glenny refers to these posters in his history *The Balkans, 1804–1999: Nationalism, War and the Great Powers* (London: Granta, 1999), 247.

4 See, for example, the following quotation from *Unfinished Peace: Report of the International Commission on the Balkans* (Washington, D.C.: Aspen Institute Berlin and Carnegie Endowment for International Peace, 1996), 68: "To be sure, the UN Secretariat did have a philosophy and an influence that tended to aggravate the failures of Western policy. One element of that philosophy was the secretary-general's firm conviction, expressed on many occasions, that the war and suffering in Bosnia had received a disproportionate share of the world's attention and moral indignation. He drew a contrast with the relatively meagre international attention given to crimes committed against non-European victims—the genocide in Rwanda being the most horrific example."

5 This attitude at the beginning of the twentieth century is well covered in *The Other Balkan Wars,* esp. chaps. 1 and 5.

6 See, for example, David Owen, *Balkan Odyssey* (London: Indigo, 1996), passim.

7 Zeljko Ivanović, "Reform as Expediency," *Transitions*, March 1998.

8 This judicial process, centered on the Hague court, was the subject of much interna-

tional criticism for its slowness or unwillingness to apprehend major indicted Serb leaders like Rádovan Karadzić and General Ratko Mladic. For a review of the Boston situation at the turn of the millennium, see the following three articles in the spring 2000 issue of the *Atlantic Monthly:* Charles Trueheart, "A New Kind of Justice"; Chuck Sudetic, "The Reluctant Gendarme"; and David Rieff, "Midnight in Sarajevo."

9 For a full summary of the Dayton Accords, see "Overview of the Dayton Peace Accords" (Washington, D.C.: Balkan Institute, December 22, 1995). See also the summary and analysis in the *Economist,* "Peace at Last, at Least for Now," November 25, 1995.

10 *Economist,* November 15, 1995.

11 Warren Zimmerman, *Origins of a Catastrophe* (New York: Time Books, 1996), 181–82. Also quoted in Phillip Corwin, *Dubious Mandate: A Memoir of the UN in Bosnia, Summer 1995* (Durham, N.C.: Duke University Press, 1999), xxi and xxii.

12 "Iszetbegovic lehnt besondere Beziehungen zu Zagreb ab," *Neue Zürcher Zeitung* (Internationale Ausgabe), November 12, 1997 (no. 263).

13 "Tudjman revidiert Dayton," *Neue Zürcher Zeitung* (Internationale Ausgabe), October 19, 1999 (no. 243). What Tudjman was aiming at was getting separate status for the Croat "State-let" of Herceg-Bosnia so that it could eventually merge with Croatia.

14 A voluminous literature has built up over the question of partition or partitions of Bosnia. Henry Kissinger became the strongest advocate of ethnic partition. In the United States, John J. Mearsheimer also argued the case forcefully. See, for example, his article, "The Only Exit From Bosnia," *New York Times,* October 7, 1997. For a balanced view of Bosnia-Hercegovina's future, see Joachim Eicher, "Die Zukunftperspektiven Bosnien-Herzogowinas," *Südosteuropa,* no. 46, 1997, 1–2. For a clear summary of expert opinion, for and against partition, see "The Bosnia Crisis and International Broadcasting" (Washington, D.C.: Radio Free Europe/Radio Liberty Fund, n.d.). For a strong argument against partition, see *Unfinished Peace,* 86.

15 Samuel P. Huntington, "The Clash of Civilization," *Foreign Affairs,* Summer 1993; *The Clash of Civilizations and the Remaking of World Order* (New York: Simon and Schuster, 1996). In this context, John le Carré's caution against "the demonization of Islam as a substitute for the anti-communist crusade" is worth bearing in mind. *Our Game* (London: Coronet Books, 1995), 78.

16 See Ehk, "Sudosteuropa's Nationalstaaten und ihre muslimischen Minderheiten," *Neue Zürcher Zeitung* (Internationale Ausgabe), August 10, 1999 (no. 183).

17 Andrić, *The Bridge Over the Drina* (London: Harvill Press, 1994), 243. Fouad Ajami in an essay for the International Commission on the Balkans in 1996 reminded me of these lines.

18 I have quoted this passage several times, most recently in *Hopes and Shadows,* p. 250. I originally took it from Ivo Banac, *The National Question in Yugoslavia: Origins, History, Politics* (Ithaca, N.Y.: Cornell University Press, 1984), 107.

19 Quoted in Sir Lewis Namier, *Vanished Supremacies* (Harmondsworth: Penguin, 1962), 150.

20 See "The Protectorate," *Economist,* February 14, 1998.

21 The figures and percentages on the problem of refugee returns are compiled from the following sources: awy, "Ungeliebte Flüchtlinge in Banja Luka," *Neue Zürcher Zeitung*

(Internationale Ausgabe), September 24, 1997 (no. 221); jpk, "Verstärkte Rückführung bosnischer Flüchtlinge," *Neue Zürcher Zeitung,* December 18, 1997 (no. 294): awy, "Vernachlässigte Menschenrechte in Bosnien," *Neue Zürcher Zeitung* (Internationale Ausgabe), January 16, 18, 1998 (no. 20).

22 awy., "Suche nach Leben in Geisterdorfern Kroatiens," *Neue Zürcher Zeitung* (Internationale Ausgabe), May 18, 1998 (no. 113). By the beginning of 1999, as many Serbs were leaving Croatia as were returning. awy., *Neue Zürcher Zeitung* (Internationale Ausgabe), February 11, 1999 (no. 34).

23 awy., "*Rückkehrprogramm für Kroatens Serben,*" *Neue Zürcher Zeitung* (Internationale Ausgabe), June 29, 1998 (no. 147).

24 R. Jeffrey Smith, "Legal Ethnic Cleansing Keeps Sarajevo Muslim," *International Herald Tribune* (Washington Post Service), February 2, 1998.

25 He promised that he would let 70,000 Croat and Muslim refugees back into Republika Srpska by the end of 1998. As of late November 1998, only 2,000 had returned. "Putting It Right," *Economist,* November 21, 1998.

26 See C.Sr., "Umstrittene Lehrbücher in Bosnien," *Neue Zürcher Zeitung* (Internationale Ausgabe), July 2, 1998 (no. 150).

27 C.Sr., "Europa's Konzeption zur Befriedung des Balkans," *Neue Zürcher Zeitung* (Internationale Ausgabe), November 10, 1999 (no. 262).

28 Andres Wysling, ed., "Das Lange Warten der Bosnischen Fluchtlinge," *Neue Zürcher Zeitung* (Internationale Ausgabe), November 13–14, 1999 (no. 265).

7. Kosovo

1 A word about names, whose symbolic, ethnic, and political importance can hardly be exaggerated. From 1945 to 1990 this province's official name reflected the nationality and linguistic preferences of the political elites in power. Between 1944 and 1967 "Kosovo" was referred to generally in Yugoslavia as "Kosovo and Metohija." ("Kosovo" in Serb means "the field of blackbirds," and "Metohija," "the land of monasteries"). In 1967, when effective control over the province fell to ethnically Albanian communist elites, the name "Kosovo and Metohija" was dropped in favor of just "Kosovo." Then, as Albanian became the first language of the province, "Kosova" became exclusively used by the Albanian population. After 1988, the old Serb term "Kosovo and Metohija" officially returned and remained till 1999. Now "Kosova" is back as the official Albanian term. But "Kosovo" is still generally used internationally, and I have used it in this book throughout. See Kyril Drezov Bulént Gokay and Denisa Kostovicova, eds., *Kosovo: Myths, Conflict, and War* (Keele University [England] European Research Centre, Southeast Europe Series, 1999), 4–5.

2 Anne Kindersley, *The Mountains of Serbia* (London: John Murray, 1976), 68, gives a marvelous account of travels through "Old Serbia." A Serb painter conveys the attachment that many Serbs feel for the medieval Orthodox monasteries when he describes them as "the title deeds of our inheritance."

3 Noel Malcolm, *Kosovo: A Short History* (London: Macmillan, 1998), brings out this point strongly; see especially 75–80.

4   "Serbian Nationalism, Slobodan Milošević, and the Origins of the Yugoslav War," *Harriman Review,* December 1995. See also Aleksa Djilas, "A Profile of Slobodan Milošević," *Foreign Affairs,* Summer 1993.

5   Gordana Igrić, "In Serbia, Tragedy Without Catharsis," *Transitions,* July 1997.

6   Ibid.

7   See Ekr, "Bevölkerungsverschiebungen in Ex-Jugoslavien," *Neue Zürcher Zeitung* (Internationale Ausgabe), August 11, 1999 (no. 184).

8   *In the Hold* (New York: Alfred A. Knopf, 1996). See also Arsenijević's article, "Notice These Students," *International Herald Tribune,* January 2, 1997.

9   These figures are compiled from official and semiofficial sources, scholarly articles, and newspapers. They apply to 1997, but some of the figures, especially those regarding Albanian migrant workers and emigrants, are unreliable or constantly shifting. The fluctuations in these numbers, in turn, affects the numbers for the resident populations, since most migrants and emigrants have to return home.

10 The University of Tetovo issue became the focal point of ethnic tensions and of Albanian aspirations. No doubt the Albanian political elite in Macedonia hoped that it would become Macedonia's counterpart to the University of Priština in Kosovo. This institution, established by Tito in 1970, was aimed at fulfilling and thereby mollifying Albanian aspirations. It became a hotbed of Albanian nationalism (see p. 171). The authorities saw the same thing happening at the University of Tetovo. Authorities subsequently allowed "unofficial" higher educational courses to be taught in private houses in Tetovo—rather as the Serbs connived at underground higher education in the framework of the "parallel state" in Kosovo. In 2000 a plan was announced for a semiprivate university in Tetovo with support from the Council of Europe.

11 These figures are taken from the article by Ekr: "Kontinuität der serbische Kosovo-Politik," *Neue Zürcher Zeitung* (Internationale Ausgabe), August 25, 1998 (no. 195). They are as accurate as possible. But Kosovo, as might be expected, has been fertile territory for minority statistical manipulation. Milošević, toward the end of 1998 claimed that Kosovo was populated with only 800,000 Albanians compared to 600,000 non-Albanians. His statement can best be explained by the fact that he was planning the mass expulsion of Albanians before the NATO offensive in March 1999.

12 On the lengths to which Čubrilović was prepared to go, see Malcolm, *Kosovo,* 284.

13 *Kosovo/Kosova—As Seen and Told,* published in Priština, December 6, 1999, by the Organization for Security and Cooperation in Europe. See also n. 11, above.

14 On the growing violence in Kosovo, see the articles by Shklezen Maliqi, "Beyond Drenica," Gordana Igrić and Gjeraqina Tuhina, "Empty Roads and Night Shooting," and the interview with Veton Surroi, "Disrupting the Balance of Fear," *Transitions,* April 1998; also the articles under the heading "Kosovo Albanians: Closing the Ranks," by Tihomir Loza, Denisa Kostović, Fron Nazi, Zoran Kusovac, and Astrit Salihu, *Transitions,* May 1998. For a brilliant analysis of the local and regional aspects and the international complexities of the escalation of violence in Kosovo, see awy, "Keine Sanktionen—Milošević triumphiert: Kosovo an der Schwelle zum Krieg Niedriger Intensität," *Neue Zürcher Zeitung* (Internationale Ausgabe), March 27, 1998 (no. 72); and C.Sr., "Kosovo is nicht Bosnien," *Neue Zürcher Zeitung,* June 5, 1998 (no. 127); "Belgrade intensifie sa

politique de harcélement militaire au Kosovo," *Le Monde,* March 28, 1998. For a constructive series of essays on Kosovo and its ramifications, see Thanos Veremis and Evangelos Kofos, eds., *Kosovo: Avoiding Another Balkan War* (Athens: University of Athens, 1998). On Greek support for Serbia, formerly political but then mainly economic, see "Why the Orthodox Are Heterodox," *Economist,* March 14, 1998.

15 "Welcome to Balkania," *Economist,* September 7, 1996.

16 See also Dusko Doder, "Listen to Kosovo's Demaci on Confederal Compromise," *International Herald Tribune,* March 26, 1998.

17 See Gazmend Pula, "The Serbian Proposal for the Partitioning of Kosovo: Accents of Albanian Reactions," *Südost-Europa,* Heft 8, 1996: also his article, "Kosova—Republic in a New (Con)federation via Refederalisation of Yugoslavia," *Südost-Europa,* Heft 3–4, 1997. (I wish to thank Dr. Pula for his advice and helpfulness during conversations I had with him.) During the Kosovo conflict, the Serbs began floating several ideas about partition.

18 On the KLA's halting progress from war to negotiations, see Christophe Châtelot, "L'UCK de la guérilla à la politique," *Le Monde,* February 7–8, 1999.

19 See "A Toothless Growl," *Economist,* May 1, 1999.

20 Both the NATO commander during the conflict, General Wesley Clark, and Strobe Talbott, the U.S. deputy secretary of state, confirmed this point in a BBC television program on August 20, 1999; Reuters, August 20, 1999.

21 Embassy, Federal Republic of Yugoslavia, Berne, press release no. 2155, March 23, 1999. Reply of the President of the Federal Republic of Yugoslavia, Slobodan Milošević, to the message of the cochairmen of the Rambouillet meetings, ministers of France and Great Britain, Hubert Vedrine and Robin Cook. (I am grateful to Dr. Cyril Steiger of the *Neue Zürcher Zeitung* for showing me this press release.)

22 St, "Kein Ausweg aus der Kosovo-Katastrophe," *Neue Zürcher Zeitung* (Internationale Ausgabe), April 1, 1999 (no. 76).

23 See *Kosovo/Kosova—As Seen and Told.*

24 Veton Surroi, one of the most distinguished Kosovars in public life, expressed his disgust and shame at the crimes against members of the remaining Serb community in a letter to the *New York Review of Books,* "Victims of the Victims," October 7, 1999. He was hounded by large sections of the Kosovar media for his courage. Figures varied of the number of Serbs left in Kosovo in September 1999. Bernard Kouchner, the UN administrator there, put the number as high as 97,000. Reuters (New York), September 11, 1999.

25 The question of at least a partial return of Serbs to Kosovo began to be raised early in 2000. One of the most interesting statements on the subject was by Oliver Ivanović, the Serbs' "strong man" in Mitrovica, the bitterly divided town in northern Kosovo. In a conversation with the *Neue Zürcher Zeitung* correspondent published in the paper's international edition on March 14, 2000 (awy, "Kosovo bleibt ein Pulverfass"), Ivanović predicted a massive, organized return of Serb refugees to Kosovo during the spring of 2000. The returning Serbs would settle in the towns of Klina, Istok, and Peć. In effect, the Serbs, already in strength in Mitrovica, would regain control of northern Kosovo and then propose partition. It was a crafty idea because both the UN authority and NATO, which were in favor of the return of Serbs in principle, could not flatly oppose the idea,

and a partition of Kosovo was still being much discussed. The problem was, of course, the Kosovars. When some Serbs returned to Istok and other towns in May 2000, this action was hotly resisted. But there was no mass return because the Serbs simply thought better of it, although the idea could of course crop up again.

26   For an extraordinary outburst on this point, see Tariq Ali's "Crimes, Lies, and Misdemeanours," *Financial Times*, April 1–2, 2000. Tariq was a vociferous opponent of the NATO action from the start.

27   "Pope's Apology Helps Advance Morality and Human Rights," *International Herald Tribune*, March 18–19, 2000.

28   "Search for a Safe Harbour," *Guardian Weekly*, March 30–April 5, 2000.

29   For an excellent analysis of the West's problems in Kosovo, see Jacques Rupnik, "Kosovo: Dilemmas of the Protectorate," *East European Constitutional Review*, Winter–Spring 2000. But Rupnik's suggested sanctions against Kosovo, if it fails to comply with the insightful conditions for peace that he proposes, are chilling: "Failure to respect these conditions would expose Kosovo to NATO's retreat, leaving the Kosovars alone against the Serb army (which has not been destroyed and could be tempted into a war of reconquest)."

30   awy, "Wiederaufbau nach den Balkankriegen," *Neue Zürcher Zeitung* (Internationale Ausgabe), August 14–15, 1999 (no. 187). See also "Kosovo Resurgent" and "The Market-Minded Kosovars," *Economist*, September 25, 1999; and Stefan Wagstyle, "Small-scale Private Enterprise Starts to Lift Kosovo's Economy," *Financial Times*, March 31, 2000.

31   Interview with *Neue Zürcher Zeitung* (Internationale Ausgabe), August 11, 1992, quoted in Brown, *Hopes and Shadows* (Durham, N.C.: Duke University Press, 1994), 258.

32   C.Ct., "La population d'Albania hésite entre solidarité et indifférence," *Le Monde*, May 28, 1998.

33   Fabian Schmidt, "What Kind of Future for Kosova," *RFE/RL Balkan Report*, December 21, 1999. Like many students of the Balkan scene, I am indebted to Fabian Schmidt's periodic analyses.

34   Ibid.

35   For an excellent overall review of East European reaction, see Stephen Holmes et al., "Eastern Europe after Kosovo," *East European Constitutional Review*, Summer 1999. See also awy, "Umstrittene Einbildung Bulgariens in die NATO," *Neue Zürcher Zeitung* (Internationale Ausgabe), May 6, 1999 (no. 103); and A. O., "Ungarn und Rumänien als Frontstaaten," *Neue Zürcher Zeitung*, May 5, 1999 (no. 102).

36   George Paul Hefty, "Kein Durchmarsch, kein Kampf Mann gegen Mann," *Frankfurter Allgemeine Zeitung*, April 23, 1999.

37   This attitude was shared by many intellectuals too; see M. F. Burnyeat, "Letter from Sofia," *Times Literary Supplement*, April 16, 1999.

38   For a background essay on Turkish attitudes to the Balkans in the 1990s, see J. F. Brown, "Turkey: Back to the Balkans?" in Graham E. Fuller and Ian O. Lesser, eds., *Turkey's New Geopolitics: From the Balkans to Western China* (Boulder, Colo.: Westview Press, for RAND, 1993).

39   See Peter Preston, "How the Earth Moved for Ankara and Athens," *Guardian Weekly*, January 27–February 2, 2000.

40　See also EBRD, transition report 1999, annex 3.2, "Kosovo Crisis and Transition Prospects in South-Eastern Europe," 82–86.

41　Cls, "Vor grossen Herausforderungen in Kosovo," *Neue Zürcher Zeitung* (Internationale Ausgabe), July 13, 1999 (no. 159).

8. Key Minorities

1　For those interested in small, forgotten minorities, see, for example, Ekr, "Die Aromunen—ein gefärhdetes Hirtenvolk," *Neue Zürcher Zeitung* (Internationale Ausgabe), July 15, 1997 (no. 161). The Aromunens (Romanian Vlachs) had some "diplomatic use" for Bucharest in the early twentieth century, but they have none now. Evangelos Averoff, Greek foreign minister immediately after World War II, was a Vlach. So were some members of the Internal Macedonian Revolutionary Organization. Their numbers now are estimated at 150,000, spread over Serbia, Greece, Macedonia, Romania, and Albania.

2　A rich literature is available on this subject. One of the most informative contemporary books for me was Gerhard Seewann (Herausgeber), *Minderheiten als Konfliktpotential in Ostmittel—und Sud-osteuropa* (Munich: R. Oldenbourg, 1995).

3　Throughout the twentieth century, much cheating has occurred over minority numbers. Central authorities have wanted to play down the numbers; minority spokesmen and irredentists have wanted to play them up. Sometimes, though, racist agitators, as well as Roma themselves, though obviously for different reasons, have been anxious to swell their numbers so as to emphasize the "threat" they are supposed to present. See Thomas S. Szayna, *Ethnic Conflict in Central Europe and the Balkans* (Santa Monica, Calif.: RAND, 1994). In this context, see especially Szayna's table on p. 20, the main source for which was Andre Liebich's article, "Minorities in Eastern Europe: Obstacles to a Reliable Count," *RFE/RL Research Report*, May 15, 1993. See also Rogers Brubaker, "Nationalising States in the Old 'New' Europe—and the New," *Ethnic and Racial Studies*, April 1996, and Iakovos D. Michailidis, "The War of Statistics: Traditional Recipes for the Preparation of the Macedonian Salad," *East European Quarterly*, Spring 1998. I am grateful to Tom Szayna for referring me to these two articles.

4　See Bianca Guruita, "Romania's Orbán Problem," *Transitions*, July 1998.

5　See Günter Klein, "Rumäniens Minderheitenpolitik im Kontext internationaler Beziehungen und der Empfehlungen des Europarates," *Südost-Europa*, nos. 11–12, 1996.

6　Fax from Turkish Embassy, Bonn, signed Haydar Berk, counselor, to International Commission on the Balkans, Berlin, May 20, 1996.

7　*Economist*, April 1, 1995.

8　Conversation in Sofia with members of the International Commission on the Balkans, November 1995. See also Zhelev's comments made in Kurdjali, June 16, 1995, at a meeting with local dignitaries; publication in English of the president's office, Sofia. For a comprehensive review and analysis of the Turks' situation in Bulgaria, see *Relations of Compatibility and Incompatibility Between Christians and Muslims in Bulgaria* (Sofia: International Centre for Minority Studies and Intercultural Relations' Foundation, n.d.).

9　"Turks and Bulgars Make Up," *Economist*, February 27, 1999.

10 Isabel Fonseca's *Bury Me Standing: The Gypsies and Their Journey* (London: Vintage, 1996) is touching and realistic. See also the series of articles on Roma in *Transitions*, September 1997. Angus Fraser, *The Gypsies* (Oxford: Basil Blackwell, 1992), is a good introduction.

11 Taken from a lecture by Dr. Zhelyazkova at the European Bank for Reconstruction and Development, London, March 31, 1993.

12 A.O. (Andreas Oplatka), "Ungarns umstrittene öffentliche Sicherheit," *Neue Zürcher Zeitung* (Internationale Ausgabe), February 17, 1998 (no. 38).

13 A.O., "Die Zigeuner—Frage als Knacknuss in Ungarn," *Neue Zürcher Zeitung* (Internationale Ausgabe), November 14, 1998 (no. 10).

14 Ibid.

15 International conference, "Towards Stability on the Balkan Peninsula," Sofia, June 6–8, 1997, organized by the Free and Democratic Bulgarian Foundation in cooperation with the Aspen Institute Berlin, Council of Europe, European Cultural Foundation, and the King Baudouin Foundation.

16 See *Unfinished Peace: Report of the International Commission on the Balkans* (Washington, D.C.: Aspen Institute Berlin and Carnegie Endowment for International Peace, 1996), 160.

17 On this issue, see Miroslav Kusy, "Autonomy as a Way of Political Management of Ethnic Conflicts: The Case of the Hungarian Minority in Slovakia," *Südost-Europa*, nos. 5–6, 1997. Much of what Kusy says about Slovakia also applies to Romania.

18 Sándor Vogel, "Sicherheitsdilemma und ethnische Konflikt aus ungarischer Sicht," in Seewan, 220.

19 Tibor Várady, "Collective Minority Rights and Problems of Their Legal Protection: The Example of Yugoslavia," *East European Politics and Societies*, Fall 1992. When I was working for the Aspen-Carnegie International Commission on the Balkans, 1995–96, I used Várady for the parts I wrote on minorities. In the final text, *Unfinished Peace*, the commission's report, he was not credited. He should have been.

20 Ibid.

21 Ibid.

9. Looking Outward and Inward

1 The most thorough summary I have seen of the "for and against" arguments is Andreas Wenger and Jeronim Perovic, *Russland und die Osterweiterung der NATO: Herausforderung für die russische Aussen-und Sicherheitspolitik* (Zurich: Technische Hochschule, 1997).

2 Kissinger also opposed the "Founding Act" between Russia and NATO and the establishment of the NATO-Russia Council on the grounds that they "seek to reconcile Russia by diluting the Atlantic Alliance into a UN-style system of collective security." *Washington Post*, June 8, 1997.

3 For a typical William Safire contribution, see "A Bigger NATO Is Better—and the Baltics Should Be in It," *International Herald Tribune*, December 17, 1996.

4 See, for example, Madeleine Albright, "Why Bigger Is Better," *Economist*, February 15,

1997; Strobe Talbott, "Why NATO Should Grow," *New York Review of Books,* August 10, 1995. More specifically on engagement with Russia, see Zbigniew Brzezinski, "The Next Big Euro-Atlantic Task Is to Engage Russia," *International Herald Tribune,* May 4, 1998.

5   Published by the Center for Political and Strategic Studies, Washington, D.C., June 1997. For a fuller expression of Mandelbaum's view on European security, see his *The Dawn of Peace in Europe* (New York: Twentieth-Century Fund, 1996).

6   George F. Kennan, "A Fateful Error," *New York Times,* February 5, 1997.

7   Letter to *International Herald Tribune,* November 15, 1997. For a strong criticism of the Clinton administration's approach to NATO, see Ronald Steel, "Instead of NATO," *New York Review of Books,* January 15, 1998.

8   For a relatively early effort to do this, see Ronald D. Asmus, Richard L. Kugler, and F. Stephen Larrabee, "NATO Expansion: The Next Steps," *Survival,* Spring 1995. (For a rejoinder in the same issue, see Michael E. Brown, "The Flawed Logic of NATO Expansion.") On the question of "unlucky" or "deferred" NATO applicants, Asmus and Larrabee offer thoughtful suggestions in "NATO and the Have-Nots," *Foreign Affairs,* December 1995. On a new concept for NATO after the agreement to accept new members, see Michael Stürmer, "Die Nato und ihre strategische Orientierung," *Neue Zürcher Zeitung* (Internationale Ausgabe), March 30, 1998 (no. 74).

9   See 272–77.

10 "Joining the Club," *Economist,* July 12, 1997.

11 *Neue Zürcher Zeitung* (Internationale Ausgabe), February 10, 1998 (no. 33).

12 Ibid.

13 *Gazeta Wyborcza* (Warsaw), October 1, 1998, reporting on a "gloomy" EU assessment of Polish agriculture. For an example of concern over Western lack of preparation, see Timothy Garton Ash, "Extend the Liberal Order to All of Europe," *International Herald Tribune,* May 4, 1998.

14 See R.Ve., "Polen gegen Isolation seiner Östlichen Nachbarn"; *Neue Zürcher Zeitung* (Internationale Ausgabe), September 3, 1998 (no. 203); also Tim Snyder, "Look East, Face West," *Transitions,* September 1998.

15 Lendvai.

16 This quotation was carried in a front-page editorial in the *Neue Zürcher Zeitung* (Internationale Ausgabe), March 28–29, 1998 (no. 73).

17 *International Affairs* (Moscow), October 1991.

18 I have learned much on this subject from conversations with Dr. Anneli Ute Gabanyi of the Südost-Institut in Munich and from her unpublished paper, "Moldova im Spannungsdreieck zwischen Russland, Rumänien und der Ukraine" (n.d.).

19 See F. Stephen Larrabee, "Russia and the Balkans: Old Themes and New Challenges," in Vladimir Baranovsky, ed., *Russia and Europe: The Emerging Security Agenda* (London: Oxford University Press, 1997), 389–402.

20 See Sophie Gherardi, "La Bulgarie voit se dissiper de rêve européen et se concretiser l'influence russe," *Le Monde,* April 7–8, 1996; C.Sr., "Sofia's zweispältige Russland—Politik," *Neue Zürcher Zeitung* (Internationale Ausgabe), April 11, 1996 (no. 84).

21 Ht, "Neues bulgarisch-russisches Gas-Protokoll," *Neue Zürcher Zeitung* (Internationale

Ausgabe), March 23, 1998. This agreement came after a period of some tension between Sofia and Moscow, partly as a result of Gazprom's heavy-handed negotiating methods.

22 See *New York Times* editorial, "Decline in Ukraine," carried in *International Herald Tribune,* April 5, 1998; also "A Truly Dreadful Prospect," *Economist,* March 28, 1998. For an overall view of Ukraine's importance, see F. Stephen Larrabee, "Ukraine's Place in European and Regional Security," a RAND reprint from Lubomyr A. Hajda, ed., *Ukraine in the World: Studies in the International Relations and Security Structure of a Newly Independent State* (Cambridge, Mass.: Ukrainian Research Institute, Harvard Papers in Ukrainian Studies, 1998).

23 Marianne Herold, "Verwirrender Wahlkampf in der Ukraine," *Neue Zürcher Zeitung* (Internationale Ausgabe), March 18, 1998 (no. 64).

24 Eg, "Weissrussland—ein blinder Fleck in Europa," *Neue Zürcher Zeitung* (Internationale Ausgabe), July 1, 1998 (no. 149).

25 Pierre Hassner, "The View from Paris," in Lincoln Gordon, ed., *Eroding Empire: Western Relations with Eastern Europe* (Washington, D.C.: Brookings Institution, 1987), 190–91.

26 Ibid., 191.

27 Ibid., 192.

28 Quoted by Andreas Whittam Smith, *Independent,* May 24, 1999.

29 See 287–88.

30 Ecs, "EU-Osterweiterung als Chance für Osterreich," *Neue Zürcher Zeitung* (Internationale Ausgabe), January 24–25, 1998 (no. 19). See also Barry James, "With Misgivings, Austria Guides Europe to East," *International Herald Tribune,* July 4–5, 1998, and "Jörg Haider, Austria's (and Europe's) Border Guard," *Economist,* July 11, 1998.

31 See B.A., "Österreichs Muhen mit dem Wachsen Europas," *Neue Zürcher Zeitung* (Internationale Ausgabe), January 3–4, 1998 (no. 1).

32 Ibid.

33 Shlomo Avineri, "Dig Deeper to Find Haider's Roots," *International Herald Tribune,* February 16, 2000. For more on Lueger, see Carl Schorske, *Fin-de-Siècle Vienna* (New York: Vintage Books, 1981), 133–48.

34 Mission "Alba" was only put in the field after unedifying wrangling among EU representatives, wrangling that, according to the *Economist,* "revived doubts about whether (the EU) can ever build a genuine foreign policy." "Quick March, Who Says?" March 22, 1997.

35 The Italian prime minister at the time, Romano Prodi, on a visit to Budapest in May 1997, assured his hosts that Italy would assume a positive role in Eastern Europe as a whole. A.O., "Rom als Anwalt der Länder Ostmitteleuropas," *Neue Zürcher Zeitung* (Internationale Ausgabe), May 22, 1997 (no. 115).

Index

economies, 36, 45, 65, 66, 67, 68, 113, 121–22, 198, 199, 202. *See also* entries for individual nations and regions

Eisenhower, Dwight D., 48

Entities in Bosnia-Hercegovina, 102, 107, 151, 153, 192. *See also* Muslim-Croat Federation; Republika Srpska

ethnic cleansing. *See* Serbia, wartime cruelty and destruction

EU. *See* European Union

European Bank for Reconstruction and Development (EBRD), 98–99

European Community (EC), 231

European Monetary Union (EMU), 197, 220

European Union (EU), 116, 120, 124, 138, 147, 160, 176, 195, 197, 199, 201, 202, 204, 212, 215, 216, 219, 222, 227, 229, 230, 231, 232, 236, 237, 238, 239, 240; Stability Pact for Balkans, 199, 239

Evans, R. J. W., 12

Federal Republic of Germany (FRG): Brandt government, 50–51; economy, 231; ethnic issue, 232; in EU, 230; immigration to, 231, 232; largesse toward GDR, 38; in NATO, 45, 147, 180, 230; negative policy toward Eastern Europe, 49–50; Ostpolitik, 50, 51, 63, 230–31; relations with Czech Republic, 113; relations with Russia, 108; relations with USSR, 50; resurgence, 231; reunification with GDR, 5, 13, 50, 51, 231. *See also* German Democratic Republic (GDR); Germany; Nazi Germany

Ferdinand, Archduke Franz, 145

FIDESZ (Federation of Young Democrats, Hungary), 122, 124, 125, 126, 127, 201

Figes, Orlando, 15

France: alliances, 14, 21, 233; diplomacy, 233–34; educational training institutions, 102–3; in EU, 147; and German reunification, 50, 233; interwar years, 13, 14; in NATO, 222; patron of Romania, 127; self-interest, 233; wavering in Kosovo conflict, 180

Freedom Union (Poland), 110, 111

French Revolution, 31, 233

FRG. *See* Federal Republic of Germany

Gambrell, Jamey, 105

Gandhi, Mohandas Karamchand (Mahatma), 88, 174

Garašanin, Iliya, 7, 245n. 5

Gauck, Joachim, 93

Gazprom, 264n. 21

GDR. *See* German Democratic Republic

Georgievski, Lupčo, 143

Gerasimov, Gennadi, 76

German Democratic Republic (GDR—East Germany), 108, 231; army, 38; collapse of, 51, 73, 78; decommunization (lustration), 92; economy, 36, 63–64; isolation from the West, 50; and Prague Spring, 35; revolt in (1953), 44; support of USSR, 37, 45, 46, 50; survival, 77. *See also* Germany

Germany, 5, 10, 18, 94, 144, 229, 230, 230–33; and balance of power, 3; collapse of German empire, 7; communism in, 14; division of (World War I), 37; Germans in Czechoslovakia, 6, 8, 17; Great Depression, 27; immigration, 110; lebensraum, 28; policy toward Poland, 7, 16, 231; in Romania, 8, 55; in Soviet Union, 8; World War I defeat, 14–15, 16; World War I, revival after, 13, 21; World War II defeat, 30; World War II, revival after, 91, 232. *See also* Federal Republic of Germany; German Democratic Republic; Nazi Germany

Gierek, Edward, 36, 40, 63, 94

Gladstone, William Ewart, 235

Glemp, Józef, Cardinal, 115

Gligorov, Kiro, 103, 142

globalization, 69–70, 71, 72, 82

Gomułka, Władysław, 34–35, 62, 94

Göncz, Árpád, 103, 127

Gorbachev, Mikhail, 35, 74–76, 77, 78, 251n. 9

GOSPLAN, 60

Great Britain, 36, 180, 246n. 29; and balance of power, 3; betrayal of Czechoslovakia (1938 Munich treaty), 14, 30; in EU, 147;

foreign policy, 234–35; and German reunification, 50; in Greece, 48; influence in
Eastern Europe, 234; interwar years, 14,
30; in NATO, 147; and Paris peace settlements (post–World War I), 6; post–
World War II years, 13; and Rambouillet
meetings, 259n. 22
Great Depression, 10, 26–27
Greater Romania Party, 130
Greece, 85, 155, 167, 205, 239; in Balkan Entente, 21; and Cyprus, 196, 197; in early
cold war, 48; economy, 222; Greeks in Albania, 8, 19; independence from Turks, 3;
and Kosovo crisis, 153, 192; and Macedonia, 163, 169; Muslims in, 196; policy
toward Serbs, 196, 197; royalty, 25; stability, 206, 224, 239; Vlachs in, 261n. 1
Grunwald, Béla, 56
Gypsies. *See* Roma

Haider, Jörg, 88, 237
Hankiss, Elemer, 86
Hanseatic League, 86
Hassner, Pierre, 233
Havel, Václav, 26, 41, 64, 84, 103, 116, 118,
253n. 9
Helsinki Initiative (1975), 51
Herder, Johann Gottfried, 223
Hitler, Adolf, 16, 21, 27, 29, 53, 235, 237. *See
also* Nazi Germany
Hobsbawm, Eric, 13
Hoffman, Karol, 95
Honecker, Erich, 38, 78, 94
Horn, Gyula, 103, 122, 125–26, 201, 209–10
Horthy, Miklós, 26
Hoxha, Enver, 38, 39, 43, 45, 94, 135, 167
Hoxha, Nexhmije (Enver Hosha's widow),
94
Hungarian Democratic Federation (Ro-
mania), 129
Hungarian Democratic Forum, 127
Hungarian Revolution: in 1848, 224; in 1956,
33, 40, 44, 126, 224
Hungarians: in Romania, 8, 18, 43, 53–54,

127, 128, 129, 200, 202, 204, 213, 229; in Serbia, 124, 163, 200, 255n. 2; in Slovakia, 200,
202, 203, 212; in Slovenia, 202; in Ukraine,
128, 132, 200, 202
Hungarian Socialist Party, 194
Hungary, 26, 38, 103, 122–28, 194, 238; Alliance of Free Democrats, 120–21; collaboration with Axis powers, 21; consumerism, 36, 41, 62, 201; criminal activities in,
99; decommunization (lustration), 30, 91,
95; democracy, 25, 120, 201; economy, 63,
65, 66–67, 86, 119, 123, 125, 232, 241; EU
membership, 201, 215, 227; Federation of
Young Democrats (FIDESZ), 122, 125, 126–
27, 201; governmental corruption, 100;
Hungarian Autonomous Region in Romania, 53–54, 56; Hungarian Democratic
Forum, 124, 127, 201; Kádárism, 41, 122,
247n. 13; and Kosovo conflict, 192, 194–95;
middle class, 86; as model state for Eastern Europe, 19, 120, 125; nationalism, 34,
200–201; NATO membership, 194, 201, 215;
and New Economic Mechanism (NEM),
62; reforms in, 34, 35, 41, 42, 123–24,
247n. 11; relations with Poland, 16; revolution of 1848, 126, 224; Revolution of 1919,
14; Revolution of 1956, 33, 35, 40–41, 44,
46, 126; Roma in, 208, 210; Romania, relations with, 18, 128, 132, 201, 212; Russians,
attitude toward, 224, 227; Slovaks in, 7–8;
Smallholders' Party, 122, 123, 201; Socialists, 125, 126, 194, 200, 201; USSR, alliances
with, 39; United States, relations with, 48,
229; Western investment in, 113, 124, 127;
World War II, devastation of, 29. *See also*
Hungarians; Kádár, János
Huntington, Samuel, 155, 256n. 15
Husák, Gustáv, 17, 38, 41, 56, 57, 78
Hussarck, Baron Max, 156–57

Igrić, Gordana, 165
Iliescu, Ion, 128–29, 202–3
IMF (International Monetary Fund), 126
IMRO-DPMNE, 143

Nazi Germany, 16, 91, 231, 236; in Albania, 167; appeasement of, 234; Aryan ideal of, 11; in Bulgaria, 58; diplomacy, 23; dominance over Eastern Europe, 21, 53, 55, 58; expansion, 28, 29, 237; Jews, treatment of, 10, 11, 85, 89, 112, 200; Molotov-Ribbentrop pact, 131–32; in Poland, 111–12; rise of, 10, 27, 231; in Romania, 53, 55, 77. *See also* Germany; Hitler, Adolf

New York Times, 216

Njegoš, Peter, 41

North Korea, 138

Novemeský, Laco, 57

Olszewski, Jan, 92

Orbán, Viktor, 103, 122, 125, 126, 194, 195, 201–2

Orthodox Church (Orthodoxy), Eastern, 10; in Serbia, 107E

Ottoman empire, 19, 58, 59, 167; decline and collapse of, 3, 7, 144; dispensation to Muslims, 167, 185; dominance of, 162, 223; remnants of, 154; "Yoke," 59, 108, 187. *See also* Turks/Turkey

Owen, David, 246n. 29

Pacem in Terris, 85

Papandreou, Andreas, 196, 197

Paris peace settlements (post–World War I). *See* entries for individual nations and regions

Partisans (Slovakia), 29

Party for Civic Accord (Slovakia), 120

Party of Democratic Transformation (Macedonia), 142

Party of Social Democracy (Romania), 80, 129

Pax Americana, 229–30

Pax Sovietica, 49

Pétain, Marshal Philippe, 29

"Petöfi-Schiller" University (Transylvania), 204

Piłsudski, Józef, 26

Plavšić, Bilyana, 157

Poland, 2, 5, 26, 32, 80, 107–12, 113, 130, 202, 215, 236, 237, 238; agriculture, 221; agriculture, collectivized, abandoned, 33; anti-Semitism in, 53, 111; Christian nationalism, 111; communism, 126; consumerism, 62, 111; decommunization (lustration), 91, 92, 95, 126; democracy in, 102, 111; economy, 26–27, 36, 63, 64–65, 66–67, 68, 81, 109, 125, 241; elections, 76, 80, 95, 102, 109, 111, 119; EU membership, 110, 215, 222; foreign policy, 224; Germans in, 7; Germany: fears of resurgent, 224, 230, 232; globalization, 71; independence, 20, 46, 81, 91, 108; immigration, 222; Jews in, 7, 108; later-day relations with, 232A, Nazi occupation of, 16, 21; martial law (1981), 39, 74; NATO membership, 215; Ostpolitik (German), 50, 51; Paris peace settlements (post–World War I), 5, 111; peasants, 42; Polish pope, 36–37, 40, 115; postcommunists, 40, 122, 126; privatization, 66; reforms, 34, 62, 64–65, 66–67, 110; repression, communist, 29, 74, 77, 109; resistance to Nazis, 28; Roma in, 208; Roman Catholic Church, 42, 111, 112; and Russia: 224, 225, 227; Solidarity (trade union movement), 37, 51, 74–75, 77; Solidarity Action (political conglomerate), 109; Soviet occupation, 16; Soviet Union, opposition to, 14, 33; Ukrainians in, 7; Upper Silesia, problems in, 67; uprisings (riots, strikes), 69: *in 1956,* 33, 44, *in December 1970,* 35, 62, *in 1976,* 40, *in 1988,* 74, 77; and U.S. popular culture, effects of, 229; Western investment in, 109; World War II, devastation, 27, 29, 111, 234

Polish October, 44

Polish United Workers' Party (communist), 40

Prague Spring, 34, 35, 37, 38, 40, 45, 50, 56, 58, 62, 74, 78

Prodi, Romano, 265n. 38

Protić, Stoyan, 156

Putin, Alexander, 223, 226, 227

Putnam, Robert D., 86–87
"Pyramid" crisis (Albania), 66, 68, 132, 173, 198, 242

Racan, Ivica, 129, 137–38
Rákosi, Mátyás, 246n. 24
Rambouillet (Kosovo peace talks), 174, 175, 177–78, 182, 255n. 43, 259n. 22
Ranković, Alexander, 171
Rateş, Nestor, 77
Reagan, Ronald, 40, 49
Red Army, 25, 108
Refugees, 59, 184, 194, 198, 237–38
Republika Srpska, 151–52, 157, 158–59, 192, 257n. 25
Rexhepi, Bajram, 186
Roma (Gypsies), 7, 11, 58, 86, 134, 138, 200, 205, 207, 208, 209–12, 246n. 10
Roman, Petre, 130
Roman Catholic Church, 10, 20, 36, 42, 56, 58, 85, 87, 115, 121, 138, 140
Romania, 3, 21, 29, 38, 39, 101, 128–32, 155, 165, 231; alliance with Poland (post–World War I), 16; conspiracy theories of Ceauşescu's fall, 76–77; constitutional democracy in, 79–80, 84, 87; criminal activities in, 99, 101, 254n. 26; Czechoslovakia, 1968 invasion, opposed to, 54; decommunization (lustration), 95; "deviation" from Soviet bloc, 44, 54; economy, 65–66, 67, 68, 129, 198, 199, 241, 249n. 12; ethnic minorities, problems with, 7, 127, 128, 153, 203, 212; EU membership hopes for, 128, 216, 254nn. 25 and 26; fascism in, 23, 25; German defeat of (World War I), 17; German minority, treatment of, 55, 248n. 22; Hungarians in, 8, 43, 54, 123, 124, 126, 200, 202, 213; Hungary, relations with, 56, 120, 128, 201; image (prestige), 71; Jews, treatment of, 53, 126; military's role, 25; and Moldova, 127, 128, 225; monarchy, illusions of restoring, 127; nationalism in, 129–30; NATO aims, suspicions of, 195–96; NATO membership, hopes for, 128, 192; re-pression, governmental, 41–42; revolution (1989), 93–94, 125, 250n. 7; Roma in, 207, 208; Russia, relations with, 130–31, 191, 224, 225; strikes, 68, 69; and Ukraine, 228; U.S. popular culture, influence of, 229; Vlachs in, 261n. 1. *See also* Ceauşescu, Nicolae
Rosenberg, Tina, 92
Rothschild, Joseph, 14
Rousseau, Jean-Jacques, 242
Rugova, Ibrahim, 173, 174, 178, 182, 186
Russia, 2, 3, 30, 75, 76, 105, 107C, 117, 149, 222–27; and Belarus, 226, 228–29; Bosnia, troops in, 192; and Bulgaria, 223, 227; communist transformation, 30; criminal activities in, 87, 96, 98, 121; and Czechoslovakia, 224; and Czech Republic, 227; diplomacy, 181; domination over Eastern Europe (post–World War II), 215, 217, 226; and Eastern Europe, 217, 224–25, 226; economy, collapse of (1998), 219; Federal Republic of Yugoslavia, support of, 109; Germany, relations with, 108, 231–32; and Greece, 223–24; Hungary, economic relations with, 227; Kosovo, 175, 191, 192; Moldova, 131, 226; Montenegro, 223; and Poland, 16, 224, 227; Revolution of 1917, 31, 79; and Romania, 131 224; and Serbia, 223; societal character, post-1989, 86; Soviet Union, revival of, 13; territorial ambitions, 43, 147; tsarism, 15, 43, collapse of, 7; and Ukraine, 226, 227–28; U.S. aims, view of, 225; West, relations with, 218. *See also* Soviet Union
Ruthenia (Carpathian Ukraine), 6, 8, 25
Rwanda, 256n. 4

Safire, William, 217
Schiffer, Claudia, 119
Schmidt, Fabian, 187
Schmidt, Helmut, 51
Schöpflin, George, 84
Schuster, Rudolf, 120
Schwartz, Herman, 93

16, 33, 35, 36–37, 44, 66, 74; and Roman
Catholic Church, 36–37, 40; and Romania, 18, 39, 44, 45, 54, 66, 77; and Serbia, 66; Stalinism, 32, 33, 41, 43–44, 167;
terror (Soviet), 31, 41, 43–44; and Tito, 45,
break with, 32, 167, death of, 38, 39; upheavals of 1989, 77; Warsaw Pact, 38;
World War I (post-), 111; World War II,
devastation of, 52; World War II (post-),
19, 29, 30, 41, 167, 224; and Yugoslavia, 32,
34, 38, 39, 40, 45, 167
"Stability Pact for South Eastern Europe,"
160, 161, 199, 239
Stalin, Joseph, 11, 12, 30, 31–33, 43, 44, 53, 54,
59, 167, 223, 248n. 14
Stalinism. *See* Stalin, Joseph
Stambolić, Ivan, 165
Steele, Jonathan, 184–85
Stoyanov, Peter, 99, 103

Talbott, Strobe, 259n.
Thatcher, Margaret, 234
Tisza, Kálmán, 56
Tito, Marshal (Josip Broz), 9, 30, 31, 32, 38,
39, 43, 48, 109, 145–46, 150, 163, 164, 168,
171, 172, 174, 189, 202, 259n. 14
Titoism. *See* Tito, Marshal
Torgyán, József, 122, 123
Trajkovski, Boris, 142, 143, 163
Transylvania, 7, 18, 19, 55, 56, 59
Treaty of Versailles, 5, 6, 7, 15, 17–18, 151
Trianon, Treaty of, 21
Tudjman, Franjo, 102, 139–41, 150, 152–53,
254–55n. 38
Tudor, Corneliu Vadim, 126
Turkey/Turks, 29, 170, 248n. 25; Albania,
167; Balkan Entente, member of, 21;
Bosnia, power in, 156; in Bulgaria, 8, 42,
58–59, 262n. 8; exodus from Bulgaria, 58–
59

UDBA (Yugoslav secret police), 171
Union of Democratic Forces (Bulgaria),
130

UN authority for Kosovo, 184
United Nations (UN), 21, 66, 147, 151, 176,
180, 260n. 26, 263n. 2
UNPREDEP (UN Preventive Deployment
Force), 142
United States, 106, 149; and Bosnian conflict,
147, 148, 151, 176; and Bulgaria, 206; cold
war politics, 48; Croatia, support of, 140;
cultural influence, 229–30; Dayton peace
talks (on Bosnia), 151; Eastern Europe,
policy toward, 46, 49, 50, 147, 228; FRG,
support of, 50, 51; global diplomacy, 226;
globalization, 230; Greece, alleged role in
1967 coup, 196; Kosovo, policy toward,
176, 179, 180; and NATO, 147, 180; and
NATO enlargement, 216–18, 222; Pax
Americana, 229–30; prestige (credibility),
177, 191, 192, 222; Rambouillet talks, actions at, 177–78, 255n. 43; Russia, policy
toward, 48, 225; and Serbia, 150, 166; superpower status, 13, 147. *See also* NATO;
Wilson, Woodrow; Wilsonianism
University of Priština (Kosovo), 171, 189, 209
University of Sofia, 208
University of Tetovo (Macedonia), 170, 189,
258n. 10
Upper Silesia, 67

Vance-Owen peace mission (Bosnia), 246–
47n. 29
Várady, Tibor, 213–14
Vasile, Radu, 130
VDNX (Soviet Exhibition of the Achieve-
ment of the People's Economy), 105
Vedrine, Hubert, 259n. 22
Venizelos, Eleutherios, 21
Vlachs, 7, 261n. 1
Vojvodina, 163, 166, 194
Vujačić, Veljko, 164

Wałęsa, Lech, 26, 78, 92, 102, 111, 238
Wandruszka, Adam, 141
War crimes tribunal. *See* International War
Crimes Tribunal

Warsaw Pact (Warsaw Treaty Organization—WTO), 44, 45
Washington Post, 216
West, Rebecca, 26, 246n. 29
West Germany. *See* Federal Republic of Germany (FRG); Germany
Wilhelm II, Kaiser, 5, 144
Wilson, Woodrow, 5, 19, 151
Wilsonianism, 18, 19, 21
World Bank, 198–99
World War I, 20, 25, 56, 107B, 108, 144–45, 167; post–World War I, 170, 232
World War II, 20, 24, 25, 27, 28, 41, 43, 46, 53, 57, 85, 112, 144, 145, 150, 155, 163, 171; pre–World War II, 145, 246n. 29; post–World War II, 53, 70, 91, 108, 121, 139, 167, 176, 184, 261n. 1
WTO. *See* Warsaw Pact

Xhaferi, Arben, 143, 170

Yalta conference of Allied leaders (1945), 30
Yeltsin, Boris, 227
Yugoslavia, 6, 15, 20, 108, 109, 110, 168, 229, 246n. 29; 257n. 1; Balkan Entente, member of, 21; and Bosnian Muslims, 156; break with Soviet Union, 32; breakup of, 9–10, 39, 42, 101, 138; communist leanings in, 24, 167; constitution of 1974, 164–65, 171, 173, 174; creation of (post–World War I), 2–3, 5, 13, 108, 145, 156, 170, 185; and Croatia, 7, 20; diversity of population, 43, 48; economy, 36, 66, 159; ethnic problems, 7, 48; pro-fascist governments in (pre–World War II), 23, 107; German occupation, 29; government of, weakening, 101, 163–64, 191; Hungarians in, 8, 200, 202; independent status and policies, 22, 34; Kosovars in, 171, 173, 178; Macedonians in, 7; military's role, 25, 190; nationhood, 9; reforms, 34, 62; Roma in, 208; Serbia, 7, 20, 171; Slovenia, 7; territorial ambitions, 19; Tito's Yugoslavia, 146, 171; trade policies, 135, 159, 198; wars of 1990s, 12, 20, 52, 66, 136, 147, 150, 237, 239; and Wilsonianism, 5, 145; World War II, losses and destruction, 27. *See also* Bosnia; Bosnia-Hercegovina; Croatia; Kosovo; Macedonia; Montenegro; Serbia; Tito, Marshal

Zeman, Miloš, 118–19
Zhelev, Zhelu, 103, 206, 262n. 8
Zhelyazkova, Antonina, 208–9
Zhirinovsky, Vladimir, 106
Zhivkov, Tudor, 38, 42, 43, 59, 78, 90, 94, 99, 132, 133, 150, 205, 241, 248n. 25
Zionism, 9
Zog I (Ahmed Zogu), 26, 135

J. F. Brown has served as an adviser to the International
Commission on the Balkans, a project of the Aspen Institute
Berlin and the Carnegie Endowment for International Peace.
He has been a Senior Analyst at RAND and has taught at the
University of California at Berkeley, U.C.L.A., and Columbia
University. In 2000 he was visiting professor at the American
University in Bulgaria at Blagoevgrad. He is the author of
several books, including *Hopes and Shadows: Eastern Europe
After Communism* (Duke, 1994); *Nationalism, Democracy and
Security in the Balkans* (1992); *Surge to Freedom: The End of
Communist Rule in Eastern Europe* (Duke, 1991); and *Eastern
Europe and Communist Rule* (Duke, 1988). He lives in Oxford.

Library of Congress Cataloging-in-Publication Data
Brown, J. F. (James F.)
The grooves of change : Eastern Europe at the turn of the
millennium / J. F. Brown.
Includes bibliographical references and index.
ISBN 0-8223-2652-3 (cloth : alk. paper) —
ISBN 0-8223-2637-x (pbk. : alk. paper)
1. Europe, Eastern—History—1989– . I. Title.
DJK51 .B74 2001
947.085—dc21   00-047655